The Rock Cover Song

ALSO BY DOYLE GREENE
AND FROM MCFARLAND

*Teens, TV and Tunes: The Manufacturing
of American Adolescent Culture* (2012)

The American Worker on Film: A Critical History, 1909–1999 (2010)

*Politics and the American Television Comedy:
A Critical Survey from* I Love Lucy *through* South Park (2008)

*The Mexican Cinema of Darkness: A Critical Study of Six
Landmark Horror and Exploitation Films, 1969–1988* (2007)

*Mexploitation Cinema: A Critical History of Mexican Vampire,
Wrestler, Ape-Man and Similar Films, 1957–1977* (2005)

THE ROCK COVER SONG

Culture, History, Politics

Doyle Greene

McFarland & Company, Inc., Publishers
Jefferson, North Carolina

LIBRARY OF CONGRESS CATALOGUING-IN-PUBLICATION DATA

Greene, Doyle, 1962– author.
    The rock cover song : culture, history, politics / Doyle Greene.
       p.   cm.
    Includes bibliographical references and index.

    ISBN 978-0-7864-7809-5 (softcover : acid free paper) ∞
    ISBN 978-0-7864-1507-3 (ebook)

    1. Rock music—History and criticism.   I. Title.
ML3534.G74 2014
781.66—dc23   2014004377

BRITISH LIBRARY CATALOGUING DATA ARE AVAILABLE

© 2014 Doyle Greene. All rights reserved

No part of this book may be reproduced or transmitted in any form or by any means, electronic or mechanical, including photocopying or recording, or by any information storage and retrieval system, without permission in writing from the publisher.

On the cover: (clockwise, from top left) Otis Redding, 1967 (Volt Records); Ronnie Wood and Mick Jagger of the Rolling Stones, 1975 (Jim Summaria); Britney Spears, 2009 (Anirudh Koul)

Manufactured in the United States of America

McFarland & Company, Inc., Publishers
  Box 611, Jefferson, North Carolina 28640
    www.mcfarlandpub.com

For Richard Leppert,
who not only provided the idea for this project
but graciously gave me permission to cover it.

Acknowledgments

My thanks to the Greene family (Earl, Hannah, and Danielle), the Lynch family (Rodney, Jeni, and Jack), Ann Klee, Matt Potts, Donn Wingate, Keya Ganguly, Gary C. Thomas, Steve Fier and Phanomvanh Daoheuang ("Nacho and Nikki"), Joe Tompkins and Julie Wilson, John "Ray" Link and Sophia Green, and especially Richard Leppert for advice, comments, and support. A thanks also to the numerous musicians I had the privilege to work with and/or discuss music with over the course of three-plus decades. Additional thanks are owed to the departments of Cultural Studies and Comparative Literature, Political Science, and History, and the Master of Liberal Studies Program at the University of Minnesota, as well as the departments of Cinema and Comparative Literature and Rhetoric at the University of Iowa.

Last, a big thanks to my late parents for their lifetime of support and patiently enduring untold hours of my stereo, MTV, and playing musical instruments.

Table of Contents

Acknowledgments   vii
Preface   1
Introduction: The Song Doesn't Remain the Same
- "Reading" through Listening   5
- Covering Cover Songs   7

Part One—Judging a Song by Its Cover

1. National Anthems: "The Star-Spangled Banner"
   - Jimi Hendrix (Woodstock, 1969)   16
   - Whitney Houston (Super Bowl XXV, 1991)   22

2. The "Anti-Cover": Punk and the Avant-Garde
   - Sid Vicious: "My Way" (*The Great Rock 'n' Roll Swindle*, 1980)   29
   - The Residents: *The Third Reich and Roll* (1976)   36
   - Hardcore and the Anti-Cover   41

Part Two—Anatomy of a Cover: "(I Can't Get No) Satisfaction"

3. "Satisfaction" and Rock: The Rolling Stones (*Out of Our Heads*, 1965)
   - The Anti-Beatles   50
   - "Satisfaction" as Manifesto   52
   - Under My Thumb: Altamont and Rock Totalitarianism   56

4. "Satisfaction" and Soul: Otis Redding (*Otis Blue/Otis Redding Sings Soul*, 1965)
   - Paint It Black: Race and Rock in the 1960s   59
   - Soul Brands: Motown and Stax   61
   - "Satisfaction" as Protest   64

5. "Satisfaction" and Punk: Devo (*Q: Are We Not Men? A: We Are Devo!*, 1978)
   - A Postmodern Protest Band (or, Anarchy in Akron) — 67
   - "Satisfaction" as Deconstruction — 70
   - Marketing Opposition — 72

6. "Satisfaction" and Pop: Britney Spears (*Oops! ... I Did It Again*, 2000)
   - The Lolita Next Door — 75
   - Blonde Alienation — 78
   - "Satisfaction" as Commodity — 79

Part Three—Signs of the Times: Cover Songs in Context

7. Music from the Waist Down: Covers, Gender and Sexuality
   - King Curtis: "Whole Lotta Love" (Single, 1970) — 86
   - Van Halen: "You Really Got Me" (*Van Halen*, 1978) — 91
   - The Flying Lizards: "Sex Machine" (*Top Ten*, 1984) — 94
   - Kim Wilde: "You Keep Me Hangin' On" (*Another Step*, 1986) — 101

8. Black Musicians, White Songs: Race and Covers in the Late Counterculture Era
   - Rufus Harley: "Where Have All the Flowers Gone?" (Recorded in 1969; Released on *Courage: The Atlantic Recordings*, 2006) — 109
   - The Isley Brothers: "Ohio/Machine Gun" (*Givin' It Back*, 1971) — 115
   - The Four Tops: "A Simple Game" (Single, 1972) — 123

9. Dance with Laibach: Covers and the Critique of the Nation-State
   - The Laibach Project — 129
   - *NATO* (1994) — 135
   - The Dilemmas of Laibach — 144

10. In with the Old: Covers and Generational Politics
    - The Midlife Crisis of Rock and Roll — 146
    - Frank Sinatra: "Something" (Single, 1970) — 147
    - "So Bad It's Good": Covers and Camp — 150
    - Pat Boone: "Smoke on the Water" (*In a Metal Mood: No More Mr. Nice Guy*, 1997) — 155
    - Johnny Cash: "Hurt" (*American IV: The Man Comes Around*, 2002) — 159

Conclusion: The Politics of Listening	167
Chapter Notes	171
Bibliography	191
Index	195

Preface

It seems that any critical discussion of popular music begins with some kind of autobiographical account, and this is no exception in order to provide some context for this project and put forth some of my own musical biases. Thanks to my older brother giving me unrestricted access to his stereo and record collection, by the time I turned 13 in the summer of 1975 I was a dedicated rock music fan. For better or worse, the first two albums that made a considerable impact were Emerson, Lake and Palmer's *Trilogy* and Jethro Tull's *Thick as a Brick*; I soon after became a devout Black Sabbath fan after seeing them on *Don Kirshner's Rock Concert*. As for the classic rock albums of the 1970s, *Led Zeppelin IV*, Bruce Springsteen's *Born to Run*, and Pink Floyd's *Dark Side of the Moon* had some great songs interspersed with less memorable moments.

During the latter half of the 1970s, my band/brand identity and loyalty became constructed around "art rock," and the artier the better. I can safely assume I was the only person in my high school who owned every Van der Graaf Generator album and no Van Halen. One purchase was *June 1, 1974*, a live album featuring Brian Eno, John Cale, Nico and Kevin Ayers. I bought it because I was a big fan of Eno's album *Here Come the Warm Jets*, but the revelation was two startling "anti-covers." John Cale reworked Elvis Presley's "Heartbreak Hotel" from smoldering rockabilly melodrama into angst-ridden, avant-gospel-metal psychodrama. (The fact that Cale learned Ayers and Cale's then-wife had sex the night before the concert may well have contributed to Cale's extremely intense vocals.) Nico performed "The End" in her trademark Teutonic vocal style accompanied by her minimalist harmonium drones and Eno's ambient synthesizer noises. The Doors' psychedelic account of Oedipal desire and revolt in the context of the counterculture and the Generation Gap—killing dad and having sex with mom—was converted into a bleak, Gothic dirge where transgression amounted to a dreary, numbing stasis. In his essay "Commitment," Theodor W. Adorno suggested that "Beckett and Kafka arouse the fear that existentialism merely talks about." While I would have hardly put it this way as a teenager listening to *June 1, 1974*, John Cale and Nico aroused the fear that Elvis and Jim Morrison merely sang about within the same song. It was the first time that I heard rock songs being covered in a way that not only radically reinterpreted the original versions musically but drastically altered my relationship to the songs as a listener. In short, I could never listen to Elvis' and the Doors' versions of the songs in the same way again.

When punk reared its ugly head ca. 1976, the controversy dominated the critical and media discourses at the time, even though it was completely absent from the local radio stations. Being an art-rock snob, I held punk in derision. However, by 1978 I was gradually losing interest in progressive rock as my favorite bands had broken up (King Crimson, Henry Cow, Van der Graaf Generator) and others were moving in more commercial directions (Can, Genesis, Gentle Giant). My overnight conversion to punk occurred on October 14, 1978, when I saw Devo on *Saturday Night Live*. All I really knew about Devo was that Eno produced their debut album, which intrigued me enough to make a point of watching the show. While the matching yellow plastic jumpsuits, robotic stage choreography, and cheap guitars made an immediate visual impact, I could hear the influence of Captain Beefheart and Krautrock amid Devo's brand of punk rock. It wasn't until Mark Mothersbaugh began yelping the lyrics that I even realized the jumbled, mechanistic tune I was hearing was a cover of the Rolling Stones' "(I Can't Get No) Satisfaction." I thought it was hilarious and innovative, but I also discerned a "political" motive behind Devo's determined desecration of the Rolling Stones and a classic rock song.

Given my art-rock leanings and becoming a punk fan well into the post-punk era, I gravitated to the Gang of Four, Pere Ubu, the Pop Group, and Wire much more than the Sex Pistols, the Ramones, the Clash, and the Dead Boys. As hardcore punk emerged in the early 1980s, my art-rock side embraced the Minutemen, Sonic Youth, and the Swans while my heavy metal side took to Black Flag, Bad Brains, and Die Kreuzen. I also became engrossed by free jazz, industrial music, and the work of John Cage. Over the course of the decade, I played bass, saxophone, and sang (read: shouted) in a number of local post-punk and post-hardcore influenced bands. During the 1990s, I worked with a number of musicians influenced by other musical genres, and in order to broaden my musical horizons, I delved into contemporary heavy metal, modern classical, the Motown heyday, and non–Western music.

Entering graduate school in the late 1990s prompted a decision to retire from performing music. My focus at the time was film studies and I began paying less and less attention to current popular music. Not unrelated, the advent of CDs entailed a huge amount of reissues and I increasingly retreated to the security of my cultural bunker of the 1970s. I adopted the attitude that with few exceptions, music after 1980 was a waste of listening time. By 2006, I sold off the vast majority of a collection that probably numbered between 1,500 and 2,000 CDs, save my personal canon of 1970s art rock, hard rock, and post-punk. The current state of American and English popular music was not a concern, and the few contemporary bands that did interest me ranged from the Mexican *música duangunese* of Los Horóscopos de Durango to the Swedish math-metal of Meshuggah.

My renewed interest in popular music came about in an unintended way. Critical interest in television comedy led into work on the teen sitcom genre. In turn, I was struck by the extensive cross-marketing of teen sitcoms and teen pop music—Disney's *Hannah Montana* franchise being the most successful example—and exploring this relationship became part of my book *Teens, TV and Tunes: The Manufacturing of American Adolescent Culture* (2012). Admittedly, I hadn't envisioned that my initial critical investigation into popular music would be through performers like Britney Spears and Miley Cyrus, but it spurred a further interest in analyzing popular music not only at the level of the text but the cultural, economic, historical, ideological, political, and social contexts that are part and parcel of popular music. The cover song became a means to this end.

Introduction

The Song Doesn't Remain the Same

"Reading" Through Listening

One primary concern from the outset of writing this book was constructing parameters that would prevent it from becoming a "best/worst" list book of cover songs—an exercise that often amounts to self-indulgent tributes to what one likes and equally self-indulgent tirades about what one hates. Rather than "record reviews," cover songs were approached in two interrelated ways. One was textual analysis of the songs themselves; second was how an examination of these songs provided a wider inquiry into the cultural, historical, political, and social pressures surrounding the production and reception of popular music.

Methodology and criticism of popular music entails a number of negotiations. One is the balancing act between text and context. Text-driven analysis can isolate music and a specific song into a "timeless" objet d'art divorced from any past or present historical or social conditions in favor of questions of aesthetic worth or cultural value: a debate which often digresses into which listener has "better taste." With context-driven analysis, the music itself can become marginalized if not bypassed amid discussion of the various factors that surround it (audience-consumers, critics and the music press, the record industry, the changing technology of producing and consuming music, etc.). The goal of this project is to provide textual interpretations of songs while also assessing them within their specific context(s).

Here "interpretation" poses its own set of issues. One is form and content and, more specifically, musical form and lyrical content. Since the 1960s and namely Bob Dylan, lyrics are elevated to the status of "rock poetry," judged by their literary quality, social conscience, and the ability to stand on their own outside a musical setting.[1] As Robert Christgau cogently stated in 1967, "Poems are read or said. Songs are sung."[2] Simon Firth similarly pointed out that "the problem with the 'poetry of rock' was its confusion of the use of words in music.... Song are more like plays than poems."[3] Patti Smith, a critically hailed "rock poet," put it more bluntly: "I started getting successful writing these long, almost rock & roll poems. And I liked to perform them, but I realized that, even though they were great performed, they weren't such hot shit written down."[4] The point being stressed is that lyrics cannot simply be read and interpreted without addressing how music functions to reinforce, problematize, or even undermine the lyrics—intentionally or unintentionally. A cover song entails analysis of *different* musical and contextual settings of the *same* song and how they can convey vastly different meanings. While the lyrical messages of specific songs are discussed, no lyrics are quoted. Song lyrics, photo images of performers, and recorded as well as live performances of the songs discussed are widely available on the Internet, specifically on YouTube.

The second problem is that formalist analysis can be daunting enough for readers with some expertise in music (i.e., ability to read sheet music, musical training on one or more instruments, familiarity with musical or technical terminology, etc.). It can be incomprehensible for readers who do not have such knowledge, much like someone trying to decipher theoretical physics without a background in higher math. Most popular music consumers "understand" music by listening to it and the affect produced, not by studying written notations; in this respect, interpretation is dependent on music as *sound* as much as the verbal "poetry" of the lyrics. Sheet music, guitar tabs, YouTube live performances and tutorials, and playing along to the recorded versions of songs on bass guitar were variously employed in order to analyze specific songs with some degree of accuracy.[5] However, the formalist discussion is limited to main riffs, chord progressions, and song structures. Any errors, discrepancies, omissions, or oversimplifications are ultimately the responsibility of the author, not the sources utilized.

A third problem is that as much as one tries to be "objective," interpretation is subjective and ultimately one listener's opinion. In their *highly* divergent readings of Led Zeppelin's "Black Dog," Simon Reynolds and Joy Press contended "[Robert] Plant is wracked with desire, shivering and stuttering like he's going through cold turkey; the turgid, grueling riff incarnates sex as agony and toil," while Susan Fast countered that "Plant's tone, which sounds like the whine of a spoiled child ... makes it fairly clear his perceived victimization is intended as a parody."[6] My interest in the debate is around the charges of sexism often leveled against Led Zeppelin and heavy metal as a whole. From my vantage point as listener-critic, I do not hear the main riff of "Black Dog" as "turgid [and] grueling" but powerful and disorientating in its sheer heaviness and highly irregular meter shifts, nor do I hear anything in Plant's wailing that "makes it fairly clear his perceived victimization is intended as a parody." My interpretation is that "Black Dog" musically manifests the desperation and disorientation of unrequited lust, and the vocals—which are largely sung a cappella between the instrumental sections to manifest a sense of isolation or "aloneness"—express the position of a male who cannot possess the object of his desire being consumed by self-pity and resentment. In this respect, "Black Dog" is sexist to the extent the song expresses a highly "masculinist" view of sexuality where the woman is represented as some form of "object-Other" who becomes idealized and/or vilified: something Led Zeppelin is hardly alone in doing as far as the schema of rock music, let alone popular music and popular culture as a whole.

Covering Cover Songs

Authorship varies in different forms of cultural production. In literature, the person who wrote the novel, play, or poem is designated as the author, although in translated works the translator becomes a kind of "co-author." In film, the director is designated the author despite the multitudes of people involved in the production of a film. Another collective form of cultural production is television where authorship is usually designated around the creator of the show (Norman Lear sitcoms, Chuck Lorre sitcoms, Dan Schneider sitcoms) or the star of the show (*Home Improvement* and *Last Man Standing* are Tim Allen sitcoms). For the most part, music is also a collective form of cultural production involving an ensemble of performers ranging from a small amateur band to a full professional orchestra, outside songwriters and arrangers, concert and studio personnel (producers, engineers, session musicians, sound and lighting techs, etc.), and people on the business end of music (managers, publicists, record company artist and repertoire staff, major label executives, etc.).[7] While classical music designates authorship around the composer—a Mozart concerto, a Beethoven symphony, or a Rossini opera—what popular music and politics share is that authorship is primarily assigned to the *performer*.[8] A singer may work with songwriters and studio producers and a politician may employ speechwriters and policy experts, but in the end, the song or political message is assigned to the messenger—be it Britney Spears or Barack Obama.

In the scope of this project, a "cover song" is defined as a different recorded version of a song against a previously recorded *standard version*. This standard version is not necessarily the original version in the sense of being the *first* recorded version of the song; it is the *best-known* version associated with a specific performer and performance of a song. For instance, the Rolling Stones' "(I Can't Get No) Satisfaction" is the original version and the standard version of the song, and can be designated the "original/standard version." However, the original version of "It's All Over Now" was recorded by the Valentinos in 1964 and soon after covered by the Stones, who had a hit single with their version. "It's All Over Now" is commonly known as a Stones song (standard version) rather than a Valentinos song (original version). For this reason, the terms "original version," "standard version," or "original/standard version" are used when and where applicable; in comparative analysis, the term "version" is used to discuss songs as a matter of convenience.

Part One examines music as an ideological product and producer of social order versus dissonance and noise as symptoms and signifiers of social disorder. Chapter 1 analyzes two well-known and decidedly different cover versions of America's national anthem, "The Star-Spangled Banner": Jimi Hendrix at the Woodstock festival in 1969 and Whitney Houston at the 1991 Super Bowl. At the immediate level, Hendrix's discordant instrumental version was performed at one of the largest counterculture music festivals at the peak of Vietnam while Houston's soul-pop vocal version backed by an orchestra was done at the biggest sporting event in America and nationally televised during the first weeks of the Gulf War. Beyond the issue of war, both Hendrix and Houston offer a musical representation of America as a liberal-democratic society in specific historical moments of crisis. Whereas Hendrix infused the national anthem with dissonance and noise to represent America cracking at the seams in the turmoil of the late 1960s, Houston's version of the national anthem as a majestic nexus of classical, pop, and soul music represented America entering the post–Cold War era of global capitalism and neoliberalism.

Jimi Hendrix's "Star-Spangled Banner" was arguably the first "anti-cover" done in rock music, and chapter 2 examines the idea of anti-covers. Covers can be replications, reverential, referential, or reinterpretations. Anti-covers are consciously overt deconstructions—and, in some cases, willful desecrations—of a previous version as far as message as well as music. For example, Fergie's cover of "Barracuda" is almost musically identical to Heart's original/standard version, the lyrics are an indictment of a male-dominated recording industry's exploitation of women, and both versions are sung by women. The post-hardcore power trio Phantom Toolbooth's version of "Barracuda" (*Power Toy*, 1988) is an anti-cover in that it is much faster, infused with an ample amount of guitar noise, and the careening rhythm section threatens the internal stability of the song rather than reinforcing it. Moreover, it is sung by a man about his subordinate status in the music industry. Rather than assailing the pervasive sexism in rock, "Barracuda" becomes an attack on the economic power and commercial control exerted by the major recording companies.

In the 1970s, the punk movement exploded as an alleged repudiation of rock and roll while at the same time relying on traditional rock form. Anti-covers became a staple of punk, and one of the landmarks was Sid Vicious' mauling of Frank Sinatra's "My Way," converting it from a self-aggrandizing MOR anthem of self-determination to an equally self-aggrandizing punk anthem of self-destruction. While unintended, the punk movement also generated greater public exposure for bands already working in areas combining rock primitivism and avant-garde experimentalism, especially as punk evolved into post-punk in the late 1970s. One such band was the Residents, who engaged in a full-scale assault on rock tradition with *The Third Reich and Roll* (1976)—a "collision" as opposed to "collection" of avant-garde butchering of classic rock songs and a none-too-subtle critique of the authoritarian aspects of rock ideology's supposed oppositional and progressive tenets.[9] This chapter also analyzes several anti-covers done by various hardcore bands in the 1980s. Emerging in the wake of the growing commercialization of punk and "New Wave," hardcore was a faster, more aggressive brand of punk and soon faced the same crisis of early punk as two strains of hardcore developed. Traditionalist "thrash music" was exemplified by the Dead Kennedys and the Circle Jerks whereas more avant-garde/experimental "post-hardcore" bands included the Minutemen, Big Black, the Butthole Surfers, and Killdozer.

Part Two provides a genealogy of the Rolling Stones' "(I Can't Get No) Satisfaction," (aka "Satisfaction"). Chapter 3 focuses on rock and the Stones' original/standard version released in 1965. On the surface, "Satisfaction" is an indictment of conformity, consumer society, and mass culture that has been canonized as one of rock's defining "oppositional" statements. However, the underlying theme of "Satisfaction"—like many of the Stones' songs—is male sexual gratification and alienation. In this respect, "Satisfaction" laid the groundwork for subsequent Stones' songs and imagery, pursuing related themes of alienation, sex, power, and apocalypse that reached a head at the disastrous Altamont festival in 1969.

Chapter 4 considers soul music through Otis Redding's cover of "Satisfaction" which was also released in 1965. As rock became the generational signifier for young white people in the 1960s, rock and its black music components developed a complicated relationship as rock consciously adopted white music elements to establish "artistic legitimacy" (i.e., American folk music with Bob Dylan, Continental modernism with the Beatles). In turn, black popular music was partially represented by Motown Records and Stax Records as rival brands of soul music. In this context, Redding's cover of "Satisfaction" translated the political implications from a rock song performed by white Englishmen in the emerging counterculture era to a soul song performed by a black, southern American during the civil rights movement.

Chapter 5 turns to punk and Devo's anti-cover of "Satisfaction" released in 1978. As a post-punk band informed by art rock as much as punk rock, Devo's deconstruction of "Satisfaction" deliberately turned the song on its head musically and ideologically; in doing so, Devo's version of "Satisfaction" represented a broader attack on rock ideology and its tenets of "authentic" American roots music sources, anti-artiness, and individualist non-conformity rebellion. At the same time, Devo became increasingly contradictory as they negotiated their cynicism toward rock music as a form of oppositional culture (namely 1960s counterculture), their own self-assumed subversive status, their blatant cultural opportunism, and their drive toward increasingly commercial music.

Conversely, chapter 6 addresses pop music through Britney Spears' much-maligned cover of "Satisfaction" released in 2000 and her controversial rise to stardom around the marketing of teen sexuality. Spears translated "Satisfaction" into a teen pop-dance number from the perspective of a teenage woman—Spears was 19 when the song was released—representing *her* alienated relationship to mass culture; by extension, it served as a response to the Stones' musical representation of alienation. To this extent, and whether intended or not, Spears' version of "Satisfaction" not only jeopardized the artificial cultural binary constructed around rock (authentic, masculine, opposition) and pop (inauthentic, feminine, conformity); it also critiqued the commodity function of *all* brands of popular music.

Part Three considers cover songs around the politics of gender and sexuality, race, the nation-state, and generations. Building on the comparison between the Stones' and Spears' versions of "Satisfaction," chapter 7 analyzes four cover songs around gender and sexual politics. The first is Led Zeppelin's "Whole Lotta Love" (1969)—arguably the archetypal cock rock song—and saxophonist King Curtis' "psychedelic soul" version from 1970. While both versions can be read as a representation of sexual intercourse from the masculine perspective, the concern of Led Zeppelin is the struggle to maintain and ultimately sustain phallic potency whereas King Curtis' version depicts intercourse from "start to finish," culminating in male orgasm and depletion of phallic might. The second is Van Halen's cover of the Kinks' "You Really Got Me." As first recorded by the Kinks in 1964, "You Really Got Me" was a rudimentary rock song about masculine insecurity and powerlessness in romantic relationships at a time when rock ideology had yet to consolidate its worldview around "hipness," where machismo, male chauvinism, and outright sexism became the norm. Covered by Van Halen in 1978, "You Really Got Me" was translated into an overbearing "cock rock" celebration of male domination over women, serving to both reinforce the sexism of rock ideology while acting as an implicit response to the feminist movement that became central to 1970s politics. The third case study is James Brown's funk classic "Sex Machine" (1971) that became the subject of anti-cover treatment by the British postpunk group Flying Lizards in 1984. While Brown's version uses the ideal of sex as a musical basis for a homosocial celebration of male sexuality, the Flying Lizards' version served as a mordant critique of the fantasy versus reality of sex. Fourth is Kim Wilde's synthpop/Hi-NRG disco version of "You Keep Me Hangin' On" (1986) in comparison to the Supremes' Motown symphonic soul original version (1966) and Vanilla Fudge's psychedelic–hard rock cover (1967). While musically quite different, both the Supremes and Vanilla Fudge versions are desperate pleas for relationship liberation from the respective positions of a dominated woman and a victimized man. Wilde's icy version becomes a resigned rumination on gender and relationship inequality that implicitly tackles the issue of domestic abuse.

Taking up issues first examined in chapter 4, chapter 8 provides three case studies of folk and rock songs initially done by white performers and subsequently covered by American black jazz and soul music performers from the years 1969 to 1972, a time span marked by intense political friction along racial and generational lines. First is jazz bagpipe player Rufus Harley's cover of the anti-war chestnut "Where Have All the Flowers Gone?" as it converted the melancholy peachiness of previous folk versions into a dissonant, jazz-funk dirge. Harley's version functioned as a critique of the human casualties of the modern military war machine and, more implicitly, the status of the American nation-state entering the 1970s with the issues that spurred the crises of the 1960s still unresolved. The second is the Isley Brothers' soul-rock cover of counterculture icons Crosby, Stills, Nash and Young's folk-rock anthem "Ohio," a denouncement of the killing of four students at Kent State University by the Ohio National Guard during an anti-war demonstration in 1970. In their cover version, the Isley Brothers paired "Ohio" in a medley with Jimi Hendrix's "Machine Gun," a song about the Vietnam War. A tense negotiation is constructed around a song originally performed by white musicians about a massacre of white students at an anti-war demonstration on the home front and a rock song originally performed by black musicians about the carnage of war where African Americans constituted a disproportional percentage of casualties. The third case study is the Four Tops' Motown reworking of English progressive rock in covering the Moody Blues' "A Simple Game." In doing so, the Four Tops changed the Moody Blues' idealistic message of achieving a better tomorrow and utopian community through heightened individual and metaphysical awareness into an anthem of racial and economic equality, rising out of the ghettos and poverty, and changing present social conditions.

Chapter 9 focuses on the Slovenian "retro avant-garde" industrial band Laibach and their album *NATO* (1994), comprised entirely of anti-covers of songs relating to the theme of war. Laibach specializes in a radical deconstruction of original and/or standard versions of songs through a *détournement* of classical music, disco, heavy metal, industrial music, military marches, punk, rock, and techno. On *NATO*, anti-covers were employed to analyze the historical and political situation of Europe in the early 1990s: the collapse of the Soviet Union, the triumph of the Western nation-states in the Cold War, the formation of the European Union, the reconfiguration of Eastern Europe, and the Yugoslav Wars. While the deliberate musical and ideological perplexities of Laibach have prompted accusations of nationalist extremism, Stalinism, and fascism, Laibach and specifically *NATO* can be read as not only a situationist study of the totalitarian aspects of popular music and society, but as commentary on both the Western and Eastern blocs in the immediate wake of a post–Cold War, post–Soviet Europe.

Chapter 10 discusses the growing crisis of rock music. Over the course of 60-plus years, rock has become part of dominant culture, and as rock becomes more "Establishment," it steadfastly self-defines itself as "anti–Establishment." Frank Sinatra's cover of the Beatles' "Something" became an initial point of convergence between counterculture and mainstream culture at a time of widespread generational divisiveness. In the context of Sinatra and the Beatles finding common cultural ground, the chapter examines how older, mainstream performers tackled pop and rock music in their own musical terms in the late 1960s and beyond. While some of the results were innovative and intriguing, others were simply woeful but redeemed around the aesthetics of Camp (e.g., the *Golden Throats* anthologies). In 1991, Nirvana's *Nevermind* was a hybrid of punk, pop, and metal that served as the dernier cri of rock rebellion, and "Alternative" soon became a dominant and profitable rock subgenre in the 1990s. In response, mainstream performers tackled rock music through vastly different approaches and receptions. One was Pat Boone's big band covers of heavy metal songs on *In a Metal Mood: No More Mr. Nice Guy* (1997), specifically focusing on Boone's cover of Deep Purple's "Smoke on the Water" and the issue of "camping" versus Camp. The other was Johnny Cash's sparse country-folk *American Recordings* series (1994–2010), with particular attention placed on Cash's celebrated cover of Nine Inch Nails' "Hurt" as it became the musical epitaph for Cash's storied career.

Over the years of pursuing independent scholarship in cultural studies, popular music has increasingly become an object of study as much as something to be enjoyed. Indeed, the study of popular music in all of its various forms has become a crucial part of the enjoyment. I can "appreciate" Laibach and Britney Spears for some very different reasons and for some of the same reasons as well. My critical approach to popular music is less concerned with the aesthetic superiority of "the old" versus "the new" and more concerned with the historical and political questions of "then" and "now." More specifically, the issue is how popular music is both a product and producer of ideology in a specific social context. From specific songs to overall genres, popular music functions as a multiplicity of competing cultural discourses, and cover songs chart the tensions between "the same old song" while the same old song can be continually reconfigured. In short, the song *doesn't* remain the same.

Part One

Judging a Song by Its Cover

1

National Anthems: "The Star-Spangled Banner"

Jimi Hendrix (Woodstock, 1969)

As the official national anthem of the United States, "The Star-Spangled Banner" is the musical signifier of America as a nation-state. The music was derived from "To Anacreon in Heaven," attributed to John Stafford Smith ca. the 1760s, and used for a number of popular patriotic songs. One was "The Star-Spangled Banner," with the lyrics being the first stanza of Francis Scott Key's poem "Defence of Fort McHenry," written after Key witnessed an unsuccessful British naval assault during the War of 1812. Hence, the lyrical subject of "The Star-Spangled Banner" is American triumph in warfare.

"The Star-Spangled Banner" raises difficulties as being a "populist" anthem musically as well as lyrically. Patriotic songs like "America the Beautiful" and "God Bless America" are written within a vocal range of slightly over an octave, and both are in 4/4 or "common time," the time signature most often used in popular music (pop, rock, punk, country, disco, heavy metal, etc.). The melody and lyrics to both songs are relatively easy to remember, and both can be completed while sung in a relaxed tempo within 45 seconds to one minute.[1] Lyrically, both songs offer general praise of America with an emphasis on landscape grandeur rather than military conflict. In contrast, "The Star-Spangled Banner" is in 3/4 or "waltz time," which is outside the 4/4 comfort zone of popular music, and requires a vocal range of approximately 1.5 octaves to perform and hit the notes correctly. The lyrics are much more poetically stylized and can be difficult to remember; they are also cumbersomely set to a preexisting song, which results in some highly forced phrasing and transitions. "The Star-Spangled Banner" is also longer than the average national anthem or patriotic song. If sung at the same tempo as "America the

Beautiful" or "God Bless America," "The Star-Spangled Banner" takes about 1'20" seconds to complete.

Even for a trained singer, the national anthem can be difficult to perform.[2] Flubbed or unconventional performances can generate national controversies. At the 2011 Super Bowl, Christina Aguilera sang a live, blues-gospel–influenced a cappella version; she botched the lyrics at a couple of points, and her performance was roundly criticized for not only being an artistic failure but a moment that dishonored America. In 1968, singer-guitarist José Feliciano performed it before game 5 of the World Series as a slow, acoustic ballad drawing from blues, jazz, and Latin music. Amid the unrest and volatility of the late 1960s, Feliciano's untraditional version was viewed as an inherently political statement and therefore unpatriotic. In short, *messing up* or *messing with* "The Star-Spangled Banner" become equally offensive acts of musical civil disobedience.

One of the most controversial and legendary performances of "The Star-Spangled Banner" was Jimi Hendrix's version at the Woodstock Festival in August of 1969—the final year of a politically turbulent decade marked by assassinations, racial strife, the Generation Gap, and the war in Vietnam. Between 300,000 and 400,000 people attended Woodstock, far more than promoters expected. Nonetheless, as William L. O'Neill wrote in 1971, "People stripped down, smoked pot, and turned on with nary a discouraging word, so legend has it. Afterward the young generally agreed it was a beautiful experience proving their moral superiority. Even the police were impressed by the public's order (a result of their wisely deciding not to enforce the drug laws)."[3] Woodstock has since been constructed as the zenith of the counterculture and Hendrix's rendition of "The Star-Spangled Banner" a defining moment.

After Hendrix worked as a backup musician for the Isley Brothers, Little Richard, and James Brown, the Jimi Hendrix Experience was formed in 1966 as a power trio drawing from hard rock, blues, funk, psychedelia, and jazz. The lineup consisted of Hendrix on lead guitar and lead vocals, Noel Redding on bass, and Mitch Mitchell on drums: a then-unheard-of arrangement featuring a black American as the star backed by white English musicians. While Hendrix was the musical and visual focal point, Redding and Mitchell were a formidable rhythm section akin to Cream or the Who. Rather than maintaining a straightforward rhythmic pace (e.g., the Rolling Stones or the Ramones), the bass and drums became auxiliary soloing instruments while they maintained driving propulsion.

Along with his sheer skill on the guitar, Hendrix used overdriven amplification and effects pedals (fuzz, wah-wah, phase-shifting, octave doubling, etc.) to produce a barrage of unprecedented sounds from the electric guitar. Rather than avoiding dissonance ("sour notes" in the riffs and solos) and potential noise that could be produced on electric guitar (feedback, string scrapings, etc.), Hendrix used them as compositional and improvisational tools. As much as his technical prowess and technological innovations, Hendrix also brought an unprecedented level of sexuality to rock. While Elvis was risqué, Hendrix bordered on the obscene. In concert, Hendrix played guitar as if he were physically copulating with it by thrusting his hips and crotch against the guitar body, playing guitar with his teeth rather than his picking hand, and playing guitar in a variety of contorted "positions" (behind his back, between his legs, etc.)—all of which produced new noise potentialities from the guitar. His cover of the Troggs' "Wild Thing" that closed his set at the Monterey Pop Festival in 1967 became one of the more intense examples.

In this respect, Hendrix was integral in constructing rock's tradition of the "guitar hero" and establishing the relationship between electric guitar, masculinity, and sexuality around what Steve Waksman termed the "technophallus":

> The electric guitar as a technophallus represents a fusion of man and machine, an electric appendage that allowed Hendrix to display his musical prowess and, more symbolically, his sexual prowess. Through the medium of the electric guitar, Hendrix was able to transcend human potential in both musical and sexual terms. The dimension of exaggerated phallic display was complemented by the new sonic possibilities offered by the instrument, possibilities he employed with aggressive creativity. Hendrix's achievement therefore rested on a combination of talent and technology in which the electric guitar allowed him to construct a superhuman persona founded on the display of musical and sexual mastery.[4]

While Waksman's analysis is productive, it does bear some examination. To be sure, Hendrix's "fusion of man and machine" entailed a degree of phallic symbolism ingrained into the electric guitar. However, the relationship between Hendrix and the electric guitar could also be read as a man-machine sexual encounter. Given the normative heterosexuality and masculinity of rock, this codes the electric guitar as the *feminine* partner to the masculine Hendrix as he stridently coaxed and prodded the guitar into producing an array of electronic sounds. While rock ideology constructed the electric guitarist as much as the electric guitar as masculine during the 1960s (an issue returned to throughout this project), the "cock rock" of the 1970s eventually placed a much greater emphasis on the electric guitar as an expressly phallic symbol and a signifier of masculine mastery and power, specifically Jimmy Page and especially Eddie Van Halen (discussed in chapter 7).

The Jimi Hendrix Experience disbanded shortly before Woodstock, and Hendrix assembled a new band named Gypsy Sun and Rainbows, consisting of Mitchell, bassist Billy Cox, second guitarist Larry Lee, and percussionists Juma Sultan and Jerry Valez. Dressed in white shirt with long-fringed sleeves, blue jeans, and a red headband—"red, white, and blue"—Hendrix and the band performed a two-hour set to close the festival with songs extended and connected by long and often jarring improvisational passages. Approximately 90 minutes into the set, Hendrix launched into an incendiary (pun intended) 3'42" version of "The Star-Spangled Banner" done as a solo instrumental save for the free-drumming interjections by Mitchell. As an "anti-cover" (a concept discussed at length in the next chapter), Hendrix converted "The Star-Spangled Banner" from a patriotic anthem celebrating military victory into a protest song against the war in Vietnam. The negation of discernible meter and use of dissonance and noise as violent disruptions in the song act as aural signifiers of gunfire, bombs, and rockets, particularly between 1'11" and 2'28", which becomes a salvo of atonal runs, drastic tremolo bar modulations, tone-cluster guitar chords, and feedback; in a touch of morbid comedy, from 2'46" to 2'50" Hendrix deftly inserts the melody of "Taps." However, it is not a piece of "noise music" per se (e.g., Merzbow or Wolf Eyes), in that the melody of "The Star-Spangled Banner" is clearly discernible as much as it is radically disfigured. In other words, there is a *collision* between music and noise.[5] Beyond the immediate critique of Vietnam, Hendrix's version addresses the status of a liberal-democratic society in America seemingly falling apart in the late 1960s and what could emerge from the potential wreckage. Paul Hegarty argued that Hendrix suggested a

> political alternative otherwise absent from the relentless positivity of the original, not only because it veers between "correct notes" and bent, feedback, or distorted sounds, but because it cuts between crisply played, discrete notes and the noise implications of those notes. It also cuts between drift and cutting, further enhanced by Mitch Mitchell's interventions on drums.... *Hendrix and the State drift into one another, signaling the potential for community Woodstock saw itself as being able to spread.*[6]

By reading "The Star-Spangled Banner" as one part of the whole of Hendrix's performance instead of isolating it and thereby constructing it into a song as art object (i.e., a track off a Hendrix "best of" CD), Hegarty contended Hendrix's performance bordered on free jazz in that the collective improvisation did not simply push songs into new musical territories but jeopardized the boundaries between music and noise, composition and improvisation, soloist and band, band and audience, and ultimately individual and community (issues returned to in chapter 8). Indeed, the matter was raised by Hendrix himself. Ten and a half minutes into an extended version of "Voodoo Child (Slight Return)"—the song that preceded "The Star-Spangled Banner"—Hendrix announced to the remaining Woodstock audience, "They can leave if they want—'we're only jamming.'"[7]

While Hegarty considers this comment "disingenuous"—Hendrix, like Cream and the Grateful Dead, developed audience expectations that extensive improvisation could and would occur in concert rather than a straight run-through of the hit songs—it is possible to read Hendrix's comment as a point of rupture. Hendrix's performance of the "The Star-Spangled Banner" is often constructed as the exclamation point concluding the festival around what Abbie Hoffman rhapsodized in *Woodstock Nation* as "the birth of the Woodstock Nation and the death of the American Dinosaur."[8] In the context of Hendrix's overall performance, one could also suggest that "The Star-Spangled Banner" ended Woodstock with a question mark. On one hand, Hendrix's appropriating the "The Star-Spangled Banner" as the symbol of the State represented a symbolic takeover and the dispersal of the Woodstock Nation back into American society as a force of political change. On the other, "The Star-Spangled Banner" represents the intrusion of the State and the dissipation of the Woodstock Nation back into their roles as students and workers in Establishment society: not as a proliferation, but a withering away.

Infusing the national anthem with dissonance and noise to thoroughly distort the music (both tonally and electronically), Hendrix musically disordered the national anthem into a representation of the social disorder that wracked America in the late 1960s. "The Star-Spangled Banner" became the moment the Woodstock Nation and the State collided and struggled in a time of immense political crisis. Shortly after Hendrix's death, Robert Hilburn eulogized him in a piece for the *Los Angeles Times* (October 4, 1970): "Hendrix's music was perfectly tied to the times. It was a troubled, violent, confused searching music on one hand; and assertive, demanding, triumphant, sensual music on the other."[9] As much as Hilburn historicizes Hendrix as "perfectly tied to the times," he points out the dialectic of Hendrix. Jacques Attali contended, "More than colors and forms, it is sounds and their arrangements that form societies. With noise is born disorder and its opposite: the world. With music is born power and its opposite: subversion."[10] The problem becomes minimizing the *noise* of Hendrix's version of "The Star-Spangled Banner" as it assails "the relentless positivity of the original" and overemphasizing the *music* of Hendrix's version of "The Star Spangled Banner" as it prescribes a "political alternative" of counterculture idealism that assumes its own relentless positivity which, over the course of history, becomes manifest as cultural nostalgia and political romanticism to sustain the counterculture myth. Put another way, instead of determining how the noise generated by Hendrix expressed a dialectical struggle between the Woodstock Nation and the State *within* "The Star-Spangled Banner," Hendrix's version is canonized as oppositional rock music to construct a binary between the State (national anthem, Establishment, American Dinosaur) versus the counterculture (anti-cover of the national anthem, anti–Establishment, Woodstock Nation). As a product and producer of ideology, music becomes the means for positing, establishing, and maintaining a "correct" social order whether liberal-democratic, communist, anarchist, or fascist (concerns directly confronted by Laibach, discussed in chapter 9).

Susan McClary wryly noted that the challenge Attali posed to orthodox Western musicology was "his penchant for sullying the purity of pitch structures with references to violence, death, and (worst of all) money."[11] If noise is the force of social disorder and music is the force of social order, the most effective conversion is turning noise into a music commodity. As Attali put it, "The Jimi Hendrix Experience inspires dreams, but it does not give one the strength to put its message into practice, to use the musician's noise to compose one's own order. One participates in a pop music festival only to be totally reduced to the role of an extra in the record or film that finances it."[12] Indeed, the manufacture of the myth of the "Woodstock Nation" was part and parcel of the marketing of Woodstock into counterculture mythology through cultural commodity.[13] In fairness, this owed to economic realities. Under pressure from activists like Abbie Hoffman and the underground press who threatened boycotts and demonstrations for what they considered a capitalist exploitation of youth culture, Woodstock promoters spent and additional $10,000 for food supplies, medical services, and political organizers to help with crowd control through consciousness raising. Realizing that security measures were woefully inadequate, promoters simply decided to make Woodstock a free concert. When services became exhausted and the roads proved impassable due to the glut of parked cars in the surrounding streets, charted helicopters maintained necessary supplies at considerable expense to the promoters. As important, the much-despised Establishment adopted a laissez-faire approach and let the festival run its course. Had this perfect storm of cooperation not occurred, Woodstock "would have become *Lord of the Flies*."[14]

In short, Woodstock made counterculture history—or, more correctly, manufactured a counterculture mythology—but the promoters lost over a million dollars. A concert film was a means to recoup some of the monetary losses.

However, the three-hour *Woodstock* (1970) glorified the festival and the historical moment while marginalizing the radical implications to the point that it became "the counterculture's *Triumph of the Will*."[15] Two accompanying soundtrack albums (the 1970 triple-album set *Woodstock* and the 1971 double-album set *Woodstock II*) were also part of marketing the Woodstock Nation. In the end, Woodstock may have represented a glimpse of a political alternative, but it was soon absorbed into the very system it ostensibly opposed. Whether or not music is oppositional cannot simply be determined by form and content, but by the degree to which the music is tied to a system it ostensibly opposes, though largely always already under the sway of a system it may oppose but cannot escape, let alone conquer.

Whitney Houston (Super Bowl XXV, 1991)

"The Star-Spangled Banner" is a staple of any sporting event, with the Super Bowl and its international TV audience being the most high-profile performance. As noted, Christina Aguilera's less-than-stellar rendition at the 2011 Super Bowl was roundly criticized as a performance that not only disgraced her, but America as a whole. In contrast, Whitney Houston's performance of the national anthem at the 1991 Super Bowl is considered one of the finest versions, if not the definitive version. In doing so, Houston's much-praised performance celebrated America at a specific moment of historical crisis: the 1991 Gulf War.

Whitney Houston's family was already established in the music industry. Her mother, Cissy Houston, was a well-known gospel singer, her first cousins were Dionne Warwick and Dee Dee Warwick, her godmother was Darlene Love, and Aretha Franklin was a family friend. In 1978, at the age of 15, Houston made her recording debut singing backup vocals on Chaka Kahn's song "I'm Every Woman."[16] Soon after, she made her lead vocal debut on the Michael Zager Band's disco song "Life's a Party." While Epic Records, Elektra Records, and Arista Records approached Huston with contracts, she gained initial career recognition as a fashion model and appeared in such magazines as *Cosmopolitan*, *Glamour*, and *Seventeen*.

In the aftermath of post-punk and the rise of postmodernism in the 1980s, eclecticism replaced traditionalism, and musicians were actively working across the diverse musical genres of avant-garde/experimental music, disco, funk, jazz, pop, punk, rock, soul, and non-western music. Material—a trio consisting of Michael Beinhorn (keyboards), Bill Laswell (bass), and Fred

Maher (drums)—were at the forefront of New York City's "mutant disco" scene ca. the early 1980s, harnessing elements of funk, rock, and free jazz. Following the departure of Maher and signing with Elektra Records, Material attempted a deconstruction of "art music" and "dance music" on their album *One Down* (1982) by drawing from a pool of well-known disco, soul, and jazz luminaries including guitarist Nile Rodgers and drummer Tony Thompson from Chic, former LaBelle vocalist Nona Hendryx, the World Saxophone Quartet's Oliver Lake, and free jazz legend Archie Shepp.

Also recruited to sing lead vocal on the song "Memories" was a then-unknown Whitney Houston. "Memories" was written in the 1960s by Hugh Hopper, best known as the bassist of Soft Machine from 1968 to 1973.[17] A melancholy 6/8 ballad, the standard version was performed by former Soft Machine drummer/vocalist Robert Wyatt and released as the B-side to his UK hit single cover of the Monkees' "I'm a Believer" (1974).[18] Known for his distinctive thin, wavering tenor, Wyatt performed the song with a backing of drums, bass, piano, string synths, and a violin solo that suggested an odd convergence of cocktail jazz and chamber music, with a haunting quality in keeping with the theme of recurring and often unshakable memories of lost love. Material converted the song from 6/8 into 4/4 with Houston's commanding soul-pop vocals alternating with Shepp's characteristically unsettling saxophone. Particularly in the latter half of the song, Houston's vocals become more "confident," and she begins to veer from the original melody in favor of her melismatic, virtuoso singing style while Shepp's saxophone responds with increasingly agitated atonal runs. While Wyatt's version suggests memory is inescapable, Material's version constructs a dialectical tension between Houston and Shepp. In what became a recurring theme in her work, Houston's soothing tonality signifies *triumph* (overcoming painful memories), while Shepp's jolting atonality signifies *struggle* (the difficulty if not impossibility of overcoming said memories).

While *One Down* failed commercially, it was critically well received and gave notice that Houston possessed immense vocal talent. Indeed, "Memories" severed as the prototype for Houston's specialty: the soul-pop ballad characterized by a tour de force vocal performance aimed at impressing listeners as much as moving them with an underlying message of personal victory over existing conditions. In 1983, Houston signed to Arista Records after being personally scouted by longtime label head Clive Davis. Working with established producers, session musicians, and songwriters, Houston's eponymous debut album was released in 1985. Embraced by record buyers and critics alike (*Rolling Stone* named it album of the year), it produced four hit singles. With the exception of the dance-pop song "How Will I Know," the hits were the lush soul-pop ballads "You Give Good Love," "Saving All My Love for You," and "Greatest Love of All," which proclaimed that the greatest love of all was the love of self rather than the love of someone else. An unabashed ode to individuality and self-determination by any means necessary at the height of Reaganism, the music video for "Greatest Love of All" served as a condensed version of the American Dream "success story." It begins with Houston in a black leather jacket performing the song in rehearsal to empty theater seats and midway through shifts to Houston performing the song in a sequined evening gown to a packed audience. Intercut is flashback footage of Houston as a child imagining a day she will be singing in the theater; in the finale, Houston's child "alter ego" walks on stage and merges into Houston as the singing star.

In November 1990, Houston's third album *I'm Your Baby Tonight* was released, and shortly thereafter Houston accepted the NFL's invitation to sing the national anthem at the 1991 Super Bowl. From the outset, Houston's version was not envisioned as a typical a cappella version but a trademark rendition along the lines of her signature ballads (i.e., "Greatest Love of All"). Working with her musical director Rickey Minor, there was a conscious effort to incorporate popular music genres like gospel, jazz, pop and soul as far as the vocals and structure; in doing so, the time signature was changed from 3/4 to 4/4. As well as providing the listener with a more familiar rhythmic pulse, this allowed extended room for Houston's patented melismatic style of singing and brief pauses between each line. Additionally, double-bassist John Clayton, an experienced musician in both classical and jazz music, was commissioned to provide an orchestral arrangement. The result was that Houston's version lasted 2'17"—noticeably longer than a typical performance.

On January 17, 1991, the United States entered the Gulf War to liberate Kuwait from Iraqi occupation with massive air strikes on Baghdad and other cities. It was the first large-scale U.S. military operation since the debacle of Vietnam, and there was considerable public trepidation that America would become involved in another lengthy military disaster. Ten days later, Houston performed the national anthem on the field of Tampa Stadium joined by members of the Florida Orchestra.[19] Like Hendrix, Houston wore "red, white, and blue" apparel although the political statement was similar yet different. Houston wore a white warm-up suit and headband with red and blue accents to not only signify patriotism but "athleticism" in terms of her characteristic vocal delivery. During her rendition of "The Star-Spangled Banner," TV cameras intercut between shots of Houston, flags representing the nation-states supporting U.S. military intervention, a close-up of a black soldier and a medium-close shot of a white soldier saluting, the stadium filled with flag-waving fans, and gigantic American flags on the stadium flagpoles. As Houston finished the song, the crowd erupted into mass cheering while Houston triumphantly pumped her fists in the air to signify victory—her vocal performance overcoming the song as well as a call for America to defeat Iraq—and a squadron of F-16 fighter jets flew over the stadium. It inevitably recalled a scene from *Triumph of the Will*.

Amid anxieties over the Gulf War, the performance was widely applauded. Even *Rolling Stone*, a magazine with decidedly liberal views as far as its journalism, placed Houston's version as the top of their "25 Most Memorable Music Moments in NFL History" list in 2003: "With America entangled in the Persian Gulf War ... Whitney Houston takes the stage and belts out a mind-blowing rendition of 'The Star-Spangled Banner,' bringing fans to their feet and tears to the eyes of many watching at home. Her singing ... stirs such patriotism that it's released as a single."[20] In fact, Houston's version hit the Billboard Top 20 and sold 750,000 in its first week of release. Amid the commercial and critical success, one of the few dissenting opinions offered was Jon Pareles in the *New York Times*:

> You've seen the timeworn 1960's image: Jimi Hendrix at Woodstock in 1969, playing "The Star-Spangled Banner" with screaming siren notes and blast of feedback that suggested the chaos of Vietnam bombing raids. Now that image has an unironic 1990's counterpart: Whitney Houston's "Star-Spangled Banner," sung live at the Super Bowl as the war against Iraq entered its second week. A full orchestra accompanies Ms. Houston's sinuous, sultry voice, which makes the national anthem voluptuous; under the last note is the whoosh of F-16 jets flying overhead.[21]

There is a considerable problem with Pareles' assessment. When Marvin Gaye performed the national anthem at the 1983 NBA All-Star Game accompanied by the drum track of his hit song "Sexual Healing," the initial controversy over the unconventional performance gave way to a much more complementary assessment that Gaye had managed to make the national anthem "sexy" and actually got people cheering, clapping, and even dancing en masse to the national anthem as a moment of collective libidinal release rather than stoically standing in ritual attention with little connect to the song or anyone else at the event. In this respect, Gaye as a male soul music icon infused the national anthem with an element of Hipness as the national anthem becomes a kind of symbolic make-out session for the body politic.

While Pareles is correct to the extent Hendrix's version can be read as an oppositional statement in using the guitar to produce noise signifying military massacres, the problem is that the "unironic counterpart" to Hendrix and his technophallic guitar becomes Houston and her "sinuous, sultry voice" that makes the national anthem "voluptuous." The upshot is that Houston's version as sung by a woman sexualizes the national anthem and by extension eroticizes military operations in the Gulf War. As a female pop icon, Houston assumes the role of "feminine" mass culture promoting acquiescent political conformity in support of a war through what amounts to political indoctrination via musical seduction (the gendering of mass culture and specifically pop music is returned to in chapter 6 and Britney Spears' cover of the Rolling Stones' "Satisfaction"). To be sure, Houston's version engages in bald ideological interpellation to the point of overdetermination, but *how* it does so is far more complicated that simply placing the blame on her vocals.

As noted, war is central to the "The Star-Spangled Banner" as a poem about a U.S. military victory during the War of 1812 set to music. The respective versions by Hendrix and Houston in two distinct historical eras provided two markedly different messages: Hendrix expressing dissent through cacophony and Houston cultivating unity through harmony. It is not that Houston single-handedly "makes the national anthem voluptuous" by the guile of her alluring vocals. Houston's version of "The Star-Spangled Banner" as a *whole* is permeated with a "seductive" grandeur where the vocal melody is continually compounded by a symphonic pomposity somewhere between John Phillip Sousa and John Williams. The organization of sound is empathetically musical and harmonious in its totality. In the context of the Gulf War, it attempts to overcome divisions between class, generations, race, and nations through a musical synthesis of musical genres within the national anthem (pop, soul, classical, gospel) in order to produce a unified home front in patriotic support for the war—a moment that the nationally televised performance more than reinforced. Musical harmony was the means, and social harmony was the end.

As much as Hendrix and Houston assess the specific issue of war in a specific historical moment of crisis, both versions offer a wider critique of America as a liberal-democratic society. Hendrix's version rejected tonality and meter in favor of feedback, microtonal bends, "wrong notes," and dissonant digressions in the song's melody while Mitch Mitchell interceded with furious drumrolls. By converting the national anthem into a piece saturated with noise, it became both a document and editorial in an era of cultural, political, and social disorder as the American nation-state was rupturing amid assassinations, race riots, mass protests, and overseas war. In its continual musical discord, Hendrix's version revealed the "real" of American life ca. 1969 rather than the ideological imaginary signified by the "relentless positivity" of the national anthem.

Conversely, Whitney Houston's rendition was a heavily orchestrated arrangement that combined symphonic force, soul passion, and schmaltz accessibility while Houston characteristically demonstrated her singing abilities not within but well *above* the musical framework. Theodor W. Adorno argued,

> *It is no accident that tonality was the musical language of the bourgeois era.* The harmony of the universal and the particular correspond to the classical liberal model of society. As in the latter, tonality, as the *invisible hand*, took over by means of the individual, spontaneous events, and over their heads. The universal resolution of tension that is effected is intended to make the sum, the balance of credits and debts, come out even. Homeostasis, balance, and the equivalency of credits and debts are immediately the same. *This model was never adequate to reality, but was to a large extent ideology.*[22]

Houston's version of "The Star-Spangled Banner" can also "correspond to the classical liberal model of society" with "tonality as the invisible hand ... never adequate to reality, but ... to a large extent ideology." With Houston's virtuosic vocal soaring above the musical setting of the national anthem, the voice signifies the superior and self-determined individual rising above the conditions of social existence to achieve personal success (i.e., "The Greatest Love of All"). Indeed, the voice becomes invested with the aura of individual triumph in private life as much as a call for national triumph in Iraq. Houston's version not only manifests collective patriotism but individual *mastery*. (In this respect, Eddie Van Halen's guitar solo showcase "Eruption" as a prelude to their cover of the Kinks' "You Really Got Me" is ideologically much closer to Houston's demonstration of mastery through technique than Hendrix's demolition of political stability through noise; see chapter 7).

While Whitney Houston emerged as one of the biggest stars in popular music during the 1980s, the dominant woman performer was Madonna, whose brands of "Boy Toy," "Material Girl," and "Blonde Ambition" feminism focused on celebrating sexual liberation along with capitalist enrichment. In doing so, Madonna could be the subversive foil to the social conservatism of Reaganism while embracing the economic ideology of neoliberalism for all it was worth. As noted, Houston was a former teen fashion model, and her marketing was around images that minimized female sexuality and even racial identity in favor of class in *both* senses of the word.[23] Houston's music and image in the 1980s signified a refined, bourgeois elegance. In 1991, Houston became synonymous with "The Star-Spangled Banner" precisely at the twilight of the Reagan Revolution, the collapse of Soviet communism, and the dawn of the

New Democrats personified by Bill Clinton, offering the electorate a "new and improved" business-friendly, centrist, reduced-government brand of progressive neoliberalism at the expense of 1960s liberalism. While Hendrix signified a counterculture era of utopian ideals coming to grips with political realities, Houston signified a post–Cold War neoliberal era of global capitalism whose utopian promise was seemingly unlimited.

2

The "Anti-Cover": Punk and the Avant-Grade

Sid Vicious: "My Way" (The Great Rock 'n' Roll Swindle, 1980)

While punk exploded onto the UK music scene in 1976, in no small part due to the Ramones' debut concerts in England that summer, the often antagonistic relationship between NYC punk and UK punk can be dated to late 1974, before "punk" technically existed. The New York Dolls' second album *Too Much Too Soon* (1974) floundered commercially and the band was in severe disarray when British fashion boutique owner Malcolm McLaren assumed an advisory role. Previously involved with the King Mob anarchist-situationist group, McLaren decided to change the band's image from an androgynous, trashy glam band to a radical Left political group by, as New York Dolls drummer Jerry Nolan recounted, "Dressing us up in matching red leather suits and playing in front of a giant communist flag. It was so stupid!"[1] Within months of McLaren's involvement, the New York Dolls were effectively finished when Nolan and guitarist Johnny Thunders quit midway through a disastrous tour of the southern states in 1975. McLaren was largely blamed for single-handedly killing a band that had become almost sacred in the NYC music community. He was vilified even more for appropriating the music and imagery of the nascent NYC punk scene upon his return to England and parlaying that into the international phenomenon of the Sex Pistols. As McLaren later admitted, "The Sex Pistols were identical to the New York Dolls."[2]

As noted, in 1974 McLaren was co-owner of the "anti-fashion" boutique SEX, and his employees and clientele became the core of the punk movement in London. Before relocating to America for his dubious stint with the New York Dolls, McLaren assisted a band called the Strand (a.k.a. the Swankers), who were regulars at SEX. At the time, the Strand's lineup was vocalist Steve Jones, guitarist Wally Nightingale, and drummer Paul Cook; McLaren introduced them to bassist Glen Matlock, a part-time SEX salesperson. Returning to England in 1975, and after continual urging from Jones, McLaren agreed to manage the Strand. He quickly exercised his authority by changing their name to the Sex Pistols and ousting Nightingale. Jones became the guitarist and John Lydon, a disheveled non-musician who frequented SEX, became lead vocalist after an impromptu audition singing along to Alice Cooper's "I'm Eighteen" that had little timbre but a lot of venom. He was rechristened "Johnny Rotten," and the rest became a controversial and convoluted history.

The UK punk scene was as musically traditionalist as NYC punk, but more explicitly left wing and class conscious. More correctly, it was consciously "proletariat" as opposed to "lower class"—the difference between the urban guerrilla imagery of the Clash and the juvenile delinquent image of the Ramones. As an exaggerated representation of class politics, Dick Hebdige noted,

> Punk claimed to speak for the neglected constituency of white lumpen youth, but did so typically in the stilted language of glam and glitter rock—"rendering" working classness metaphorically in chains and hollow cheeks, "dirty" clothing (stained jackets, tarty see-through blouses), and rough and ready direction. Resorting to parody, [punk] described itself in bondage through an assortment of darkly comic signifiers.... Despite its proletarian accents, punk's rhetoric was steeped in irony.[3]

As much as class representation, UK punk self-defined itself as a complete historical break from the rock dinosaurs. In this respect, Hebdige pointed out that the subculture of British punk was produced by "combining elements drawn from a whole range of heterogeneous youth styles.... Punk reproduced the entire cultural history of post-war working-class youth culture in 'cut up' form, combining elements which had originally belonged to completely different epochs."[4] However, another "irony" of punk was that its incongruent assemblage of "heterogeneous youth styles" from "completely different epochs" quickly coalesced into a hegemonic movement demanding conformity and exclusive adherence to punk subculture regulations. Punk "anarchy" was saturated with codes of conduct in regard to what kinds of music could and could not be listened to—yet alone performed—as far as a select proto-punk and punk canon. Punk fashion was strictly codified as well: no long hair, no facial hair, and requisite fashion statements (leather jackets, torn jeans, combat boots, chains, spiked collars, and kitsch attire like dated suits, go-go boots, leopard skin, and miniskirts). Not coincidentally, McLaren's boutique became the premier place to buy punk fashion and accessories. Matlock later recounted, "When we started the Sex Pistols, we said we wanted loads of bands like us, but we didn't mean *exactly* like us."[5]

The great contradiction of punk was that it rejected the rock tradition while simultaneously embracing it. Early punk did not recognize the dilemma of tradition as expressed by Adorno: "To insist on the absolute absence of tradition is as naïve as obstinate insistence on it. Both are ignorant of the past that persists in their allegedly pure relation to the objects; both are unaware of the dust and debris which clouds their allegedly clear vision."[6] Punk categorically rejected the previous decade of rock ca. 1965–57 by nostalgically retreating to rock ca. 1955–65—excepting proto-punk bands like the Stooges and New York Dolls—rather than pursuing new musical directions. In this way, the role of tradition (as Adorno had it) was better expressed by the ethos of post-punk and how Gang of Four guitarist Andy Gill described the band's relationship to the 1970s hard rock band Free: "You could say that Free influenced the Gang of Four, but our approach was to take *that bit* but leave *that other ridiculous* bit out, or take that cliché and turn it inside out."[7] In the case of the Sex Pistols, if one subtracts Lydon's vituperative vocals and inflammatory lyrics, it becomes difficult to hear "Anarchy in the U.K." and "God Save the Queen" as much more than 1970s hard rock anthems.

Instead, the shock effect of punk, and especially the Sex Pistols, was manifest around the theory and praxis of the Situationist International—not surprising given McLaren's situationist background. The SI defined a "constructed situation" as "a moment in life concretely constructed by the collective organization of a unitary ambience and a game of events."[8] Moreover, the SI contended, "There is no such thing as situationism, which would mean a doctrine for interpreting certain conditions.... In this sense there can be no situationist painting or music, but only a situationist use of those means."[9] As a "situationist use of music," the Sex Pistols were a "game of events" in the theater of real life that ruptured the current status quo of rock music, rock ideology, and the record industry. Indeed, the "noise" produced by the Sex Pistols largely owed to their "situationist use of music" and a relentless execution of what McLaren pathetically attempted in his brief stint with the New York Dolls.[10] Rock has always been defined and self-defined as rough and rebellious, irreverent and insolent, and the Sex Pistols became a grotesque "serious-parody" of a rock-and-roll band. They exaggerated and exacerbated rock's imaginary subversive self-image into a repulsive real where, as Andrew Hussey suggested, "a perfect series of negative reversals had replaced politics with art ... the spectacle disrupted and faced with its own negative reflection."[11] Part of this "negative reversal" entailed a rejection of the rock ideology of the 1960s. "Peace and love" gave way to "anarchy," and "utopianism" gave way to "nihilism."

Drawing from the Stooges, the Sex Pistols converted concerts from spectacles to situations that could be unpredictable and even uncontrolled. The unwritten contract between performers giving the audience their money's worth and the audience passively enjoying the show was obliterated. As important as the onstage performance of punk, the *offstage* performances of punk by the Sex Pistols generated an ongoing public furor. In 1976, EMI terminated the band's contract after a profanity-laced BBC interview and reportedly badgering people at Heathrow Airport. After signing to and then being dropped by A&M in the same week, the music press floated rumored reports that other artists on the A&M roster pressured the label to dismiss the band; one name that repeatedly came up was progressive rock keyboardist Rick Wakeman, who consistently and vehemently denied the charges. In the process, the Sex Pistols pocketed around $250,000 in advance money from EMI and A&M. When a frustrated Matlock quit in early 1977, it was announced he was sacked for "liking the Beatles" and replaced by early UK punk-scene stalwart Sid Vicious, whose skill on bass was rudimentary (at best) but who was notorious for once assaulting *New Musical Express* journalist Nick Kent. The change guaranteed that the Sex Pistols would be more about generating controversy than producing music.[12]

Ironically, or perhaps not so ironically, the band next signed to Virgin Records, England's leading progressive rock label.[13] As much as capitalizing on the Sex Pistols controversy, it was Virgin's first major step in successfully rebranding itself into a punk-based label, well aware that many punk fans were previous art rock consumers rather than hard rock consumers (something confirmed by Lydon in his Capital Radio interview, discussed shortly). Released in June 1977, the infamous "God Save the Queen" single coincided with Queen Elizabeth's silver jubilee celebrations, and another inevitable media furor ensued after a situationist incident. A riverboat aptly named *Queen Elizabeth* was chartered to cruise the Thames River while a PA system blasted "Anarchy in the U.K." and "God Save the Queen." When the festivities got out of hand, the captain of the boat contacted police, who escorted them to shore and arrested several members of the Sex Pistols' entourage for disorderly conduct.

The ongoing pandemonium surrounding the Sex Pistols also delayed production of their long-anticipated album. *Never Mind the Bollocks, Here's the Sex Pistols* was not released until October of 1977, well after the debut records of other frontline UK punk bands the Damned and the Clash.[14] In fact, *Bollocks* appeared scarcely a month before the release of Wire's *Pink Flag*, arguably the first "post-punk" album as cogently reviewed by Robert Christgau (*The Village Voice*, 1978): "From a formal strategy almost identical to the Ramones, [Wire] deducts most of the melody to arrive at music much grimmer and more frightening." Moreover, the use of the word "bollocks"—the English equivalent of "bullshit"—violated the Indecent Advertisements Act of 1899; it generated more controversy and outrage but also limited the album's promotion in England. In a typical McLaren stratagem, rumors quickly circulated that the album was going to be recalled and issued with a different title and cover which immediately made *Bollocks* a potential "collector's item" that fueled demand even further (Virgin Records filed a court petition over the album cover title and eventually won a judgment that permitted wider advertising). Amid the hoopla, *Bollocks* topped the album charts in the UK. However, even though punk was front and center in rock's critical discourses in America, in particular *Creem* magazine, punk was only generating a small but dedicated following. *Bollocks* failed to crack the Top 100 in America.[15]

By the time the American tour started, the growing stagnation of early punk as a musical genre and the continual need to intensify the "shock effect" virtually guaranteed that the entire project would end in bedlam. McLaren booked much of the tour in southern cities where they had little if any fan base and performances were played in the close confines of smaller clubs. Jim Mendiola described the show at Randy's Rodeo in San Antonio, Texas, on January 8, 1978:

> Johnny Rotten wore a T-shirt depicting two cowboys having sex [and] taunted the crowd, calling them all "fucking cowboy faggots." Aluminum cans and Lone Star longnecks instantly rained the stage and continued throughout the entire set. One irate fan attempted to climb the stage and assault [Sid] Vicious [who] cracked his bass guitar over the fan's head.... Forget the Alamo. On January 8, 1978, real San Antonio history was made.[16]

As well as the hostility directed at the audiences (fans and foes alike), Vicious was barely able to perform on stage, let alone tour, due to a debilitating heroin addiction. An irritated and increasingly ostracized Lydon was at considerable odds with McLaren and the rest of the band. The tour culminated with a dismal performance at San Francisco's Winterland Ballroom that famously concluded with Lydon asking the audience a rhetorical question—"Ever get the feeling that you've been cheated?"—before storming off the stage. Lydon effectively quit the Sex Pistols that night.

Undeterred, McLaren stated that "if Rotten is the voice of punk, then Vicious is the attitude." Indeed, Vicious was more than willing to perform punk offstage as much as onstage until the inevitable final curtain. Vicious' girlfriend Nancy Spungen was found stabbed to death on October 12, 1978; Viscous was arrested and charged with second-degree murder (he died before the case could go to trial). A week later, Vicious attempted suicide and was committed to Bellevue psychiatric hospital. Following his release, Vicious was arrested on another assault charge in December and spent almost two months in Riker's Island until he was released on bail. The next morning, Vicious was found dead of a heroin overdose. As cliché as it sounds, his death on February 2, 1979, also signified the end of the early punk era.

Amid the eventual tragedy of Sid Vicious, there was a morbid farce in Vicious' punk anti-cover of Frank Sinatra's "My Way" as part of the Sex Pistols' mockumentary film *The Great Rock 'n' Roll Swindle*. Much of the filming and recording was done in the first half of 1978, and Vicious' single version of "My Way" was originally released that summer. However, the project was effectively shelved in the wake of Vicious' considerable legal and personal difficulties. The soundtrack was eventually released by Virgin in 1979—three weeks after Vicious' death—and the film in 1980. It largely amounted to McLaren's soapbox for how he masterminded the whole Sex Pistols' project and effortlessly manipulated the whole of the recording industry, the media, and the audience.[17] In this context, the version discussed is the one that appears in *Swindle* in that the visual performance of "My Way" is equally important to the music as far as encapsulating the early punk era.

Opening with marquees of the Olympia Theater in Paris advertising a performance by Sid Vicious, after being introduced by an emcee in a tuxedo, Vicious staggers down a neon staircase until he reaches a microphone stand at center stage. This is intercut with bourgeois concertgoers dressed like they are attending an upscale supper-club concert or the opera. The song begins with piano and lush strings as Vicious intentionally (one hopes) warbles the first verse hopelessly out of tune; his abysmally humorous crooning is almost drowned out by the enthusiastic sounds of the cheering audience. The song then shifts into a straightforward punk version of the song with Vicious adopting the sneering, shouting vocal style that became a staple of early punk. Musically, it also reflects the strengths and limitations of punk. It is exhilarating in its ferocity and hilarious in its flippancy while it is extremely unadventurous musically and demonstrates the extent to which punk had become predictably formulaic by 1978: the requisite eighth-note guitar and bass barrage driven by a steady backbeat as it otherwise faithfully follows the chord changes and song structure of the Sinatra version. The key difference is that the string accompaniment continues throughout "My Way" to deftly parody the swelling orchestra in the Sinatra version, and the lead guitar parodies heavy metal guitar soloing.[18] The juxtaposition of the guitar-bass-drum punk attack and the schmaltzy strings produces a sardonic and sinister tension as a convergence of punk and MOR that ultimately commented on the problematic status of punk. Indeed, "My Way" as performed in *Swindle* became a commentary on how rapidly punk nihilism as oppositional culture was assimilated into bourgeois culture and how punk could react.

At several points there are improvised deviations from the original lyrics, including obscenities which are obscured by boosting the sounds of the cheering audience. Vicious' performance is intercut with reaction shots of members of the audience—including a woman who more than resembles Queen Elizabeth—marveling at Vicious' rendition of "My Way" while a man dressed in the closest thing to standardized "punk" fashion watches with an incredulous stare. After Vicious finishes the song, he pulls a pistol out of his unkempt dinner jacket and fires it into the audience, killing several concertgoers. He then gives them the two-finger salute (the British equivalent of giving someone the middle finger) and saunters offstage.

The final irony is not simply in the punk defilement of "My Way" but how *both* versions of the song became crucial in constructing a cultural mythology around the performer. Sheldon Shiffer noted,

> Both songs personify a subject telling his story of punishment for his originality and the failure to earn fair rewards for his efforts.... [Sinatra] invest[s] the listening-subject ... with hope of eventual prosperity, loyalty to socially established ideas, and respect for the listener as judge. The Vicious recording however, disparages those past ideas for failing to deliver, and as the victim of failure, his character wants vengeance.[19]

Frank Sinatra's version solidified his mystique as the unrepentant individual pursuing the American Dream on his terms, and his victory amid failure was that there were no compromises and no regrets. Sid Vicious' version constructed its own inscrutability of the equally unrepentant punk hell-bent on a nihilistic death trip. A leading theorist of the Situationist International, Raoul Vaneigem, wrote,

> Razonov's definition of nihilism is best: "The show is over. The audience gets up to leave their seats. Time to collect their coats and go home. They turn around ... no more coats and no more home." Nihilism is born of the collapse of myth. When a mythical system enters into contradiction with economic and social reality a gulf opens between the way people live and the prevailing explanation of the world, which is now completely inadequate. All traditional values are sucked into the abyss and destroyed.[20]

Simon Frith noted that the shared interest of the situationists and punks was the "politics of everyday life, the aesthetics of boredom. McLaren sought to turn spectacle—the passively experienced structure of reality that we, as consumers, live—into situation, the structure blown up, the rules made clear, the possibilities for action and desire exposed."[21] The Sex Pistols' mission—or at least McLaren's—was demolishing a rock mythology that by the 1970s had become an imaginary dead end rather than a real avenue for youth rebellion (dismantling the structure of rock music form was quite another matter). Constructed as rock's "negative reversal," the Sex Pistols exposed the extent to which rock was an integral part of the system rather than inherently opposed to it.

As the Sex Pistols ceased being situation and became part of the spectacle, Vicious' performance of "My Way" in *Swindle* became a moment where punk had to establish its own mythology around Vicious as the nihilistic supra-rebel obliterating the status quo until death do them part. While Vicious became punk's tragic hero, McLaren used *Swindle* to explode the myth of punk as subversive culture by cynically claiming it was all a situationist scam to line his wallet from the outset. If the Sex Pistols' project began by proclaiming "Anarchy in the U.K.," McLaren's concluding axiom became "cash from chaos." McLaren ended the situation with swindle, and in demystifying the punk movement as it was becoming a new myth of youth culture, punk became the highest form of cultural opportunism as much as cultural opposition.[22]

The Residents: **The Third Reich and Roll *(1976)***

One unintended aspect of the punk movement and especially the shift toward musical experimentation with post-punk by the end of the 1970s was that it produced a more hospitable cultural climate for avant-garde rock bands. However, the term "post-punk" is something of a misnomer as far as establishing a definitive break between the early punk era ca. 1975–78 and a post-punk era ca. 1978–81 dominated by punk bands working in more avant-garde, experimental, and, yes, "arty" musical terrain. In England, "post-punk" in theory if not praxis originated in July of 1977. With the Sex Pistols nothing short of Britain's international popular music disgrace, Capital Radio aired a 90-minute special, *The Punk and His Music*. It featured an extended interview with John Lydon, who bemoaned the current state of punk as an already formulaic and largely exhausted genre, and he played selections from some of his favorite albums which included art rock by the likes of Can, Captain Beefheart, and Peter Hammill. As Simon Reynolds put it, "Just about everything Lydon played on Capital Radio contradicted the punk myth of the early seventies as a musical wasteland. If that wasn't treasonous enough, Lydon broke with his Malcolm McLaren-scripted role as [a] cultural terrorist by effectively outing himself as an aesthete."[23] Lydon's subsequent band, Public Image Ltd. (officially abbreviated "PiL"), eventually recorded one of the landmark post-punk albums, *The Metal Box* (1979). The influence of Can could charitably be described as pervasive in PiL's use of simple, repetitive bass-drum rhythm patterns (highly influenced by disco and reggae), atonal guitar and keyboard interjections, and vocals that were not so much sung but chanted, moaned, and caterwauled.

Echoing Lydon's criticism of punk traditionalism was Mark Perry, a young bank clerk who was profoundly affected by the Ramones. In 1976, Perry founded the fanzine *Sniffin' Glue*, which was to the London punk movement what the fanzine *Punk* was to the NYC punk scene, and subsequently formed his own band, Alternative TV (ATV). While the first single "How Much Longer?" was fairly standard—or standardized—punk when released in late 1977, lyrically it was a vicious attack on the internal conformity of the punk movement (by this time Perry had abandoned *Sniffin' Glue*). ATV rapidly evolved into an avant-garde band by way of punk, with Perry citing Frank Zappa, Can, and free jazz as primary influences. Their debut album, *The Image Has Cracked* (1978), included a cover of Zappa's "Why Doncha Do Me Right?" and a ten-minute song titled "Alternatives"—a tape montage from a live show in which audience members were invited onstage to vent into the microphone. Indeed, ATV's live shows were highly unpredictable and confrontational, as Al Spicer noted: "[ATV] boomed around the hall, colliding with tape cut-ups and other sound effects ... a concise three-minute statement at one gig could turn into a twenty-minute harangue the following evening."[24]

The follow-up to *The Image Has Cracked* was *Vibing Up the Senile Man* (1979), by which time ATV was essentially Perry with assistance from Dennis Burns and Throbbing Gristle's Genesis P-Orridge, the latter contributing percussion on two tracks. Songs became vignettes using a variety of sounds as disturbing aural scenery. The lengthy "Radio Story" features Perry's third-person recount of a man's plight when he discovers his girlfriend has suddenly moved out and summarily ended their relationship. The musical accompaniment of "Radio Story" is a slow, repeated bass line treated with reverb which is rhythmically accompanied by an electronic knocking sound. At approximately 2'00" it becomes apparent that the knocking is a radio, and it begins to tune in and out of various frequencies, producing a loud array of static, whines, bleeps, and snippets of talk. It serves as a backdrop for the man's overwhelming desperation trying to make sense of his drastically changed situation. At 6'15" the bass line abruptly stops and a free jazz saxophone duet erupts accompanied by the electronic noises produced by the radio, increasingly treated with effects like echo, phase-shifting, and panning across the stereo speakers. By 7'15", the saxophones fade out and the song concludes with an onslaught of radio noises at 7'52". It was a far cry from the Ramones.

What Lydon and Perry revealed was that the "Fuck Art, Let's Dance" sloganeering of early punk was largely a façade.[25] Colin Newman, vocalist/guitarist for Wire, described the relatively sudden evolution from punk to post-punk:

> London 1975: the prevailing aesthetic is '50s retro, pub-rock holds sway ... playing the standards or updating them in an uninspiring way. Then in '76 UK punk exploded in London.... The Pistols were a generational signifier, we all understood what they said, the previous generation didn't. It was quite simple BUT the main problem with the music of punk in '76 and '77 was that it implied all this newness that it didn't actually deliver.[26]

As stressed, the fundamental problem of punk was its unwillingness or inability to strive toward "newness" and unfamiliar musical territories as part of an emergent new youth culture, but retreat to "the old" of traditional rock 'n' roll. The strength of the punk explosion was that it introduced crucial elements lost in the malaise and excesses of rock in the 1970s in a return to democratization, directness, simplicity, even aggression and transgression. However, unless and until punk broadened its musical vocabulary and began to radicalize *form* as much as *content*, it was quickly destined to lapse into generic exhaustion. Simon Frith termed this as a break between

> *punk populism* versus *punk vanguard*. The punk populists remain locked in their original position.... The punk vanguard became more interested in musical meaning itself, in the stylistic assumptions that bound subcultures together. These musicians—the Gang of Four were the most articulate—began to explore textual structures in ways familiar in other media (in Godard's films, for instance), distancing themselves from their own performances, juxtaposing terms from different genres (*musical montages* of rock/reggae/funk).[27]

In America, punk bands like the Talking Heads, Suicide, Pere Ubu, Devo, the Screamers, MX-80 Sound, Chrome, and the Residents were working in the more experimental musical territories of "post-punk" *concurrent* with the initial punk explosion.[28] Active since the early 1970s, the Residents began as a multi-media project encompassing film, theater, and music that incorporated elements of Dada, Surrealism, Pop Art, and kitsch. Musically the Residents were highly influenced by sources ranging from Frank Zappa, Captain Beefheart, Harry Partch, free jazz and musique concrète; however, popular music genres like exotica and commercial jingles could be discerned as well. Early practitioners of the punk DIY ethos, the Residents used their limitations to their advantage: nominal musical skill, inexpensive equipment, and releasing their product from their own independent label, Ralph Records. Live performances were akin to avant-garde musical theater, making extensive use of props, staging, masks, and costumes. One of the more enduring images of the Residents was the band identically dressed in top hats and tuxedos with giant eyeball masks covering their heads. The Residents also cultivated an underground air of mystery, up to having all contact between the band and the outside world filtered through an entity known as the Cryptic Corporation, which ostensibly handled band management and public relations.[29]

In 1976, the Residents embarked on a concerted assault on rock music through anti-covers on their album *The Third Reich and Roll* (henceforth *TRR*). The front cover, done entirely in red and black, featured a caricature of Dick Clark in a Nazi uniform holding a carrot, which one can interpret as the carrot being rock music as consumer music and the (unseen) stick being authoritarian order. Each side of the album—one side titled "Why Hitler Was a Vegetarian" and the other side "Swastikas on Parade"—contained a medley of classic rock songs radically rearranged and performed using vocals, keyboards, guitar, saxophone, drums, tuned percussion, found objects, and sound effects modified with effects like distortion, echo, reverb, ring modulation, and phase-shifting. "Songs" vary in length—some little more than a recognizable riff repeated a few times with others lasting two or more minutes—and assembled through tape edits into abrupt montages bordering on cut-up methods. Given it was performed and recorded on equipment that was less than "state of the art," *TRR* is decidedly "lo-fi" and sounds much like one is listening to an AM radio rather than experiencing full stereophonic sound—an aural effect which may have been intentionally exaggerated by the Residents.

"Swastikas on Parade" opens with a drum backbeat and the opening lines of "Let's Twist Again" shouted in German, which after 15 seconds suddenly cuts to clanking machine sounds juxtaposed with percolating percussion rhythms. The opening wordless vocal hook of "Land of a Thousand Dances" begins followed by a distorted, guttural lead vocal heaving out the song's first verse, with the horn punctuations in the original replaced by dissonant organ blasts. In turn, "Land of a Thousand Dances" breaks down only to reorganize in a different mechanistic drum rhythm. A piano begins the 12-bar riff of "Hanky Panky" with an effect-laden, snotty-sounding lead vocal. Over the course of two minutes, several more pianos are multi-tracked, with each playing the riff (in part or in whole) in different tempos and different ascending key signatures. "Hanky Panky" collapses as the vocals go from repeatedly chanting the title into extended moans and gibberish as the pianos and drum rhythm stops entirely. Choral vocals then enter languidly singing the wordless vocal hook of "Horse with No Name" while another set of effect-saturated vocals sing the opening lines of "Double Shot of My Baby's Love" accompanied by almost random, sporadic electronic noises culminating in the sounds of an aerial dogfight and a plane plummeting to the ground. This cuts to distorted saxophones playing an intermittent two-note riff while the vocals grunt the opening verse of "The Letter" which ends with a volley of electronic noise. The distorted guitar riff to "Psychotic Reaction" follows and is soon joined by a detuned and equally distorted rhythm guitar strumming away but not quite in time or in tune with the other guitar. This is augmented by burbling electronic noises and saxophone blurts, and an echo-saturated vocal is relatively buried in the mix. The song snippet ends with a sound effect recording of a car crash lasting several seconds before giving way to a short duet between atonal saxophone and the sound of gunfire. A drum beat begins, and the sound of continuing gunfire can be heard underneath a truncated version of "Little Girl" emphasizing processed keyboards and a crass, effects-treated vocal. This cuts to a rendition of "Papa's Got a Brand New Bag," although off-key lounge saxophones play what appears to be the melody of "Little Girl" while a male falsetto operatically sings in German. The song also contains a quasi-sample of the James Brown version: a tape edit of the horn blast that cues the verses is inserted twice into the Residents' version. This shifts to a brief foray into "Talk Talk" with the requisite components of distorted and detuned guitar, out-of-tune keyboards, and garbled vocals before "Swastikas on Parade" appropriately closes with "Wipeout." The famous drum rhythms are electronically treated to have a deadened, wooden quality, and the equally famous guitar riff is played on a keyboard that, for lack of a better description, sounds like a harmonium submerged underwater. For added measure, an almost unrecognizable version of "Telstar" is played simultaneously to "Wipeout." Total time of "Swastikas on Parade": 17'30".[30]

"Swastikas on Parade" typifies the Residents at their best as well as their worst. On one hand, it demonstrates the degree to which the Residents could effectively deconstruct popular music and avant-garde/experimental music into unsettling yet humorous assemblages. "Songs" become a ground-up assemblage of rock-and-roll songs spewed back out as dissonance and noise while still retaining their recognizable "essence" with vocal melodies and instrumental riffs as the hooks that made them hit songs and marketable musical commodities. On the other hand, the Residents not only were influenced by Frank

Zappa musically, but had a predilection for adopting the "attitude" as well. While not as condescending as Zappa, the Residents were more than capable of succumbing to a degree of smugness as far as their efforts to be self-consciously avant-garde. Put differently, as effectively as the Residents could manage the balancing act between accessible popular music and inaccessible avant-garde music, there was often a pervasive sense that they were congratulating themselves in the process.

Not unrelated, the second issue is the political aspirations of *TRR*. Simon Reynolds hailed it as "a darkly comic satire on pop as totalitarianism."[31] While Reynolds is correct at a certain level, *TRR* ultimately fares better as musical satire than political satire. Beyond *TRR*'s overt content specifically referencing Nazi Germany—the album title, the titles of each side, the cover art, and the occasional use of aural signifiers like German vocals and militaristic sound effects—there is little that makes a direct "connection" between rock and fascism. Indeed, the listener is effectively handed the intent of *TRR* before they open the shrinkwrap and listen to it. Pop totalitarianism can just as easily be revealed through closer reading and inspection of rock music itself. As Lester Bangs pointed out, "Rock 'n' roll is power music ... with undercurrent themes of almost fascist domination and subjection running ... through the Stones to Alice Cooper" (the Rolling Stones discussed at length next chapter).[32] Conversely, the Residents' critique becomes limited in comparison to Laibach's musical-political project as a similar essay on "pop totalitarianism" that becomes willfully complicated and problematic for the audience both musically and ideologically (discussed at length in chapter 9). Ultimately, *TRR* operates through fairly "orthodox" oppositional strategies and provides a product tailored to easy consumption for an assumed audience with avant-garde tastes and leftist politics. These criticisms aside, *TRR* succeeds as far as it exposes that the culturally constructed "binary" of music in a capitalist-consumer society is actually between the difficult listening of avant-garde and experimental music versus popular music as a whole—be it rock, pop, or other genres. It is *not* found in the traditional binary that rock ideology constructs between subversive rock and conformist pop.

Hardcore and the Anti-Cover

By the early 1980s, the hardcore punk movement emerged with its epicenter in Los Angeles as a reaction to laid-back 1970s "West Coast rock" like the Eagles and Fleetwood Mac, a frustration with the sanitation of punk into the commercial sound of New Wave, and a seeming rejection of the avant-garde "artiness" pursued by post-punk. In short, early hardcore was early punk played much faster, more aggressively, and with a heavier sound. However, the strict genre conventions of hardcore music soon resulted in the hardcore movement experiencing the same crisis of early punk and post-punk and becoming similarly divided into two strains. Paraphrasing Simon Frith's terminology, one was "hardcore populism" represented by thrash music, and the other "hardcore vanguard" represented by more experimental post-hardcore bands. The overall problem of thrash and hardcore populism was unintentionally laid out by Steve Blush: "The music wasn't avant-garde, experimental, nor did it have unlimited possibilities.... That insistence on speed imposed limitations, which soon turned to assets."[33] These "limitations as assets" in part owed to hardcore populism's emphasis on egalitarianism and individualism as part of an anarchist ideology. The strict rules of thrash formalism allowed less-skilled musicians to move from the audience to the stage while the breakneck tempos and shouted vocals could and would obscure limitations as far as technical skill. The contradiction was that standardization of thrash music became central to hardcore populist "anarchy."

Two bands at the forefront of thrash music were the Dead Kennedys and the Circle Jerks who defined thrash as traditional punk with short songs played as fast as possible topped with polemical leftist statements.[34] In fairness, the DKs had a more expansive musical vocabulary than most thrash bands, with surf music, rockabilly and even the early Mothers of Invention being discernible influences. However, Jello Biafra's self-righteous political lyrics and haranguing yodel could be hard to take beyond small doses. One DKs anti-cover was a thrash version of Elvis Presley's "Viva Las Vegas" reframed as a satirical attack on American materialism. Another was an anti-cover of the Bobby Fuller Four's "I Fought the Law."[35] The original lyrics are about a man who is now serving a prison sentence of hard labor for bank robbery and realizing the futility of his struggle against the law. Biafra rewrote the lyrics into a protest song about the reduced manslaughter conviction Dan White received after he assassinated San Francisco mayor George Moscone and city supervisor Harvey Milk based on his infamous defense that eating too much junk food resulted in diminished mental capacity at the time of the murders (i.e., the "Twinkie Defense"). The problem is that Biafra's rewrite of the lyrics is, like the original version, in the first person, with Biafra assuming the "persona" of Dan White, rather than rewriting the song in the third person and singling out White by name (which would have greatly clarified the meaning from the outset). The chorus is reconfigured so it is not the outlaw defeated by the law, but the outlaw who overcomes the law. Given that the song is in the first person, unless or until the listener understands that Biafra is recounting a specific travesty of justice, the chorus comes off as a self-aggrandizing statement of Biafra's anti–Establishment struggles and proclaiming himself the victor.[36]

The Circle Jerks' 1980 debut album, *Group Sex* (14 songs with a total time of 15 and a half minutes) was one of the definitive thrash albums: high-octane punk with elements of metal and pop that attacked the military ("Paid Vacation"), the rich ("Beverly Hills"), and the federal government ("Red Tape") while reflecting a male adolescent view of sex (the title track, "I Just Want Some Skank"). *Wild in the Streets* (1982) was the follow-up, the title track a cover of a song written and originally recorded by Garland Jeffreys in 1973. Jeffrey's version was musically reminiscent of the Rolling Stones, with the lyrics a commentary on how the pressures of urban poverty result in drug abuse and gang violence while America society remains indifferent to such problems. The Circle Jerks' anti-cover of "Wild in the Streets" was done in typical punk/thrash style of distorted eighth-note guitar/bass fury, the backbeat pushed to its limits as far as barely containable velocity, and requisite hoarse, screamed vocals. At one level, it can be read as a celebration of drug abuse and gang violence—a second verse about the joy of using beer to wash down barbiturates was added by the Circle Jerks—and the repeated title of the song in the chorus becomes an anthem to no-holds-barred teenage rebellion. However, sophomoric comedy and satire was a component of the Circle Jerks' style, as opposed to the seriousness of later Back Flag or the DKs (the latter's penchant for heavy-handed sarcasm notwithstanding). Whether intended or not, "Wild in the Streets" could also be read as less of a vociferous glorification and more of a satirical critique of hardcore pseudo-rebellion as pointless exercises in substance abuse, vandalism, and violence.

In contrast to hardcore populism and thrash, "hardcore vanguard" or "post-hardcore" was represented by hardcore bands that adopted elements of 1960s and 1970s rock (hard rock, heavy metal, psychedelia, even pop and progressive rock), black music (funk and jazz), and avant-garde/experimental music influences (dissonance and noise). They ranged from Black Flag, Big Black, Butthole Surfers, Flipper, the Meat Puppets, the Minutemen, Saccharine Trust, Sonic Youth, and the Swans.[37] As noted, post-punk bands like Devo and the Residents were active before punk became an international musical movement ca. 1976. Likewise, post-hardcore as historically defined beginning ca. 1984—specifically with the releases of Black Flag's *My War*, the Minutemen's *Double Nickels on the Dime*, and Hüsker Dü's *Zen Arcade*—fails to take into account that numerous hardcore bands were already working in more eclectic and experimental musical territories outside the dominance of thrash music in the early 1980s (e.g., Flipper formed in 1979, the Meat Puppets and the Minutemen in 1980, and Sonic Youth in 1981). One of the pioneer early hardcore bands, Black Flag, became one of the leading post-hardcore bands by utilizing slower tempos, odd time signatures (3/8, 5/4, 7/4), abrupt tempo and structural changes, dissonant riffs that bordered on 12-tone music (the G–C–C♯–F♯–F/A♯ progression of "Drinking and Driving"), and guitarist Greg Ginn's atonal, free-from solos. By their final album *In My Head* (1985), Black Flag sounded like a convergence of Black Sabbath, King Crimson, and Captain Beefheart.

The Minutemen drew on classic rock ranging from Creedence Clearwater Revival, Blue Öyster Cult, and Steely Dan as well as post-punk bands like Wire, the Pop Group, and especially the Gang of Four. In his *Village Voice* review of the Minutemen's debut album *The Punch Line* (1981), Robert Christgau hilariously described the Minutemen's emphasis on abstract political commentary over political polemics as "not Fredric Jameson, but better than the skinheads they play for," and their fragmentary jazz-funk-punk style marked by quick-fire structural changes as "not Ornette Coleman, but better than the Circle Jerks they play with." Indeed, the Minutemen were hardcore punk by way of harmolodics and critical theory, a musical-ideological project best realized on *Double Nickels on the Dime* (1984). The double-album set included a 0'38" cover of Van Halen's "Ain't Talkin' 'Bout Love" that condensed the song into a scratchy funk guitar intro of the main riff, Beat poet–meets–drill sergeant vocals barking the opening lines over the flailing bass-drum rhythm section while the guitar drops out completely, a sudden burst of scribbly guitar solo, and a brief final restatement of the main riff by the full band. In this way, Van Halen's chronicle of the continual hunt for male carnal satisfaction was musically deconstructed by the Minutemen into a concise statement of male sexual satisfaction as the ethos of "Wham, bam, thank you, ma'am."

Big Black was a trio with an unorthodox lineup of two highly distorted guitars (what the band once termed a "smash" guitar favoring the bass end and a "klang" guitar with an abrasive treble bias), a clunky bass guitar, and a drum machine. They covered Kraftwerk's synthpop classic "The Model" and the power pop band Cheap Trick's "He's a Whore" with equally harsh intensity on their final album *Songs about Fucking* (1987). "The Model" is an evocative song about society's objectification of women, where men desire women and women accept their status as objects of desire. In the Big Black version, the drum machine provides an unwavering backbeat while the synthesizer parts were replicated by a clanking bass, washes of distorted guitar noise, piercing lead guitar lines, and vocals treated to have a tinny, megaphone sound. Voyeurism is represented as an "inhuman" ordeal of suffering for both the seer and the being-seen. "He's a Whore" is about a male gigolo willing to have sex with any woman if the price is right. In Big Black's version, the drum machine backbeat propels an abrasive grind of distorted guitars and chunky bass while the vocals are delivered in a blasé but sinister monotone representing the "male whore" as an emotionless sexual predator. Big Black's versions of "The Model" and "He's a Whore" became the "industrial" variants of the original versions where, as Gilles Deleuze cogently put it, "the unconscious isn't a theater but a factory."[38] Big Black depicted desire as something that was always seething and capable of exploding as some form of uncontrolled and uncontrollable outburst where sex and violence were not differentiated a priori. In this way, the lyrics of Big Black's songs could also veer from a seeming repulsive misogyny to statements of radical feminism.

The Butthole Surfers were influenced by punk, 1960s psychedelia, 1970s hard rock, and the avant-rock of Captain Beefheart and Krautrock bands; at their most experimental ca. 1986–89, the Butthole Surfers were hardcore's answer to the Dada minimalism of Faust. On *Rembrandt Pussyhorse* (1986), the Butthole Surfers anti-covered the Guess Who's 1970 hit song "American Woman" with a vengeance. "American Woman" encapsulated the counterculture mentality of the era by conflating its lyrical attack on the Vietnam War and economic inequality with a highly chauvinistic lyrical assault on women. Arguably one of the *least* "politically correct" rock critics, Lester Bangs witnessed the Guess Who perform an extended version of "American Woman" filled with vulgar slurs against women and later stated, "I never have been more offended by a concert."[39] The Butthole Surfers eviscerated "American Woman" into a repetitive and reverb-saturated backbeat, fragments of the main guitar riff, howling variations of the lead guitar line infused with dissonance and feedback, disruptive percussion and piano intrusions, a jarring use of studio tape edits, and treated vocals that alternated between high-pitched gibberish and proclamations being shouted through a megaphone as a sardonic commentary on the song's dated and highly questionable political thinking.

Killdozer recorded numerous anti-covers including Neil Diamond's "I Am, I Said," Jessi Coulter's "I'm Not Lisa," and a nine-minute version of Led Zeppelin's "When the Levee Breaks" that tested the limits of human listening endurance to the point of Karlheinz Stockhausen. They also released *For Ladies Only* (1989; the A-side was "The Romantic Side" and the B-side "The Side of Love") that included anti-covers of Deep Purple's "Hush," Bad Company's "Good Lovin' Gone Bad," Elvis Presley's "Burnin' Love," and Don

McLean's "American Pie." While they bordered on joke band territory, Killdozer specialized in sluggish dirges that at times sounded like the record was being played at the wrong speed (i.e., a 45-rpm record played at 33 rpm). Characterized by bludgeoning drums beats, bulky fuzz bass, heavily distorted noise guitar, and vocals that sounded like the lyrics were not being sung but retched, Killdozer's anti-covers sounded like the band was regurgitating noise out of the popular music it was trying to digest.

The anti-cover represents the most overt strategy and tactics for turning previous versions of songs on their head musically and politically. What needs to be stressed is that anti-covers are overt and *intentional* deconstructions and, in some but not all cases, outright desecrations of songs. They are not unintentional Camp in the form of sincere but pathetic renditions of pop and rock songs by mainstream stars—for instance, Jack Webb's utterly emotionless recitation of "Try a Little Tenderness" accompanied by generic, easy-listening music—nor are they intentional camping along the lines of Pat Boone's *In a Metal Mood* (issues discussed in chapter 10). Anti-covers can range from the Residents' sarcastically humorous "comedic parody" to Laibach's grimmer but equally humorous "serious parody." However, they are not "joke songs" by gimmick bands like Dread Zeppelin, whose repertoire consisted of reggae-style versions of Led Zeppelin songs sung by an Elvis impersonator (another example of deliberate camping). Poklaholix, a German punk-polka octet whose repertoire ranges from traditional polka songs to originals like the ska/speed metal–infused "Berlin Polka" to punk-polka covers of Kraftwerk's "Das Modell" and Rammstein's "Pussy," proves much more difficult as far as the distinction between joke band and avant-garde band, especially given that the musical video for "Pussy" features graphic montages of copulating animals and footage of the Berlin Wall's destruction.Ultimately, a strict differentiation between Camp, joke song, and anti-cover can be highly vague and often subjective. Part of the commercial success of the Flying Lizards, namely their anti-cover of "Money" that became a hit single, was the extent to which it was received as a quirky novelty song rather than a post-punk indictment of upper-class avarice (discussed in chapter 7). The Ramones covered the Beach Boys' "Do You Wanna Dance?" (*Rocket to Russia*, 1977), and it was a reverential rather than irreverent punk cover version of a classic rock song; indeed, it demonstrated the degree to which the Ramones and early punk were well within the rock tradition that punk allegedly rejected. Conversely, the Dickies were a Ramones-influenced, fairly ordinary punk band who covered several famous rock songs ranging from Barry McGuire's "Eve of Destruction," the Moody Blues' "Nights in White Stain," and Black Sabbath's "Paranoid." While they came off as joke covers–and the joke got old quickly—these were anti-covers in the sense that they overtly besmirched the originals, and it was not coincidental that the respective songs came from the genres of 1960s folk-rock, progressive rock, and heavy metal—three genres held in particular contempt by early punk. Returning to the Circle Jerks, *Golden Shower of Hits* (1983) closed with an anti-cover medley of six songs running 5'12" titled "Golden Shower of Hits (Jerks on 45)." The overt satire was Stars on 45, a Dutch studio band that had a chart-topping hit in 1981 with a medley of songs–mainly the Beatles—played at the same tempo with an unwavering backbeat designed for dancing in clubs as much as radio listening. While "Golden Shower of Hits" could easily be termed a joke song, its punk battery of songs across the genres of rock, pop, MOR, and country constructed a tragicomic narrative:

- "Along Comes Mary"—the Association: first encounter
- "(They Long to Be) Close to You"—the Carpenters: romantic courtship
- "Afternoon Delight"—the Starland Vocal Band: sexual intercourse
- "(You're) Having My Baby"—Paul Anka: unplanned pregnancy
- "Love Will Keep Us Together—the Captain and Tennille: forced marriage
- "D-I-V-O-R-C-E"—Tammy Wynette: bitter divorce

As a medley of anti-covers, "Golden Shower of Hits" became an "anti-love song" that not only mocked the "rock opera" format but subverted rock ideology's perpetuation of social fantasies around love and sex.

In the context of the anti-cover, particularly expressed in the punk and avant-rock genres, the issue is the extent to which more conventional cover versions can have the same effect as anti-covers as far as drastically configuring a song in different historical conditions and shifting political struggles.

Part Two

Anatomy of a Cover: "(I Can't Get No) Satisfaction"

3

"Satisfaction" and Rock: The Rolling Stones (Out of Our Heads, 1965)

The Anti-Beatles

Jacques Attali asserted that "both [John] Cage and the Rolling Stones, *Silence* and "Satisfaction," announce a rupture in the process of musical creation.... They are not the new mode of musical production, *but the liquidation of the old.*"[1] This statement is testament to the status, if not the mythology, established around the Rolling Stones and their 1965 song "(I Can't Go No) Satisfaction"—more commonly known as "Satisfaction"—as one of the defining moments of rock as oppositional culture. However, John Cage and the Rolling Stones are antithetical as far as their respective musical-ideological projects.

One of the most influential figures in twentieth-century experimental music, John Cage challenged the essential tenets of Western music. As Cage put it, "If the word, music, is sacred and reserved for the eighteenth and nineteenth century musical instruments, we can substitute a more meaningful term: *organization of sound.*"[2] Examples ranged from Cage's invention of the "prepared piano" in which various objects were inserted between the piano strings (dowels, screws, etc.) to produce an array of percussive sounds to compositions like *Imaginary Landscape No. 4* (24 performers in teams of two operating the tuning and volume knobs of twelve radios simultaneously) or *4'33"* (a performer sitting at a piano for four and a half minutes without playing it and the music becoming the random noises generated in the venue).

Formed in the early 1960s, the Rolling Stones were highly influenced by American popular music genres like blues, R&B, country-western, and fifties rock and roll; watching early performances of the Stones, the cynic could suggest Mick Jagger was doing his best to imitate James Brown while Keith

Richards was trying to mimic Chuck Berry.[3] Over the course of their 50-year career, the Stones remain steeped in popular and rock music traditions as well as contemporary popular music trends (for instance, the noticeable disco influence on their 1978 hit "Miss You"). While they have evolved and updated their musical style, the Stones have always operated through the traditional rock-and-roll format of merging American black music (blues, R&B) and white music (country-western), with *Exile on Main Street* (1972) the archetypal example. To this extent, the Stones have engaged in an assimilation and recapitulation of the old modes, and not any sort of deconstruction, yet alone liquidation, of established popular musical constructs.

As part of their marketing, the Stones also cultivated an image of being the "anti-Beatles" of the British Invasion in the early 1960s. At the time, the Beatles were still known for their matching gray suits, "mop top" haircuts, pleasant and polite stage demeanor, and bouncy pop-rock songs like "She Loves You" and I Want to Hold Your Hand" (both 1963). While the Beatles were tidy, the Stones were tawdry. As Irwin Stambler noted,

> Rightly or wrongly, the general media associated the Beatles with an aura of boyish light-heartedness, while the Stone were seen as reflecting the darker, surlier side of human nature.... Some of the disparity between the two groups was based in musical roots. The Beatles took their lead originally from ... Presley, Holly, and the Everlys, and rock is recognized as essentially a blend of watered-down blues and country music. The Rolling Stones evolved from the British skiffle craze, which received its incentive from the more brutal, seamier zone of "roots" blues, a music form that reflected the bitterness and indignities of American ghetto life along with the exuberance Negros still maintained despite their troubles.[4]

In this respect, The Stones did not simply draw from black American popular music genres but American black subculture—or at least a romanticized version of it—perpetuated by Norman Mailer's essay "The White Negro" (1957). For Mailer, the struggle revolved around whether "one is Hip or one is Square ... one is a rebel or one conforms, one is a frontiersman in the Wild West of American night life, or else a Square cell, trapped in the totalitarian tissues of American Society."[5] The escape from Square society was becoming "Hip" and the white male was adopting (read: appropriating) an idealized "blackness." More so than other rock bands of the British Invasion (e.g., the Beatles, the Who, the Kinks, etc.), the Stones embodied Mailer's glorification of the "white negro" as Hip rebellion against Square conformity—in particular Jagger, whose singing style was highly influenced by black R&B vocalists like Don Covey and his stage moves clearly informed by James Brown. However, Mailer's "White Negro" essay is ultimately less concerned with racial equality than with the struggle for male sexual liberation. "The hipster moves through his life on a constant search with glimpses of Mecca ... (Mecca being the apocalyptic orgasm), and if everyone in the civilized world is at least in some small degree a sexual cripple, the hipster lives with the knowledge of how he is sexually crippled and where he is sexually alive."[6] The Stones sang about sex rather than romance ("Let's Spend the Night Together"), reveled in male chauvinism and outright misogyny ("Heart of Stone," "Under My Thumb"), and celebrated revolutionary machismo ("Jumpin' Jack Flash," "Street Fighting Man," and "Satisfaction"). In short, the Stones presented themselves as rock music's popular threat to the Establishment in the tumult of the 1960s, and some consider the Stones the first "proto-punk" band.[7] As Peter Shapiro described them ca. 1965, "This was the Stones at their most punk: lyrically baiting the audience while [they] overloaded their amps, creating a tightly-packed distortion that strained the technological brink."[8]

"Satisfaction" as Manifesto

> It has a very catchy title. It has a very catchy riff. It has a great guitar sound, which was original at the time. And it captures the spirit of the times, which is very important in those kinds of songs ... Alienation. Or it's a bit more than that, maybe, but a kind of sexual alienation. Alienation's not quite the right word, but it's one word that would do.[9]—Mick Jagger

A Jagger/Richards composition, "Satisfaction" was a pivotal change for a band whose recorded output included a substantial amount of blues, R&B, and fifties rock covers. A *Rolling Stone* critics' poll named "Satisfaction" the second-greatest song in rock history, bested only by Bob Dylan's "Like a Rolling Stone." "Satisfaction" is indicative of the Stones' rough-around-the-edges merger of R&B and country music—Brian Jones played acoustic rhythm guitar in contrast to Richards' lead electric guitar—and it is structured somewhat differently than the traditional verse-chorus format of many songs; for example, "Jumpin' Jack Flash" has a standard intro-verse-chorus-verse-chorus-bridge-verse-chorus-outro structure. Instead, "Satisfaction" is structured as follows and anchored by the song's signature guitar riff:

Intro (riff)
Pre-chorus (no riff)
Chorus (riff)
First verse (riff)

Pre-chorus (no riff)
Chorus (riff)
Second verse (riff)
Pre-chorus (no riff)
Chorus (riff)
Third verse (riff)
Chorus/outro (riff)

In fact, "Satisfaction" contains one of the most famous guitar riffs in rock music. Early rock songs had "hooks" mainly built around vocal melodies while the instrumental accompaniment played driving chord progressions (e.g., "Great Balls of Fire," "Hound Dog," "Johnny B. Goode," or "Tutti Frutti"). The Kingsmen's "Louie Louie" (1963) was one of the first rock songs where the A-D-Em-D guitar riff in the chorus was a central part of the song while the vocal is relatively buried in the mix and the lyrics are all but indecipherable (prompting accusations that the song was filled with obscured obscenities). One recognizes "Hound Dog" by singing the vocal line; one can identify "Louie Louie" by humming the guitar riff as well as singing the vocal line.[10]

"Satisfaction" was also built on the guitar riff—albeit unintentionally. Keith Richards recorded the two-bar, B–C♯–D guitar line as a "scratch track" with the plan being that a horn section would use it as a guide for an overdubbed track and then Richards' guitar riff would be removed from the final mix. In order to replicate a saxophone-like sound, Richards used a Gibson Maestro fuzz box to greatly distort and increase the sustain on the guitar. As Steve Waksman noted, "Relying on an appended fuzz box [Richards] generated something that sounded much more like an *effect*, more piercing and single-mindedly fuzzy."[11] However, producer Andrew Loog Oldham insisted on leaving Richard's guitar scratch track in the final mix and forgoing the horn section.

"Satisfaction" is written in E-major, so the D is an accidental note that would be D♯ if played in accordance to the E-major scale; in effect, Richards plays a B-minor riff within an E-major song. In a song about individual alienation and the denial of satisfaction in consumer society, the D is a slightly dissonant note that becomes the musical signifier of "discord" while Jagger shouts (as opposed to sings) the title of the song in the chorus and vents on the mass media—and ultimately women—in the verses. The D is also the highest note in the riff and suspended between the two bars, beginning on the last upbeat of the first bar and held 1.5 beats into the second bar. The anticipation and building tension of the ascending notes and the dissipation and release of tension in the descending notes of the riff "peaks" on a note that literally "falls flat" as far as resolution or attainment of satisfaction.

Moreover, a close listening of the guitar riff reveals an extraordinarily sloppy performance by Richards, keeping in mind it was not intended to be included in the final mix. Beginning the chorus–first verse, the listener can hear Richards step on the fuzz-box switch on the one and enter 2.5 beats late (playing B–C♯–D); beginning the chorus–second verse, Richards enters three beats late (playing C♯–D); beginning the chorus–third verse, Richards plays a muffled eighth note (B) midway in the bar before the riff begins and then enters 2.5 beats late (playing B–C♯–D). Rather than "mistakes," one can consider the sheer nonchalance of Richards' performance of the guitar riff as manifesting a kind of "indifference," or, more simply, an "I don't give a damn" attitude. In terms of the riff's dissonance and sloppiness, an element of "noise" appears in "Satisfaction." Here the issue becomes reading "Satisfaction" as musically revolutionary around the "newness of noise" and the role of the guitar riff. Ultimately, the riff functions as the melodic hook of the song as much as Jagger's slurred half-sung/half-shouted vocals. The distorted guitar riff may act as a kind of aural "rebellion" against musical convention, yet the overall "organization of sound" falls very much within traditional musical constraints of melody, harmony, and meter as well as recognized popular music genres and their conventions.

In this respect, the Stones' rhythm section of bassist Bill Wyman and drummer Charlie Watts also need to be considered. The drive of "Satisfaction" is insistent and unwavering, with Watts' snare on every beat throughout the song providing a martial quality. Wyman and Watts were a traditionalist rhythm section that provided a stable anchor for the other instruments as opposed to contemporaries like Cream, the Who, and the Jimi Hendrix Experience where the rhythm sections were much more adventurous and explosive. However, Watts and Wyman had *deceptively* simple approaches. Watts' straightforward drumming was infused with a jazz influence and contained subtle syncopations and variations. Wyman's walking bass style drew from blues and R&B; moreover, Wyman removed the frets from his bass guitar and held it vertically rather than horizontally while using a pick rather than his fingers. While many bassists in the 1960s were emphasizing the guitar potential of the bass guitar (e.g., Jack Bruce, John Entwistle), Wyman approached the bass guitar as an extension of the upright bass. In this way, the Stones' musical style became defined around a seething hostility manifested by Jagger's vocals and Richards' electric guitar propelled by the swinging precision of the Watts-Wyman rhythm section. In short, the Stones' musically manifested *swagger*: a projection of masculine confidence (if not arrogance) and Hip individualist defiance of all aspects of Square society that assuredly strolled as much as it aggressively rocked.

Another crucial aspect of "Satisfaction" was that it signaled Jagger's move into social commentary lyrics, manifesting the Stones' anti–Establishment image into anti–Establishment song statements. Indeed, "Satisfaction" was one of rock's first overtly political songs as far as its surface attack on consumer culture and its expression of alienation at a time when most rock songs were primarily concerned about falling in or out of love. However, like many Stones songs, the core issue is gender and sexual politics. The lyrics of "Satisfaction" are written in the first person, and the first verse details Jagger's boredom listening to the radio and worthless bits of advertising. The second verse is the point at which Jagger begins to assert his Hip rebel masculinity against the Square TV pitchman with an implied reference to race: he dismisses the man promoting a laundry product that promises to make Jagger's clothes and appearance "whiter." This gives way to the third verse, which is not about the mass media and consumerism but Jagger bemoaning the fact that he is a globetrotting rock singer still having a difficult time getting laid, with one line often interpreted to mean that a woman can't put out for Jagger because she is having her period. The attack on a conformist, consumer society ends up being a complaint about a lack of individual satisfaction, namely male sexual gratification being denied by women. Hence, there is a binary conflict represented in "Satisfaction": the Square, mass society, conformity, sexual repression, and the woman versus the Hip, individuality, rebellion, sexual liberation, and the man.

In *The History of Sexuality, Volume 1*, Michel Foucault offered a radical critique of how sex is thought of in Western society. The long-held ideology is that sex and society are locked in a monolithic struggle of sexual liberation versus sexual repression, what Foucault termed the "Repressive Hypothesis." Foucault examined the historical proliferation of multiple competing discourses around sex and how they constructed cultural norms of sexuality that necessitated determining the "sexually aberrant" (adultery, homosexuality, taboo sexual practices) in order to determine "sexual normalcy" (monogamous marriage, heterosexuality, acceptable sexual conduct). In the 1950s, sexual politics and the "Sexual Revolution" were largely rooted in the myth of the Repressive Hypothesis and proponents like Norman Mailer and Hugh Hefner, who began publishing *Playboy* in 1953. They became the antecedents to the 1960s counterculture whose views on sexual liberation largely echoed the Repressive Hypothesis. Indeed, the glaring contradiction for the counterculture was that the battle for male sexual liberation entailed the sexual domination of women as a central tenet of rock ideology. As MC5 guitarist Wayne Kramer candidly recounted, "We were sexist bastards.... We had all this rhetoric of being revolutionary.... The boys get to go out to fuck and the girls can't complain about it. And if they did they were being bourgeois bitches ... counterrevolutionary."[12]

Under My Thumb: Altamont and Rock Totalitarianism

Throughout the 1960s, the Stones continued to cultivate their anti–Establishment Hip mystique while perilously flirting with authoritarian ideology, whether intended or not. Songs like "Satisfaction," "Jumpin' Jack Flash," "Street Fighting Man," "Sympathy for the Devil," and "Gimmie Shelter" upped the ante where the Stones' recurrent themes of alienation, death, power, sex, and violence became infused with a sense of pending catastrophe. They also resonated with the revolutionary machismo that permeated the counterculture, the growing impatience with the lack of significant political change, and a growing belief that violent direct action was the only viable option (an issue returned to in chapter 8). As William L. O'Neill put it, "Romanticism has never worked well in the past. It seemed to be doing as badly in the present. The hippies went from flower power to death tripping in a few years. The New Left took only a little longer to move from participatory democracy to demolitions."[13]

By the end of the decade, the Stones' increased emphasis on decadence, destruction, and domination was exacerbated by the underground press after the Beatles released "Hey Jude/Revolution," their first single on their self-run Apple Records. A John Lennon composition, "Revolution" called for social change while explicitly denouncing violence and Mao Zedong. The Beatles were dismissed as counterrevolutionaries; *Barb* hailed "Street Fighting Man" as rock's politically correct response to the times, and Liberation News Service (LNS) ran an article with the dead-serious headline "LNS Supports Rolling Stones in Ideological Split with Beatles."[14] While the Beatles moved from apolitical love songs to political "peace and love songs," the Stones were elevated to the status of rock revolutionaries. Writing in the 1970s, Jacques Attali hailed "Street Fighting Man" by proclaiming, "The commodity is absolutely incapable of filling the void it created by suppressing ritual sacrifice ... living in a void means admitting the constant potential for revolution, music, and death."[15] Perhaps Attali did not get the memo about Altamont.

In 1969, the Stones' released the cryptically titled *Let It Bleed* and commenced their first concert tour of America in three years. As Peter Shapiro described it, "*Let It Bleed* was no celebration of the Woodstock nation.... The Stones became an apocalyptic juggernaut. Richards' guitar riffs fused with the bass and drums to achieve an edginess that went beyond functional propulsion. The savagery of the music perfectly echoed the brutality of Jagger's lyrics."[16] In turn, the imagery matched the music. Allen Rinde described Jagger the opening night of the tour in *Rock* magazine (December 8, 1969): "Studded black pants, with a studded silver belt and black full-sleeve jersey, an Uncle Sam red, white, and blue hat and grey and black scarf hanging down between his legs, looking like a crown prince of darkness."[17]

While the Stones may have represented the antithesis of the Woodstock Nation, they were impressed enough with the profit potential of a Woodstock event, and they hastily organized their own free concert festival to end the tour, replete with a film crew that would document the event. Santana, the Flying Burrito Brothers, Jefferson Airplane, the Grateful Dead, and Crosby, Stills, Nash, and Young (CSNY) agreed to perform. Altamont, a racetrack outside San Francisco, was the last-second choice for the venue. There was extremely poor planning and preparation from the outset, not the least of which being the decision to hire members of the Hell's Angels as stage security (reportedly for $500 worth of beer). Three hundred thousand concertgoers descended onto Altamont, and fueled by drugs and excruciating conditions, a tension-filled atmosphere was soon punctuated by outbreaks of violence that interrupted the concert. Turmoil quickly escalated after Jefferson Airplane's singer Marty Balin was punched in the face and knocked unconscious by a Hell's Angel after going into the audience and confronting them over their increasingly aggressive approach to maintaining order. An onstage argument followed between Jefferson Airplane guitarist Paul Kanter and a Hell's Angels member that left little doubt as to who was now in charge at Altamont: the Hell's Angels began to mill about the crowd to quell any real or imagined threat to their authority with pool cues. As the situation deteriorated, Jagger was also socked in the face by an irate concert attendee moments after he disembarked from his helicopter, and the "clown prince of darkness" was visibly unnerved by what was transpiring when the Stones took the stage and meekly pleaded with everyone to "just be cool." A melee broke out in the crowd during "Sympathy for the Devil" that forced a lengthy delay. The worst was yet to come. As the next song, "Under My Thumb," drew to a close, Meredith Hunter—an African American high on amphetamines—got into an altercation with several of the Hell's Angels, brandished a pistol, and was stabbed to death by Hell's Angel Alan Passaro.[18] It was all captured by the film crew the Stones hired, and a chronicle of the grisly day at Altamont was released under the title *Gimmie Shelter* (1970).

As discussed last chapter, specifically citing the Stones as an example, Lester Bangs contended that rock and roll "is power music ... with undercurrent themes of almost fascist domination and subjection." Norman Mailer himself conceded that the politics of the Hip contained a potentially catastrophic consequence:

> Whether the hipster's desire for absolute sexual freedom contains any genuinely radical conception of a different world is of course another matter, and it is possible since the hipster lives with his hatred, that many of them are the material for an elite of storm troopers ready to follow the first truly magnetic leader whose view of mass murder is framed in a language which reaches their emotions.[19]

In the aftermath of Altamont, the *Los Angeles Free Press* was less florid and more direct in their assessment by publishing an editorial cartoon of "Mick Jagger with an Adolf Hitler moustache, arms draped around a Hell's Angel, while long-haired kids gave them a Nazi salute."[20] In the end, Altamont provided an essay on "rock totalitarianism" just as effectively as the Residents' *The Third Reich and Roll*. The point of departure, as Charles Bukowski once observed, is that "the difference between art and life is that art is more bearable." While the Residents' confined their critique to musical farce, the Rolling Stones actualized it as historical tragedy.[21]

4

"Satisfaction" and Soul: Otis Redding (Otis Blue/Otis Redding Sings Soul, 1965)

Paint It Black: Race and Rock in the 1960s

In the early 1960s, the British Invasion of rock bands—at the forefront, the Beatles, the Rolling Stones, and the Who—conquered the American popular music market and established rock as the dominant genre for a younger generation of music consumers. The contradiction was that while they drew extensively from blues and R&B sources, rock music became the all-but-exclusive domain of white, male musicians with a predominately white, male, middle-class audience. Appropriation was now admiration, and cover songs were crucial to this process. Simon Frith pointed out that during the 1950s, cover songs were generally viewed as uniformly inferior to the original versions, with Pat Boone's covers of Little Richard's "Tutti Frutti" and "Long Tall Sally" the infamous examples; however, by the late 1960s, cover songs were viewed as a means by which an original version could be reinterpreted and be just as good—if not better—than the original version.[1] It is not coincidental that this critical shift coincided with the British Invasion. While Pat Boone was vilified, there was little if any criticism when the Beatles covered the Isley Brothers' "Twist and Shout" or when the Rolling Stones covered Howlin' Wolf's "Little Red Rooster" to great commercial success. Indeed, a decade that began with numerous white pop and rock performers covering blues and R&B songs ended with numerous black soul performers covering pop and rock songs by the likes of Bob Dylan, the Beatles, and the Rolling Stones.

By the late 1960s, rock's relationship to black music became rather difficult. Despite Keith Richards' definition of rock as "music from the neck down,"

Simon Frith contended that rock music was predicated on the Cartesian "mind-body" dichotomy, where black music became the "body" of rock music based on "the *assumption* ... that while black music was important as an expression of vitality and excitement—was, in other words, good to dance to—it lacked the reflective qualities needed for genuine artistic expression."[2] Or, in what was intended as praise but amounted to a backhanded compliment, Dave Marsh contended, "Disco isn't listening music. Disco is active dancer music. That's what it's there for."[3] Given this mind/listening and body/dancing dichotomy that became central to rock ideology, rock embarked on becoming a legitimate form of "art" in two highly different ways and through two legendary figures: Bob Dylan and the Beatles.

In 1965, Dylan entered the rock market by performing a set with electric instruments at the Newport Folk Festival, a move that infuriated the folk community at the time but made Dylan a rock star. On *Bringing It All Back Home* (1965), *Highway 61 Revisited* (1965), and *Blonde on Blonde* (1966), Dylan defined rock as a musical genre steeped in American "roots music" (folk, R&B, country, blues, etc.), enigmatic but unpretentious lyrics, anti–Establishment sentiments, and recorded performances that had the right feel rather than flawless technique to signify emotional "sincerity." Close listening to Dylan's rock songs in the 1960s such as "Like a Rolling Stone," "Rainy Day Woman Nos. 12 & 35," or "Positively 4th Street" reveals an overall slackness as far as ensemble playing, unsteady tempos, lax transitions, awkward vocal phasing of lyrics, and other musically "incorrect" techniques that nonetheless work in the overall effect generated by the songs.

Dylan was also crucial as far as folk music displacing—but far from replacing—country music as the artistic and politically conscious "mind" component of rock music. More specially, the role of folk music was as much an ideological shift as a musical shift in the 1960s. Folk music was historically associated with progressive left-wing politics (Woody Guthrie, Pete Seeger, Phil Ochs), whereas country was increasingly perceived as conservative, pro–Establishment music (namely Merle Haggard, although rock and the counterculture's relationship to country and Haggard proved quite complicated, as discussed in chapter 10). During the latter half of the 1960s, bands like the Buffalo Springfield, the Byrds, Country Joe and the Fish, Jefferson Airplane, and Crosby, Stills, Nash, and Young combined psychedelic rock, folk, and political lyrics into a brand of rock music particularly favored by the counterculture audience (CSNY is addressed further in chapter 8).

In Britain, the Beatles were pursuing rock as "artistic expression" through other directions. By the mid–1960s, the Beatles were breaking away from pop-rock conventions and seeking to expand the musical and lyrical vocabularies of rock music on their albums *Rubber Soul* (1965) and *Revolver* (1966). "Norwegian Wood (This Bird Has Flown)" was in 12/8 and featured a sitar, "Eleanor Rigby" eschewed the rock band for a classical string quartet, and "Tomorrow Never Knows" incorporated numerous studio effects like backwards tracks, tape loops, and other electronic music effects associated with musique concrète rather than rock. The influences of Indian, classical, and electronic music would become crucial as far as the Beatles' subsequent musical development. Not related, concerts became impossible for the Beatles, who were playing packed stadiums filled with screaming fans to the point that the band could not be heard over the din of the crowd. Deciding to focus on recording and abandoning live performances, the Beatles were freed from the constraints of having to replicate their recordings onstage and could utilize the studio as a compositional tool rather than a glorified stage with recording equipment.[4] The result was one of rock's first "studio albums" *Sgt. Pepper's Lonely Hearts Club Band* (1967). As well as drawing from and merging disparate genres (rock, pop, classical, music hall, Indian, electronic, experimental, etc.), songs were meticulously assembled in the studio around the initial performances and modified with a plethora of overdubs and studio effects.

Despite their musical differences, what Bob Dylan and the Beatles shared was a core idea that rock music was no longer just for energetic dancing but intent listening. In short, rock became art with contemplation value. The upshot was that white music became the mind of rock—be it Dylan's folk Americana or the Beatles' modernist Continentalism.[5] Black music genres became the body of rock, which within the Cartesian distinction entails the primacy of the mind over the body. One might say, "I listen, therefore I am" replaced "I dance, therefore I am."

Soul Brands: Motown and Stax

In this context, popular music and race developed another knotty relationship during the 1960s. On one hand, rock music and soul music became "segregated" into different genres and different markets, with rock's assumed audience being young white popular music consumers and soul's assumed audience black popular music consumers. On the other hand, soul music became a highly popular crossover music product, namely the different brands of soul offered by Detroit-based Motown Records and Memphis-based Stax Records. Johnny Otis contended, "Motown is more urbanized, while Memphis [Stax] is closer to the gospel roots of soul. Put another way, Motown Sound is essentially a pop-soul sound, while Memphis [Stax] Sound is a heavier, black soul sound."[6] While Otis concedes that this is a general distinction, it is indicative of a long-standing critical view distinguishing Motown and Stax.

Motown as "pop-soul"—or what could be termed "symphonic soul"— was deemed a commercialized, manufactured, standardized, even sanitized brand of soul that lacked the "authenticity" of Stax. To be sure, Motown was focused on maximizing the commercial potential of soul music. Motown's in-house team of Brian Holland, Lamont Dozier, and Eddie Holland (H-D-H) wrote and produced many of Motown's biggest hits for performers like the Supremes, the Four Tops, and Martha and the Vandellas until they left Motown over an acrimonious royalty dispute with Motown head Berry Gordy, Jr., in 1967. Along with the trademark vocal harmonies and R&B foundation, H-D-H frequently utilized strings and other orchestral instruments; in this respect, Motown infused soul with elements of pop, MOR, and even classical music. H-D-H also had a distinct songwriting approach that gave Motown its signature sound as well as manifesting an overall similarity between Motown performers. Indeed, songs had a degree of "interchangeability" in that they could be assigned to any number of performers. The Four Tops' first hit "Baby I Need Your Loving" (1964) was initially intended as a song for one of the label's female acts (the Supremes recorded a cover version of the song in 1966). Hence, the "individual" style of Motown acts was primarily distinguished through the performers and, more specifically, the lead vocalists: Diana Ross' sweet soprano, Martha Reeves' forceful alto, Smokey Robinson's smooth tenor, or Levi Stubbs' gutsy baritone. As well as Motown's musical formula, there was a concert formula. Male performers wore matching suits or tuxedos while female performers wore matching evening gowns; as well as singing, performers had highly choreographed dance moves (notably the Temptations).

As important, Gordy's management emphasized "quality control," which meant little if any deviation from the Motown brand identity. Intent on making Motown's roster of performers into stars—Diana Ross the most overt example–and keeping Motown a relatively mainstream label, Gordy barred Motown acts from appearing at the Monterey Pop Festival for fear the label would be associated with the anti–Establishment counterculture. Rock music did not emerge from Michigan until the late 1960s—well after Motown was established in 1959—with hard rock bands like Grand Funk Railroad, the Amboy Dukes (featuring Ted Nugent on lead guitar), and proto-punk bands the MC5 and the Stooges. Any rock influences were minimal (at best) in the Motown sound until ca. 1970 when Motown rebranded itself from love-song-based "symphonic soul" to politically conscious "psychedelic soul" (assessed further in chapter 8).

In the mid–1950s, rock and roll was arguably born at Sun Studios in Memphis, whose roster included Elvis Presley, Jerry Lee Lewis, Roy Orbison, and Johnny Cash. White music and black music were already becoming "integrated" in Memphis, and it was in this environment that Stax Records began operations in 1960 as Motown's market rival for soul music; moreover, this closer proximity to rock music may have accounted for Stax's "heavier" sound. The first Stax house band was the Mar-Keys, an integrated group composed of black and white musicians. In 1962, four members of the Mar-Keys—keyboardist Booker T. Jones, guitarist Steve Cropper, bassist Lewie Steinberg, and drummer Al Jackson, Jr.—recorded a jam session during a break from session work that produced the 12-bar R&B/rock instrumental "Green Onions," one of Stax's first major hit records. Booker T. and the M.G.s was also a racially integrated quartet. Jones and Jackson were black, and Cropper and Steinberg were white; Donald "Duck" Dunn, who replaced Steinberg as bassist in 1963, was also white—which puts the whole idea that Memphis soul was a "blacker" soul sound into some jeopardy.[7]

Booker T. and the M.G.s also served as the primary house band for Stax Studios and worked extensively with Otis Redding. In 1962, Redding was employed as a driver and occasional backup musician for the Pinetoppers. The band auditioned for Stax and recorded some demos, and as the session drew to a close a reluctant Redding was prodded to sing two songs: a fast R&B song titled "Hey Hey Baby" and a slow ballad titled "This Heart of Mine." Stax was not particularly impressed but decided to release the Redding recordings as a single. "This Heart of Mine" became an unexpected hit, and Stax quickly signed Redding to a contract. However, Redding had relatively moderate success throughout much of the 1960s. While Motown performers accumulated over 100 Top Ten hits from 1959 to 1972 and Aretha Franklin had several Top Ten hits in the late 1960s, none of Redding's hit songs cracked the Billboard Top 20 during his lifetime. Arguably his best-known song from the era was "Try a Little Tenderness," a slow-burn soul version of a big band song written in 1932 and recorded by Bing Crosby in 1933 and Mel Tormé in 1946. The song became synonymous with Redding and a case where Redding's cover version became the standard version subsequently covered by other pop and rock performers rather than the original version (e.g., Three Dog Night).

Redding's breakthrough to a wider audience occurred at the Monterey Pop Festival (June 16–18, 1967). As noted, Berry Gordy, Jr., forbade Motown acts from appearing at the festival. Redding became soul music's main representative at Monterey; by extension, Stax became the brand of soul music exclusively featured at Monterey as well. Backed by Booker T. and the M.G.s and a horn section made up of members of the Mar-Keys, Redding gave a dynamic performance that was widely hailed as one of the festival highlights. Moreover, a key aspect of Redding's concert performances was his "body language" and the fact that he was not an accomplished dancer like James Brown or the Temptations; Redding could appear rather awkward and unsteady on stage. Instead of slickly moving about, Redding prowled the stage, stomped his feet, gyrated his upper body, waved his arms, and belted out songs is an intense, husky baritone. In this way, Redding's stage presence and mannerisms compared to the intensity of an evangelical preacher delivering a sermon rather than a musical performer, and the fact that Redding was over six feet tall and well over two hundred pounds also contributed to his formidable stage presence. Monterey was also Redding's last major concert performance; he was killed in a plane crash in transit to a concert on December 10, 1967. By the time of his death and especially afterward, Redding was one of the more famous performers in the soul music genre, in no small part due to his crossover popularity with pop and rock audiences.

"Satisfaction" as Protest

Among the songs that Redding performed at Monterey was "Satisfaction," which he initially covered on his album *Otis Blue/Otis Redding Sings Soul* (henceforth *Otis Blue*). Recorded in two days at Stax Studios, *Otis Blue* was co-produced by Isaac Hayes, who also played keyboards, and the backing band was the M.G.s (Cropper, Dunn, and Jackson) and a horn section composed of members of the Mar-Keys. As discussed last chapter, the Stones' version of "Satisfaction" has an unorthodox but well-defined structure; it also has caviler looseness as far as Jagger's vocals and especially Richards' guitar riff while propelled with a controlled velocity by Wyman and Watts. Otis Redding's version is tightly performed but has a frantic quality amid the interplay of instruments and especially Redding's largely improvised vocals after the first verse, which Redding admitted was the result of unfamiliarity with "Satisfaction" in that the Stones' version was only released a month earlier as an advance single off *Out of Their Heads*. Instead, Redding delivered a kind of steam-of-consciousness, at times indecipherable fragments of verbal and non-verbal statements about wanting and not attaining satisfaction punctuated with grunts, moans, and shouts that manufactured "meaning" just as much as the lyrics. As Simon Frith argued, "In black music, singers articulate awe and fervor through an apparently spontaneous struggle *against* words ... [and it] can only be described in terms of sound, not *what* is sung but *how* it is sung."[8]

"Satisfaction" begins with the M.G.s playing the riff collectively in a stop-start rhythm. After the riff is played twice, Jackson switches to a swinging backbeat and the trumpets play a jazzy variation on the riff in a higher register for four bars. Redding then begins singing while Cropper plays crisp quarter notes on guitar—in effect mimicking Watts' insistent snare beat rather than Richards' guitar. Where Richards begins the riff in the first chorus–first verse, the horns provide a staccato version of the riff rather than guitar—an ironic change in the arrangement as Richards intended the guitar riff to be used as a scratch track to guide an eventual overdubbed horn section.

The strict pre-chorus/chorus/verse structure begins to break down as Redding's version progresses while still maintaining its tense drive while Redding largely improvises the remaining lyrics. After the horns drop out, the guitar begins the B–C♯–D riff, and soon after the horns punctuate the song with a two-note, two-bar blast on the one and two of every other bar while Redding begins his vocal ad-libs. When Redding begins the second pre-chorus, the guitar returns to the quarter-note rhythm, and at the point where the second verse "should" appear Cropper briefly plays the B–C♯–D riff while Redding does not sing any lyrics. This produces a momentary "shock" for the listener in the form of a "silence" with the sudden absence of known lyrics replaced by spontaneous vocal interjections. The horns enter with the two-bar, two-beat blast and then the band transitions as a whole. The horns modify the pattern to a three-note, two-bar pattern (on the two, upbeat between three and four, and one of the next bar) while the baritone saxophone plays a line of notes against Dunn's walking bass guitar part and Cropper resumes the quarter-note riff to end the song.

Despite the looseness of the vocals and guitars, the Stones' version of "Satisfaction" is lockstep in its persistent quarter-note rhythm and unconventional but well-organized song structure to the point it carries itself with assured defiance precisely at the point the counterculture was emerging as a potent force in American society. In contrast, Redding's version increasingly roams about in agitated musical desperation as the quest for satisfaction was continually denied during the contentiousness of the civil rights movement. Indeed, this becomes a central political component as far as Redding—a black, southern American—performing "Satisfaction" during the civil rights movement while Jagger—a white Englishman—attacked consumerism, mass media, and ultimately women in an affected singing style borrowing from American black and southern dialects. Redding's emphatic vocal bursts (verbal and nonverbal) backed by an integrated soul band from Memphis translated the Stones' version from a manifesto of the alienated and defiant counterculture "white negro" into a protest song and document of the turbulent struggle for racial equality.

5

"Satisfaction" and Punk: Devo (Q: Are We Not Men? A: We Are Devo!, 1978)

A Postmodern Protest Band (or, Anarchy in Akron)

> Individuality and rebellion were obsolete.[1]
> —Devo co-founder Mark Mothersbaugh

Although they largely digressed into an unintentional synthpop parody of themselves by the 1980s, in the late 1970s Devo rivaled the Talking Heads as America's leading post-punk band, and even seemed poised to become the dominant post-punk band of the era. Devo shared a degree of stylistic similarity to the Talking Heads in the jumpy rhythms, skeletal melodies, and strangled vocals but contained considerable differences as well. As David Byrne described it, "I wanted [the Talking Heads] to sound like a well-oiled machine where everything was transparent, all the working parts visible.... Nothing hidden in a big murk of sound. Somehow that seemed more honest. And probably more arty as well."[2] While Devo was equally mechanistic and "arty," Mark Mothersbaugh summarized their deconstruction of "Satisfaction" as the sound of "some sort of stupid, perpetual motion machine clanking around the room that we couldn't stop."[3]

Before discussing their cover of "Satisfaction" and how it exemplified Devo's musical-political project, it is necessary to provide some context. If punk rejected the 1960s counterculture, Devo was very much rooted in disillusionment with the era. Devo founders Mark Mothersbaugh (vocals, keyboards, guitar) and Gerald Casale (bass, keyboards, vocals) met at Kent State University and were present at the anti–Vietnam War demonstration on May 4, 1970, that ended with four students killed by the Ohio National Guard.

The band was originally based in Akron, Ohio, "the rubber capital of the world"; the city was the headquarters of Firestone, Goodyear, and Goodrich, and the local economy was almost entirely dependent on the tire industry and, by extension, the auto industry. To this extent, the environment that produced Devo was not only the death of the counterculture dream at Kent State, but the decline of American industrial capitalism in the 1970s as Akron became one of several northeastern and midwestern "Rust Belt" cities.

The pressures of counterculture disenchantment and economic entropy fueled Devo's central concept of "de-evolution." At one level, de-evolution was a satire of pseudo-science that mixed Christian fundamentalism, conspiracy theory, and science-fiction. Yet there was something quite serious in the concept as well. Devo was a critique of the paradox of modernity as rational and scientific progress paralleled by humanity's increasing regression into barbarism, a concept which resonated with Frankfurt School philosophers like Herbert Marcuse and particularly Max Horkheimer and Theodor W. Adorno's *Dialectic of Enlightenment*. Rather than simply being a postmodern musical-comedy act (e.g., Blue Man Group), Casale stated Devo was an assault on the "kind of emptiness and pinheadedness and distortion with which we face modernity and what we call civilization leading to post-nuclear life and disaster."[4]

From the outset, Mothersbaugh and Casale envisioned Devo as a multimedia performance art project where, as Casale noted, "we were a self-contained conceptual unit where the visuals, the theatrics, and the ideas and staging were as important as the music itself.... A postmodernist protest band."[5] Musically, Devo drew from garage rock, surf rock instrumentals, Captain Beefheart, early Roxy Music, Krautrock bands (especially Kraftwerk's minimalist synthpop), and Frank Zappa; in certain respects, Devo could be described as a convergence of the Sex Pistols and the Residents. Out of these influences, Devo developed a highly clinical and mechanistic style. "Robotic" inevitably became the word synonymous with Devo, not only musically but visually. One of the theatrical components in Devo's concerts entailed the band dressing identically in work-themed attire and moving about onstage like highly agitated androids (the idea, according to Casale, coming from Russian Constructivist ballet).[6]

Devo developed little if any fan base in Akron. Confrontations at the infrequent live shows were common as enraged audiences and venue proprietors routinely halted shows in mid-performance. Taking a cue from Man Ray's maxim that the goal of Dada was to "try the spectators' patience,"[7] Devo extended songs to an interminable length, played well past their allotted set time, and baited the audience as much as the audience heckled them. Mothersbaugh recalled,

> At the time, we were a lightning rod for hostility.... We'd play "Jocko Homo" for 30 minutes, and we wouldn't stop until people were actually fighting with us, trying to make us stop the song. We'd just keep going "Are we not men? We are Devo!" for like 25 minutes, directed at people in an aggressive enough manner that even the most peace-lovin' hippie wanted to throw fists. We were in a negative-energy vortex back in the mid–1970s.[8]

"Jocko Homo" became the unofficial Devo anthem. The title was taken from a virulent anti-evolution religious pamphlet, while the song's chorus and bridge question-answer exchange cited by Mothersbaugh was referenced from the *Island of Lost Souls* (1932), a film where scientific experiments speed up the evolutionary cycle of various animals to create semi-humans. Musically reminiscent of Frank Zappa, "Jocko Homo" is in a brisk 7/8; midway through, it uncomfortably transitions into a martial 4/4 bridge call-and-response chant and then back to 7/8 to end the song. The odd time signature and shifting sets of descending riffs makes "Jocko Homo" rhythmically rigid and robotic even by Devo's standards. Reducing rock music to simple yet complex mechanical sounds and rhythms, Devo reflected a social reality of modern life that denied individuality, humanism, and rebellion but represented modernity as a process of automatically going through the motions.

Amid the early punk rock explosion, Devo relocated to Los Angeles in 1977 and the band's fortunes improved markedly. Iggy Pop was so impressed he wanted to do an album of Devo songs with Devo as the backing band (in effect, joining Devo as the lead singer while maintaining his solo artist status). David Bowie, Brain Eno, and Robert Fripp all expressed interest in producing the band. A more unlikely supporter was Neil Young, who was synonymous with counterculture "hippie music." Young featured Devo in his surreal comedy *Human Highway* (1978, released 1982), and a highlight was a cacophonous ten-minute performance of "Hey Hey, My My (Out of the Black)" by Young and Devo featuring Young singing in a comical clipped voice, a motorik backbeat, copious synthesizer noises by Mark Mothersbaugh, and Young taking his trademark discordant guitar soloing to extremes.

While major record labels including Warner Bros., Island, and Virgin Records competed for Devo, Stiff Records swooped in, licensed the early Akron independent singles Devo had recorded and released on their self-operated record label Booji Boy (pronounced "Boogie Boy"), and released them in Europe in spring of 1978 as a 12" 45 titled *Be Stiff*. One of the songs was "Satisfaction" which nearly made the UK Top 40. Amid industry politics,

Brian Eno was eventually chosen as the producer, and Devo's debut album, *Q: Are We Not Men? A: We Are Devo!* (1978, Warner Bros/Virgin), recorded in Germany at engineer Conny Plank's studio (not coincidentally where Kraftwerk recorded *Autobahn*). Released in fall of 1978, it also proved to be Devo's most intriguing album and included new versions of "Jocko Homo" and "Satisfaction."[9]

"Satisfaction" as Deconstruction

Devo's anti-cover of "Satisfaction" contains two things that become quite conspicuous in their absence. One, it is not anchored by a steady snare drumbeat; second, it almost completely dispenses with the song's signature riff. Instead, drummer Alan Myers provides a repetitive, robotic, "one-two-three-and-four" pattern of clomping drums save for the three, which is accented by hitting the bell of a ride cymbal. One rhythm guitar produces a pattern of atonal, brittle eighth notes with the strings muted by dampening them with the palm of the picking hand. The other rhythm guitar produces a cycle of repetitive notes augmented by effects to the point they become plunking blurts, as comical as they are mechanical. Gerald Casale's bass serves as the closest thing to a melody instrument in the song. Fairly loud in the mix and with a thick, treble bias, the bass alternates between a repetitive, growling riff and a four-bar pattern of D–A–D–G during the end of the pre-chorus sections that provide the most tonal variation in the song. The lead guitar supplied by Mothersbaugh only appears in the intro of the song, playing an extremely atonal, ascending short solo before the vocals. As far as the singing, Mick Jagger's defiant drawls and shouts are replaced by Mark Mothersbaugh's desperate barks and yelps; while Jagger's vocals project righteous frustration at his inability to attain any satisfaction in a consumer culture, Mothersbaugh coveys anxious resignation that any such satisfaction in said culture is impossible. In one of the more hilarious moments of the song, Jagger's use of the word "baby" in the final verse is carried to extremes when Mothersbaugh repeats "baby" over 30 times and extents it eight-and-a-half bars rather than the one beat in the Stones' version. Only in the final 40 seconds of the song does any substantial musical change occur. A highly distorted guitar adds a truncated variation of the first three notes (B–C♯–D) of the "Satisfaction" riff while electronically altered vocals chime on the last word when Mothersbaugh chants the full title to close out the song until it abruptly stops (total time: 2′41″).

Two things are striking in Devo's version of "Satisfaction." One is that the song is extraordinarily busy within its interlocking yet disjointed parts, but it does not seem to go anywhere. While Devo's version of "Satisfaction" has an urgent nervousness, there is no sense of "teleology" or even "drama." Here the Krautrock influence on Devo and bands like Can and Kraftwerk becomes crucial. Paul Hegarty suggested Krautrock bands could be loosely categorized by their

> exploration of repetition, statis and a machinic quality exemplified in the "motorik" beat.... A style of playing that refused blatant virtuosity.... Linear beats in bars and the possibility of expressive climaxes are lost.... In short, little changed, and when it did, on glacial time scales compared with either classical or rock expectations. The result is a driving beat that manages to convey total movement and stasis.[10]

The other issue is the extent to which rock music places a premium on individual experience and authenticity through a passionate expression of emotion or "feeling." There was something acutely cold and perfunctory in not only Devo's music but their representation of a rock band as workers cranking out a rock song the same way they would dispassionately produce any other consumer item on the assembly line—precisely why Devo moved like robots onstage and dressed identically in various industrial workplace outfits. Robert Christgau suggested in regard to punk that "the underlying idea of this rock and roll will be to harness late industrial capitalism in a love-hate relationship whose difficulties are acknowledged, and sometimes disarmed, by means of ironic aesthetic strategies: formal rigidity, role-playing, humor."[11] To this extent, Devo's love-hate relationship to industrial capitalism was manifest in the "formal rigidity" of mechanistic punk music, "role playing" as identical robotic musicians, and often condescending "humor" that could be as sophomoric as the Ramones and as acerbic as the Sex Pistols.

Nevertheless, it is not so much punk but Kraftwerk that better compares to Devo. Kraftwerk represented an embrace of the human-machine assemblage on *Autobahn* (1974), *Radio-Activity* (1975), and *The Man-Machine* (1978). Hegarty suggested, "There are two levels of subversion: firstly, in the rejection, through use of processing, synths, and so on, *of rock's claim to authentically represent the individual,* second, that the machine and human are intertwined, not as a result of industrial society, but as a *natural* necessity."[12] The similarity was that Devo also offered a rejection of rock ideology's "claim to authentically represent the individual." The difference was that Kraftwerk's anti-humanism entailed a well-ordered, even utopian world of humans and machines working in mutually productive "harmony" and "rhythm." Devo's human-machine relationship was the *unnatural* consequence of industrial capitalism that resulted in a dystopian, technocratic society—especially when "humans" entered into relationship with "machine."

What Devo also shared with Kraftwerk was the mechanistic and (increasingly) synthesizer-dominated music, the emphasis on visual uniformity, and the anti-humanist position resulting in accusations that they were fascists.[13] Devo openly ridiculed the principal tenets of rock ideology and rock myths constructed by its critical discourses: the premium on individual agency, social rebellion, emotional expression, and progressive political messages. In doing so, Devo effectively declared open season on itself for the rock press.[14] Dave Marsh's *Rolling Stone* review of Devo's second album, *Duty Now for the Future* (1979), amounted to a vitriolic diatribe against the band and its audience:

> Devo is sort of the rock equivalent of Kurt Vonnegut, taking off from premises that it only half understands. These guys synthesize trenchant experimental trends into a hodgepodge that's compelling only to those without the intellectual vigor to penetrate the band's surface pose to find the real pose underneath [read: Marsh being the possessor of said "intellectual vigor" versus Devo's ignorant herd of fans].... As rock & roll, this sort of stuff is a horror show that dispenses with backbeat, melody, and raw emotion—i.e., all the things that ever made rock worthwhile.[15]

It was not surprising that *Rolling Stone*, one of the main purveyors of rock ideology, assailed Devo. Marsh's highly traditionalist position posits that anything that does not conform to "authentic rock" defined by the holy trinity of "backbeat, melody, and raw emotion" necessarily allies itself with the enemy, and why Bruce Springsteen as Marsh's ideal of the rock and roll "working-class hero" represented the antithesis to Devo in all respects.

Marketing Opposition

While the fascist charges were bogus–whether the critics or the band themselves wanted to admit it, Devo was well within the tenets of traditional American liberalism—there were substantial problems with Devo's brand of cultural opposition. In the 1970s, Devo was at the frontline of the music video revolution, long before MTV debuted in 1981 and made music videos for songs—usually the ones released as singles—standard operating procedure.[16] The music video for "Satisfaction" bears some elaboration. Devo is shown on a green-lit soundstage performing the song in yellow plastic jumpsuits on cheap guitars, moving around like high-strung androids. There is an inner narrative where Mark Mothersbaugh is trying to cop a feel of his date in the backseat of a car only to be prevented by the father in a suit and military helmet (the first verse), or watching TV on the couch and having his advances interrupted by the mother in curlers and nightclothes brandishing a rolling pin (the second verse).[17] While Devo exposes the underlying theme of "Satisfaction" as rebellion through male sexual liberation, it also demonstrates the degree to which Devo shared the Repressive Hypothesis view of the Rolling Stones where male sexual liberation is quashed by sexually repressed authoritarian figures.

The third verse constructs a montage sequence. One series of shots depicts the Devo character of "Booji Boy"—a grotesque rubber mask of a baby that symbolized all that was stupid and infantile in modern society—in a crib sticking a fork into a smoking toaster and summarily electrocuting himself.[18] This is intercut with a punk dancing spasmodically before he does a back flip and lands flat on his back and continues writhing. The gestures of punk rebellion and self-explanatory dances like "the pogo" and "the worm" are the domain of a false *pseudo-rebellion* with unfree *pseudo-individuals* engaged in aimless *pseudo-activity*, as described in Adorno's vivid description of Jazz Age "jitterbug" dancers where "their ecstasy is without content ... [and] takes possession of its object by its own compulsive character.... It has convulsive aspects reminiscent of St. Vitus' Dance or the reflexes of mutilated animals. Passion itself seems to be produced by defects."[19]

Like their stance that the advancement of modernity was matched by the regression of humanity, Devo's view of cultural rebellion resonated with the pessimism of Frankfurt School theorists like Adorno and Marcuse over the oppositional potential of mass culture and the possibilities of oppositional culture operating within the bounds of capitalist production and consumption. Marcuse contended that all forms of cultural resistance are negated "by being absorbed by what they refute ... entertaining without endangering."[20] In this way, Devo's overall attack on rock pseudo-rebellion was extended into a pointed critique of punk pseudo-rebellion in the "Satisfaction" music video. Mothersbaugh put it more directly: "We thought the punks never learned from the failure of the hippies. *Rebellion always gets co-opted into another marketing device.*"[21]

To this extent, Devo's project proved untenable as they sought to remain "a postmodern protest band" while asserting that "rebellion always gets co-opted into another marketing device." In his 1981 *Village Voice* article "Devo Take a Stand," Robert Christgau effectively outlined the paradox of Devo:

> The Devo Philosophy is no more coherent than the Playboy Philosophy, opposing the most commonplace boho-modernist no-nos—conformity, technocracy, etc.... But it's always been harder to tell whether Devo thought the

world (or the weirdoes) worth saving; like Frank Zappa ... they purvey a sour satire in which the audience is sometimes indistinguishable from the target. This is a band that has always reveled in contradictions. Deploring conformity, they wear uniforms and hustle more groupie gear than Kiss. Skeptical of technology, they're on their way to an all-keyboard [band].... And what could be more conformist-technological than the robot moves they've always mocked so assiduously?[22]

The crucial issue was how Devo dealt with their contradictions. If the avant-garde and cultural subversion of today become the cultural commodities of tomorrow, Devo simply froze the clock and made the Devo brand of commodified subversion the product du jour. By 1979, a wide array of Devo fan paraphernalia was being brazenly marketed. The inner sleeve for *Duty Now for the Future* was a parody of magazine and comic book mail-order ads, but the plethora of merchandise was quite real.

At one level, the Devo marketing machine could be interpreted as another aspect of their overall mockery of the music industry, a situationist use of music and merchandising beyond the usual fare of T-shirts and posters to include items like plastic golf shirts emblazed with atomic logos. At another level, the glut of Devo products smacked of pseudo-subversion and Malcolm McLaren's situationist use of music as "cash-from-chaos" cultural opportunism as much as cultural terrorism with his stint with the Sex Pistols. Mark Mothersbaugh recounted, "Devo was ... obsessed with the fine line between commercial and fine art and also the juxtaposition of highbrow and lowbrow.... We were equally obsessed with TV commercials as we were with the fine arts of our times."[23] It is this ethos that ultimately summed up Devo's mission as a "postmodern protest band." Like Andy Warhol, Devo realized that art, labor, and consumerism were inseparable in modern capitalism; also like Warhol, Devo made their brand of avant-garde eminently consumable popular culture.

6

"Satisfaction" and Pop: Britney Spears (Oops! ... I Did It Again, *2000*)

The Lolita Next Door

Since her debut album ...*Baby One More Time* and title track respectively topped the album and singles charts in 1999 when she was 17 years old, Britney Spears remains one of the more controversial and occasionally maligned figures in American popular music and pop culture. Not only was she at the forefront of the late 1990s "teen pop" movement, but Spears was blatantly marketed around teen sexuality. "...Baby One More Time" combined a half-time funk rhythm with male heavy breathing audible in the mix, saccharine vocal harmonies, and Spears' cooing, gasping, and occasionally groaning vocals. If the song sounded like a calculated cross between bubblegum pop and porn film music, the music video for "...Baby One More Time" did little to dissuade that impression. Variously dressed in a disheveled schoolgirl's outfit or sweatpants and a sports bra, Spears did not so much dance but prowled the hallways, parking lot, and gymnasium of a high school while giving the camera an array of suggestive facial expressions.

As the title suggested, the follow-up album, *Oops! ... I Did It Again* (2000), was very much designed to replicate the controversy; the title track was also the first single and sounded more than similar to "...Baby One More Time." However, another controversy ensued over Spears' teen-pop cover of "Satisfaction" that also appeared on the album. In the traditionalism of rock ideology, it was bad enough that a decade that began with Nirvana's *Nevermind*, the grunge movement, and "industrial" bands like Nine Inch Nails ended with the commercial triumph of the Spice Girls, Christina Aguilera, and boy bands. Even worse for rock purists, Spears had the audacity to cover a song all but sacred in the classic rock canon, although none other than Mick Jagger gave Spears' version his seal of approval when they were co-interviewed at the

2001 MTV Video Music Awards (VMAs). Whether Jagger's endorsement had more to do with enjoying the song or the royalty checks can be left open to debate.

Considering it is one of the standard bearers of rock ideology, *Rolling Stone* gave *Oops!... I Did It Again* a surprisingly positive review. Rob Sheffield proclaimed, "Underneath its cheese surface, Britney's demand for satisfaction is compelling, fierce, and downright scary, *making her a true child of the rock and roll tradition.*"[1] As discussed last chapter, as far as the "rock-and-roll tradition," *Rolling Stone*'s criterion is "ideological" in the sense that it largely revolves around certain tenets: a genuine respect for rock's roots music, an adherence to "backbeat, melody, and raw emotion," a rejection of pretentious "artiness," and a humanist celebration of individual rebellion and social protest—the rationale that allows Bruce Springsteen as well as Britney Spears to be part of the "tradition" and why Devo was so vehemently reviled. However, *Rolling Stone* readers tend to think of "rock-and-roll tradition" less around formalism and ideology but the ordained performers that constitute the tradition versus those that do not deserve inclusion in the tradition. When *Rolling Stone* conducted a readers' poll of the "Top Ten Worst Covers of All Time," Spears had the dubious honor of making the list twice, coming in fifth with "Satisfaction" and seventh with her cover of "I Love Rock 'n' Roll." In fact, five of the top ten (so-called) worst covers of all time were done by young women associated with teen pop. As well as Spears' two placements, Jessica Simpson's cover of "These Boots Were Made for Walking" was ninth, Avril Lavigne's cover of "Imagine" eighth, and Miley Cyrus' cover of "Smells Like Teen Spirit" topped the list.[2]

To this extent, rock music and its ideology are indicative of the historical gendering of mass culture, which Andreas Huyssen pointed out became especially pronounced in the late 1800s and early 1900s.

> In the age of nascent socialism and the first major women's movement in Europe, the masses knocking at the gate were also women knocking at the gate of male-dominated culture.... The political, psychological, and aesthetic discourse around the turn of the century consistently and obsessively genders mass culture and the masses as feminine.[3]

Critical theory on mass culture, namely Adorno's work on the culture industry, defined mass culture around capitalist production. For Adorno, true culture critiqued social conditions of existence, exemplified by the avant-grade modernism of Arnold Schoenberg, Alban Berg, Franz Kafka, and Samuel Beckett.[4] Mass culture was culture reduced to standardized commodities by the culture industry designed for easy cultural production and consumption that sustained social conditions rather than questioning them. However, for Adorno the central issue was cultural production, not cultural consumption: "If the masses have been unjustly reviled from above as masses, the culture industry is not among the least responsible for making them into masses and then despising them."[5]

As rock ideology developed in the 1960s, it relied on the historical gendering of mass culture while bastardizing Adorno's culture industry argument to blame the music consumer rather than the record industry, specifically by constructing the stereotype of the young, female "teenybopper" record buyer. Norma Coates suggested,

> Although rock culture, as it emerged in the late 1960s, was largely populated by upwardly-mobile, white, middle-class youth, it embraced and honed an oppositional relationship to mainstream culture. It was not enough to designate women as low Others and to ignore their contributions to rock culture. They had to be actively distained and kept in their place…. Women and teenage girls came to be deemed the "outsiders" of rock culture.[6]

Extrapolating from Coates' critical work, Charles Allen Muller argued, "Most audiences cling to media-driven stereotypes … that rock music signifies masculinity, authenticity, honesty, and rebellion while pop holds connotations of femininity, dishonesty, ephemerality, and trashiness … synthesizers and most digital technology are also coded as feminine."[7] In fact, rock music "needs" the Spice Girls, Britney Spears, Hannah Montana, Miley Cyrus, and even boy bands or Justin Bieber as the examples of what constitutes the "inauthentic feminine" of pop with an assumed audience of conformist teenyboppers in order to construct its canon of the "masculine authentic" of rock with an assumed audience of rebellious rock fans (e.g., the Rolling Stones, the Who, Bruce Springsteen, etc.). Hence, the ideology of rock culture is predicated on a series of binaries:

Rock	Pop
Authentic	Inauthentic
Masculine	Feminine
Art	Commodity
Oppositional Culture	Mass Culture
Individualist	Conformist
Hip	Square
Fans as mature connoisseurs	Fans as immature consumers
Anti-Establishment	Establishment

The subversive element of Spears' version of "Satisfaction" is the extent to which it ruptures rock ideology around its binaries of masculinity and femininity, rock and pop, oppositional culture and mass culture.[8] More specifically, what comes under scrutiny is the myth of rock's oppositional status around the "masculine authentic" personified by the Rolling Stones and the myth of teen pop's conformist status around the "feminine inauthentic" personified by Britney Spears through a teen pop cover of a canonical rock song indicting mass culture and women.

Blond Alienation

As discussed in chapter 3, the overt message of the Stones' "Satisfaction" is an attack on consumer culture, but the hidden message is the championing of rebel Hip masculinity and male sexual liberation. This element was not lost on Spears when she performed a medley of "Satisfaction" and "Oops! ... I Did It Again" at the 2000 VMAs. Spears began by performing "Satisfaction" in a man's black suit with sequined pinstripes and a fedora. After the pre-chorus and chorus, Spears sang the *second* verse with altered lyrics. While the Stones' version entails Jagger dismissing the Square male TV announcer pitching laundry products promising to improve the "whiteness" of his appearance (hence maintaining Jagger's "white negro" Hip rebel persona), in Spears' version she is offended by a female TV announcer selling clothes that will enhance Spears' sex appeal, playing on the marketing of Britney Spears with an ironic assertion that she won't conform and dress sexier to improve her popularity and sacrifice her individuality. However, the performance of the second verse effectively contradicted the defiant lyrical statements when Spears tore off the man's suit to reveal a sequined, see-through bodysuit and then performed "Oops! ... I Did It Again" surrounded by half-naked male dancers while Spears provided her patented Michael Jackson–meets–strip clubs array of moves. By performing "Satisfaction" in male attire it became a statement in which Spears, as a woman dressed as a man, still cannot attain satisfaction in a man's world. However, by self-consciously reverting to her controversial teen sexpot image, it became an acknowledgement that Spears' identity is her designated role as a mass-culture "commodity fetish."

Spears' covering a song originally sung by Mick Jagger, one of rock's more iconic male vocalists, also suggests an inherent "gender politics" when a cover song is sung by a woman or a man. Assuming a heterosexual dynamic— although the songs could also be heard and read from a same-sex relationship perspective—Linda Ronstadt's cover of "You're No Good" (*Prisoner in Disguise*, 1975) becomes a song where a woman castigates a man, whereas Van Halen's cover of "You're No Good" (*Van Halen II*, 1979) becomes a song where a man belittles a woman. In an admittedly simplified reading, Ronstadt's version becomes a feminist statement and Van Halen's version a chauvinistic response (the sexual and gender politics of Van Halen is discussed further next chapter). "I Love Rock 'n' Roll" was originally a minor 1975 hit single by the Arrows, an all-male power trio. Joan Jett's fairly similar cover became the standard version when it topped the singles charts in 1982. The key difference was that it was sung by a woman—Jett has a raspy voice and a "tough chick" punk image— and "I Love Rock 'n' Roll" became a defiant message to the rock community that it was no longer an all-but-exclusive "men's club" at a time when women were becoming a greater percentage of rock performers in the wake of punk and beyond. It is not coincidental that the song was covered by later generations of female popular music performers like Britney Spears and Miley Cyrus. However, John Shepherd pointed out the potential pitfalls of this kind of reframing:

> The vocal sheen and vocal hardness that characterizes the woman-as-sex-object and the woman moving toward a male location in the social structure can become exaggerated to stridency when the woman singer as rock artist attempts to carve a niche for herself. Although the stridency of Janis Joplin has represented a clear challenge to the status quo, this stridency as a form of cultural resistance is also doomed to failure because it derives from the same splintered notions of "sexuality" that also give rise to "cock" rock.... The masculinity appropriated in the process of actively generating a "sexually desirable" female image steps over into the masculinity adopted in actively becoming "one of the boys."[9]

In short, the issue Shepherd raises is that women in rock not only have to adopt the role of "sex object" but frequently have to adopt the trappings of traditional rock masculinity as "one of the boys" to be accepted in rock culture.[10] To be sure, Britney Spears exemplified the woman-as sex-object in late–1990s pop. However, Spears did not implement the strategy of cultural resistance by becoming "one of the boys" in rock culture, and this does not necessarily lead to a conclusion that Spears remains complicit in her marketing around the (teenage) woman as a sexually desirable ideal. Rather, it is precisely how Spears covered "Satisfaction" around what rock ideology deems "feminine" that allows it to be read as a point of cultural resistance, a representation of female alienation in "feminine" mass culture that ultimately becomes a critique of rock music's role as a commodity in consumer society housed in the cover of a canonical rock song denouncing consumer society.

"Satisfaction" as Commodity

Spears' version of "Satisfaction" begins much slower and quieter than the Stones' version. In the intro, a jazzy acoustic guitar treaded with chorus effect plays the B–C♯–D riff with a bass drum on the one and finger snapping on the three of every other bar. As far as the signature riff, in Otis Redding's version it becomes variable and intermittent, whereas in Devo's version it is all but excluded. In Spears' version the riff is marginalized and played on a shimmering acoustic guitar as opposed to distorted electric guitar. As touched on in chapter 1, Jimi Hendrix's highly sexualized relationship with the electric guitar was one of foreplay and copulation as much as phallic symbolism. In terms of rock's normative heterosexuality, this suggests the electric guitar is feminine in relationship to Hendrix. Conversely, if the electric guitar is deemed masculine, the relationship metaphorically becomes a homoerotic relationship as far as sexualized musical performances. Either way, the heterosexual and masculine dynamics of the electric guitar are jeopardized. In response, rock ideology engaged in a binary reductionism that defines the acoustic guitar as inherently "feminine" and the electric guitar as inherently "masculine." The "guitar heroes" of 1960s rock included Hendrix, Eric Clapton, and Jimmy Page whereas women guitarists were generally associated with folk and usually played acoustic guitars: Joan Baez, Joni Mitchell, Emmylou Harris, Buffy Sainte-Marie, Judy Collins, and Melanie Safka. As John Strohm observed, "While the [female] folkie acoustic players flourished, the electric guitar remained a boy's club. This reinforced the idea that electric guitars were for boys and acoustic guitars for girls."[11] In this context, one could argue that the signature riff in Spears' version is rendered feminine given the status of the acoustic guitar in rock ideology.[12] As important, the intro establishes an atmosphere of melancholy whereas the Stones' version establishes a tone of menace.

When the dance beat kicks in, it is a metronomic backbeat, although periodic studio editing and drum programming alterations occasionally interrupt the flow of the song. Languid string synthesizer plays the rhythm guitar chord progression, and horn synthesizers add punctuations. Guitars are relatively submerged in the mix. As noted, the acoustic guitar plays the main riff and an electric guitar adds a wash of heavy metal power chords in the pre-chorus leading into the chorus, which is to say the "masculine" component trying to emerge out of the dance-pop mix only to be suppressed in the chorus. Spears' vocals are the only sounds that match the volume of the backbeat accompanied with an array of background vocals reiterating the title in a soul-gospel style while Spears also punctuates the song with numerous non-verbal vocal interjections. Indeed, if the core of rock and roll is, as Dave Marsh insisted, "melody, backbeat, and raw emotion," Spears' version of "Satisfaction" distills it into melody (vocals), backbeat (drum program), and raw emotion (Spears' performance).

To this extent, Spears' version of "Satisfaction" compares to Otis Redding's version, as much as it may be an affront for some to even mention Spears and Redding in the same sentence. Like Redding, there is a reframing of "Satisfaction" politically by the very act of covering the song. Redding sang "Satisfaction" from the perspective and position of a black, southern American in 1965 amid the civil rights struggle. Spears reconfigured "Satisfaction" by singing it from the perspective and position of an American teenage woman in 2000 and *her* alienated relationship to consumer mass culture—the irony being that Spears also represents consumer mass culture in public consciousness. Also like Redding's version, there are a number of lyrical modifications in Spears' version. The first verse is left intact where Spears, like Jagger, is listening to incessant commercials on the radio. As discussed with regard to her 2000 VMA performance, the second verse changed the lyrics from a TV commercial for laundry detergent to a TV commercial for women's fashion, and Jagger's rejection of a product that will enhance the "whiteness" of his appearance changes to Spears' ironic claim that she won't follow fashion trends to be sexier and more popular. The third verse where Jagger is bemoaning his sex life (or lack thereof) is omitted entirely in favor of a pre-chorus reprise which goes into an extended finale of a continual dance beat over which the full title of the song is sung and Spears provides numerous non-verbal vocal ad-libs.

In rock ideology, the degree to which a white performer demonstrates having "soul" is often assessed by the extent to which they can effectively "pass for black"—be it a singer, a band, a producer, or what have you. As discussed in chapter 4, soul performers such as Otis Redding "articulated" songs though the frequent use of non-verbal vocals juxtaposed with lyrics. In contrast, white music genres such as country and folk primarily articulate meaning through lyrics, with little if any use of non-verbal sounds; indeed, sections of spoken-word recitation are far more likely to be used than non-verbal interjections. In Spears' version of "Satisfaction," there is an inordinate amount of non-verbal lead vocal punctuations throughout the song (sighs, grunts, moans, etc.), clearly derived from Michael Jackson's singing style. To be sure, two criticisms could be leveled, if a bit simplistically. One is that Spears blatantly copies Michael Jackson in a failed attempt to pass for black; the other is that Spears' non-verbal interjections were often used to spice up a song with sexual innuendo, and therefore "Satisfaction" becomes yet another song perpetuating Spears' "Lolita next door" image. However, the Stones' version of "Satisfaction" contains an overt message of anti-consumerism and a hidden message of male sexual liberation. To a certain extent, Britney Spears not only becomes a retroactive target of the Stones' version as a symbol of mass culture but an object of sexual conquest. As much as translating "Satisfaction" into a different era, genre, and lyrics to address the alienation of young women in mass culture, Spears' non-verbal vocal interjections become signifiers of a frustration that words cannot fully express.

The omission of the third verse in Spears' version also reconfigures the song into an extended finale of steady dance backbeat, repeated statements of the full title by background vocals, and the string of vocal ad-libs by Spears. There is little if any variation, and while Spears' version lasts 4'26", it effectively runs its course by the 3'00" point of the song. From the perspective of rock ideology, Spears' version ends up "good to dance to" but offers little if any reward as far as serious listening and contemplation value (see chapter 4). In fact, the "contemplation value" afforded by Spears' version is *how* the musical framework of "Satisfaction" becomes a critique of popular music and mass culture (intentionally or unintentionally). The protracted conclusion with the steady and relentless thud of processed drum backbeat conveys a deadening monotony matched by Spears' repeated and repetitious verbal and non-verbal proclamations about the inability to attain satisfaction in the mass culture of a consumer society she is perceived to epitomize. This markedly contrasts to the underlying restlessness of previous versions of "Satisfaction" variously conveyed by the driving swagger of the Stones, the shifting intensities of Otis Redding, or the nervous rigidity of Devo. In effect, Spears' cover of "Satisfaction" *converts* it into generic teen dance-pop. It amounts to little more than a repetitive, electronic dance backbeat over which Spears could just as easily have sung "Jumpin' Jack Flash" or "Gimmie Shelter."

This is precisely the complaint of the rock traditionalist: Spears co-opted an oppositional classic rock song denouncing consumerism and debased it into an all-purpose and innocuous musical product. Another way to consider it is that Spears turns "Satisfaction" on its head. The contradiction is that over the course of the Rolling Stones' 50-year career they have become synonymous with rock rebellion as well as one of rock's most financially successful bands; indeed, the Stones are effectively a multi-national corporation producing music with a brand identity of being anti–Establishment. "Satisfaction" becomes a timeless statement of opposition divorced from past and present historical and social conditions to maintain its own myths. While they took vastly different approaches, both Devo and Spears ultimately critique "Satisfaction" around Marcuse's assessment that points of cultural opposition are inevitably "absorbed by what they refute ... entertaining without endangering." Devo's eventual failure was trying to have it both ways as far as maintaining the increasingly unsustainable subversive status of Devo while insistently marketing Devo as oppositional culture. Britney Spears' version reveals the contradiction of "Satisfaction" as a song condemning mass culture while it generates capital through its continual circulation in the mass culture marketplace. It was not so much that the Stones' "Satisfaction" was absorbed by what it refuted. It was always already absorbed by what it refuted the moment it was released and became a hit single for the Stones. The trajectory from the Rolling Stones to Britney Spears is ultimately not a question of the co-optation of rock as oppositional culture, but the cultural and economic logic of popular music in capitalist society.

Part Three

Signs of the Times: Cover Songs in Context

7

Music from the Waist Down: Covers, Gender and Sexuality

King Curtis: "Whole Lotta Love" (Single, 1970)

As discussed in chapter 3, the Rolling Stones were central to constructing rock ideology around, for lack of a better term, "cocky" anti–Establishment defiance that adopted white identification with black subculture, the mythic Repressive Hypothesis of sex, and a valorization of masculinity over femininity to the point of overt male chauvinism. By the late 1960s the gender and sexual politics of rock ideology were in contradiction to the progressive if not revolutionary façade being built around rock music as oppositional culture. Amid the feminist movement of the 1970s, rock reacted with reactionary gestures epitomized by the "cock rock" clichés of hard rock and heavy metal as "a masturbatory celebration of penis power."[1] Led Zeppelin's concert film *The Song Remains the Same* (1976) became notorious for the camera's fetishistic attention to Robert Plant's crotch and prompted the Who's lead singer Roger Daltery to comment that the film's intent was to "make Robert Plant's dick look big."[2]

Led Zeppelin was initially formed in 1968 by Jimmy Page (guitar) and John Paul Jones (bass, keyboards). Both were already well known in the rock music industry in that Page was a highly sought-after session musician and member of the Yardbirds while Jones was a respected session musician and arraigner. Having worked together on recording sessions—notably Donovan's hit song "Sunshine Superman"—Page and Jones decided to form a band after the Yardbirds' dissolution. Vocalist Robert Plant and drummer John Bonham rounded out the quartet and they became one of rock's most influential and popular bands until they disbanded in 1980 after Bonham's death.

While "Stairway to Heaven" is Led Zeppelin's best-known song, "Whole

Lotta Love" is arguably the archetypical Led Zeppelin song. Page's famous guitar riff is a blues-derived, two-bar B–D–B–D–E progression matched by Jones' bass and Bonham's characteristically ponderous but propulsive half-time drum patterns. Structurally, the song revolves around the repetition of the riff punctuated by disruptive breaks.

Intro (riff)
Verse 1 (riff)
Chorus (riff, drums enter)
Verse 2 (riff)
Chorus (riff)
Break 1 ("free-form" section)
Break 2 (guitar solo)
Verse 3 (riff)
Chorus (riff)
Break 3 (a cappella vocals)
Outro (riff, ad-libs vocals)

As Susan Fast analyzed the role of the riff in "Whole Lotta Love," "[It] might be experienced metaphorically as the body being jolted during the pickup and released by the tonic. Because the riff is so short and because it repeats throughout.... The body is continually—relentlessly—hit by the intensity of the pick-up ... [and] kept in a fairly constant state of intensity or arousal."[3] Another, somewhat cruder way to consider the riff to "Whole Lotta Love" is as a signifier of sexual intercourse. Given that Led Zeppelin is often a band synonymous with cock rock, "Whole Lotta Love" is frequently read as a song extolling male sexual prowess and the "whole lotta love" Plant is singing about is a sizable penis.[4] To be sure, Fast concedes the male gender specificity and unmistakably phallic references in the lyrics; what she instead emphasizes is how "Plant's over-the top vocal delivery of the lyrics contradicts masculine gender stereotypes of hardness and control ... the taunting/teasing/flirting delivery ... these are the flirtatious sounds a young girl might make."[5] Indeed, Fast reads "Whole Lotta Love" around female sexuality as opposed to cock rock, and the song, in effect, represents a woman achieving intense pleasure during sexual intercourse, where the high-pitched moans, groans, and screams in "Plant's performance suggest ... multiple climaxes."[6]

While Fast offers a productive alternative to the rote cock rock assessments of Led Zeppelin, the masculine alignment of rock music cannot be overlooked.[7] Steve Waksman suggested "Whole Lotta Love" contains an internal tension expressed by the free-form section's "interruption of the throbbing, single-minded riff ... [that] enacts a crisis in the representation of phallic potency," whereas the guitar solo following the free-form break is an attempt at "resuscitation ... hemmed in by the wall of sound produced by the band as a whole."[8] The free-form break, lasting from 1'19" to 3'05", is a cymbal-driven drum solo by Bonham overlaid by electronic effects as well as studio-treated instruments and vocal interjections. However, "free form" is something of a misnomer. While the section is tumultuous as far as the intermittent, churning waves of electronic noises and Plant's brief ecstatic howls, it is not arrhythmic in the sense of free jazz or modern classical. Bonham's hi-hat retains a strong sense of 4/4 meter drive throughout, and his ride-cymbal patterns are highly syncopated rather than seemingly random punctuations. The continuous beat of the song is still maintained, and the rhythm of sexual intercourse is presented as a different "tension and release" around percussion rather than the guitar riff. This is immediately followed by Page's guitar solo lasting from 3'05" to 3'20". The only accompaniment by the rhythm section is heavily accentuating the one and the upbeat between two and three of every other bar while the 4/4 drive is steadily maintained by Bonham's hi-hat as a continuance from the first break into the second break. Drawing from Waksman's analysis, "Whole Lotta Love" becomes a metaphor of *male* performance of sexual intercourse, with the main riff in the verse/chorus signifying sexual potency (sustaining an erection during intercourse) and the breaks lapses in said potency (the danger of losing an erection or premature climax). Hence, the guitar solo is followed by a restatement of the main riff in a third verse–chorus section representing a reinvigoration of phallic power before a third break lasting from 3'59" to 4'26" in which Plant reprises lines from the verses a cappella. His vocals become rawer and lustier while the lyrics are gender specific as far as Plant directing them at a woman. Moreover, Plant asserts that he can provide the sexual pleasure the woman not only wants but needs, and the full band provides a brief, two-note descending chord progression in the otherwise a cappella break; this is crucial in that they underscore in unison Plant expressing his male sexual prowess that promises to satisfy the woman. "Whole Lotta Love" ends with an outro where the band returns to the "throbbing, single-minded riff" while Plant ad-libs the vocals which become much more direct and even somewhat lewd. The outro provides reassurance that "phallic potency" remains the same as the song fades out.

King Curtis was a saxophonist with an illustrious career as both a solo performer and backing musician until his untimely death on August 13, 1971, when he was stabbed to death during a street altercation in Harlem. Born in Fort Worth, Texas, Curtis played saxophone in high school with classmate

Ornette Coleman and began a professional music career playing in jazz vibraphonist Lionel Hampton's backing band. In 1952, Curtis moved to New York City to work as a session musician, playing on records ranging from Buddy Holly to Andy Williams; he also played the saxophone on the Coasters' hit "Yakity Yak" (1958) while his final session work was on John Lennon's *Imagine* (1971). In 1967, Curtis had a Top 40 hit single with his self-composed instrumental "Memphis Soul Stew" which indicated Curtis had more affinity for the Stax brand of "southern soul" over Motown's "symphonic soul." The same year, King Curtis released the album *King Curtis Plays the Memphis Hits*.

In March of 1971, Aretha Franklin performed three nights of concerts at the Fillmore West, and Curtis headed an all-star backing band consisting of Billy Preston (organ), Cornell Dupree (guitar), Jerry Jemmott (bass), Truman Thomas (electric piano), Bernard "Pretty" Purdie (drums), Pancho Morales (percussion), and the Memphis Horns (Wayne Jackson, lead trumpet; Roger Hopps, trumpet; Jack Hale, trombone; Andrew Love, tenor saxophone; Jimmy Mitchell, baritone saxophone).[9] Curtis and the band also served as the opening act, performing a set of instrumental covers released as *Live at the Fillmore West* (1971). They included rock, soul, and even country songs like Procol Harum's "A Whiter Shade of Pale," Stevie Wonder's "Singed, Sealed, and Delivered," Bobbie Gentry's "Ode to Billie Joe," Buddy Miles' "Them Changes," Jerry Jeff Walker's "Mr. Bojangles," and a short but highly intense version of "Whole Lotta Love." Curtis also recorded a studio version of "Whole Lotta Love" that was released as a single in 1970, which is the version discussed.[10] One immediate difference between the Led Zeppelin and King Curtis versions of "Whole Lotta Love" is the "pace." The vast majority of rock songs are not only in 4/4, but are driven by a backbeat (snare on the two and four), a half-time beat (snare on the three), or a quarter-note beat (snare on the one, two, three, and four). While the Curtis version is slightly faster, the half-time drum beat on the Led Zeppelin version is replaced by what can be termed a "reversed backbeat" with the snare on the one and three. This not only "accelerates" the velocity as far as two snare beats per bar instead of one, but it is also a somewhat disorientating pattern for the listener to "get into the groove" comfortably.[11] Moreover, the Led Zeppelin version begins with a build, the guitar beginning the song alone playing the main riff and soon after joined by bass while the drums do not enter until the chorus after the first verse. In this way, Led Zeppelin establishes anticipation (foreplay) before the song locks into its ensemble driving rhythm (intercourse). King Curtis' version begins with a bang—double entendre intended—with heavily distorted lead guitar playing the first four pickup notes and the rhythm section immediately entering on the one of the next bar of the song and, as noted, the reversed backbeat driving the song with a careening, almost chaotic volatility. Curtis plays Plant's vocal melody on saxophone, and the horn section joins in to play the vocal line in the chorus while the trombone emphatically punctuates the tonic as the "release point" by loudly playing a sustained note each time it appears in the riff.

As an instrumental cover, there are no lyrics or voice that specifically "genders" the song although music is *culturally* coded into masculine and feminine components that are established as "natural" differences (e.g., electric guitars or drums as "masculine" and acoustic guitars or synthesizers as "feminine").[12] In turn, hard rock and heavy metal, genres dominated by male performers and electric guitar, are often critically interpreted as "inherently" masculine or even masculinist genres (i.e., cock rock). Led Zeppelin's "Whole Lotta Love" can be read as representing the masculine struggle to sustain phallic power or "staying power" over the process of sexual intercourse (the main riff versus the interruptive breaks), with a kind of phallic omnipotence attained as the song concludes through the outro's reiteration of the main riff and sexual intercourse continuing indefinitely as the song fades out. King Curtis' cover can also be read as an aural representation of sexual intercourse itself. Ironically, the song lasts 2'46" from start to finish.

Not meant as facetious, Curtis' version as a collision of hard rock and southern soul not only parallels Motown "psychedelic soul" of the era (discussed next chapter) but invites comparison to porn film soundtracks. The difference is that most porn film music of the era was "smooth music" like light funk-jazz, lounge music, or easy listening instrumental that was highly incongruent to the graphic visuals of sex acts captured on grainy film. King Curtis' version is anything but smooth; it is tense and frenetic, trying to rein itself in and maintain the rhythm of sexual intercourse as long as possible before male climax is achieved and the sex effectively ends. Here the "breakdowns" in the King Curtis version can be compared to Led Zeppelin. The free-form section appears as a percussion-dominated, Latin-influenced groove while the guitar solo section is done as a kind of big-band rave up; as important, the third verse-chorus and break with Plant's a cappella vocals are omitted. As noted, Steve Waksman characterized these first two breaks in the Led Zeppelin version as respective moments of "crisis" followed by "resuscitation" while the main riff states "phallic potency" during intercourse. The effect is different in the King Curtis version which goes directly from the second break into the outro. If the main riff suggests the rhythmic drive of sex, the first break suggests the transition from a steady "thrusting" to a more "irregular" syncopated rhythm that does not provide a point of relaxation but increased agitation in the rhythmic drive coupled with the "entwinement" of the horns as they continually rise in pitch.

It is the second break of the Led Zeppelin version—Page's guitar solo—that becomes the pivotal moment of "crisis" in the King Curtis version. The full band with particular emphasis on the horn section mimics the stop-start accents of the Jones-Bonham rhythm section while the guitar solo is manifested by twisting saxophone runs. It collapses the rhythmic drive as "the point of no return" and the onset of male climax. Indeed, to signify that the male orgasm is reached, the second break immediately shifts to the outro. Over the reversed backbeat the main riff is played by the horn section while the guitar plays a *descending* four-note pattern on guitar as a "release of tension," and Plant's outro vocal ad-libs are replaced by Curtis' grunting saxophone using a wah-wah pedal to drastically modulate the tone. This is followed by the "guitar solo" as a single plaintive note played a few times that is sustained for several beats and modulated in tone via sharply bending the string. The King Curtis version of "Whole Lotta Love" becomes a narrative of the sex act structured as

> Main riff/verse/chorus (coitus)
> Latin break (approaching male orgasm)
> Big band break (inevitability of male orgasm)
> Outro of main riff (male orgasm reached and onset of post-coitus)

Whereas the Led Zeppelin version ends with the returned emphasis on the thrusting main riff and a restatement of phallic power, in Curtis' version the main riff representing sex becomes overwhelmed by sounds representing male orgasm, the primal noises produced by the saxophone and the bluesy and almost mournful guitar representing "the little death" of orgasm as the song fades out. While Led Zeppelin's version concludes with the outro as a statement of endless coitus and phallic power immune to the threat of orgasm, the outro in the King Curtis version signifies the moment when coitus ends and post-coitus begins. The song becomes "spent."

Van Halen: "You Really Got Me" (Van Halen, 1978)

While well known in the U.S., the Kinks failed to match the superstar success of British Invasion contemporaries like the Beatles, the Rolling Stones, and the Who. One key factor was the Kinks being denied work permits by the American Federation of Musicians (AFM) from 1966 to 1969, reportedly as a result of several onstage and offstage "incidents" during the Kinks' first U.S. tour in 1965. With their presence in the American counterculture and popular music market severely restricted—they had to decline an invitation to play the Monterey Pop Festival due to the AFM dispute—the Kinks focused on the European market and especially England. Not surprisingly, the Kinks were one of the most "English" rock bands of the 1960s British Invasion in two respects. One was that the Kinks were highly influenced by the British music hall as much as American R&B. The second was that Kinks' songs were political but not in the sense of anthems or protest songs. Rather, the Kinks tended toward ironic vignettes chronicling the foibles of everyday modern life in tension with British attitudes concerning the bourgeois lifestyle ("A Well-Respected Man"), mass culture ("Dedicated Follower of Fashion"), or romance ("Lola," a song about a male virgin who falls in love with a transvestite).

In any event, the Kinks' place in rock history was secured with their first hit single "You Really Got Me" (1964), a shambolic garage-rock song that might be termed "proto-punk" in terms of its elementary F–G–G–F–G rhythm guitar riff repeated throughout much of the song. The lyrics are a first person account of a man hopelessly dependent on his girlfriend for his happiness, and his pleas for her not to exercise her own power in the relationship and possibly break up with him. Indeed, she could summarily strip him—or symbolically castrate him—of what makes him a man: the masculine status that he invests in himself through her being his girlfriend. Ray Davies' singing is fairly calm in the beginning of each verse and develops a noticeable agitation by the time he reaches each chorus (here one could contrast the impassioned vocals of soul music addressing similar subject matter, such as Percy Sledge's "When a Man Loves a Woman" or the Four Tops' "Bernadette"). The bridge after the second verse–chorus is a guitar solo consisting of a discordant and choppy flurry of notes that escalates tension into the third and final verse–chorus. A recurring and precarious cycle develops in "You Really Got Me." There is the continual repetition of the one-bar, stop-start riff operating with and against the backbeat and Davies' relaxed-to-distressed vocals interrupted only by a frantic and somewhat slipshod guitar solo. This not only mirrors the relationship as it teeters on the brink of collapse but male self-esteem that is also endangered.

Amid the punk and post-punk movements, progressive rock became virtually extinct whereas heavy metal survived in no small part due to Van Halen taking the genre to new levels of musical virtuosity, visual flamboyancy, and masculine vitality with their eponymous debut album. Steve Waksman pointed out that,

> however much of this new virtuosity strove for artistic progress, it shared much with the earlier forms of guitar heroism, including its unabashedly mas-

culine orientation. With the rise of the guitar hero in the 1960s and 1970s, the virtuosity of musicians was enhanced and amplified by the technological trappings of the electric guitar, which assumed the status of ... "technophallus," fusing human and technological capabilities in a way that reinforced the historical coupling of virtuosic performance and masculine potency.[13]

"Eruption" (*Van Halen*) is a showcase solo guitar piece where Eddie Van Halen does not merely demonstrate his considerable skill as a guitar player, but his *mastery* of the guitar through a minute-and-a-half run-through of his signature guitar gymnastics: thirty-second- and sixty-fourth-note arpeggios, tremolo bar finesse to execute drastic pitch changes, and "double tapping" (the picking hand playing hammer-ons and pull-offs on the fretboard in tandem with the fingering hand). In terms of the technophallic symbolism constructed around the guitar, "Eruption" and its double-entendre title becomes a masturbatory exercise in masculine power and prowess where full confidence in "technique"—musical and sexual–is fully demonstrated and displayed on the technophallus.

However, the "money shot" is not in the copious and seemingly endless flow of guitar orgasm unleashed throughout "Eruption" but the extended coda as a full-band heavy metal reworking of "You Really Got Me." The guitar launching into the rudimentary riff of "You Really Got Me" is an abrupt contrast to the virtuoso showcase of "Eruption." The effect is that, having demonstrated his full capabilities as a guitarist, the transition to a simple and well-known two-chord riff is not only well within Eddie Van Halen's means, but *below* them. In this way, Robert Christgau's *Village Voice* review of Van Halen's *Woman and Children First* (1980) defined what had been Van Halen's raison d'être from the outset: "[T]he message of the music isn't the exuberance of untrammeled skill, it's the arrogance of unchallenged mastery. They're kings of the hill and we're not." Indeed, the "untrammeled skill" exhibited in "Eruption" transitions to "unchallenged mastery" of "You Really Got Me."

In terms of studio production, the clattering sound of early 1960s garage rock is updated to the overkill of late 1970s stadium rock. Drummer Alex Van Halen maintains a backbeat that not only rocks, but in its subtle syncopations, confidently saunters. Michael Anthony's bass largely restates the main riff to provide the steady undercurrent of masculine "primitivism." Throughout the song, Eddie Van Halen frequently fills the awkward gaps produced by the stop-start main riff with his patented guitar acrobatics to provide further evidence of his prowess on the guitar-technophallus. Ray Davies' introverted and anxious delivery is replaced by David Lee Roth's leering, lurid, self-assured drawl that manifests a sarcastic conceit. Moreover, the masculine effect was heightened by Roth's concert performances which combined acrobatic athleticism with exaggerated cock rock posturing, although defenders of Roth contend that his almost overdetermined cock rock "persona" was consciously ironic if not a full-scale parody of metal machismo and/or laced with an androgynous element.[14]

Unlike the cyclical unsteadiness of the Kinks' original, the drive of Van Halen's version becomes linear and infused with self-confidence. Drums, bass, guitar and voice continually reassert masculine authority to reconfigure the lyrics so the song no longer manifests the threat that the woman might leave and emasculate the man, but an implicit promise offered by the man that if she does leave, there will be consequences.[15] Put more bluntly, if the Kinks' version expresses a man pleading with the woman not to break his heart, Van Halen's implies a warning that his broken heart may well lead to her broken nose. To this extent, the advent of Van Halen signified a transition in heavy metal from a *phallocentric* to *phallogocentric* cultural discourse.[16] As Terry Eagleton suggested,

> Modern society, as the post-structuralists would say, is "phallocentric"; it is also ... "logocentric," believing that its discourses can yield us immediate access to the full truth and presence of things. Jacques Derrida has conflated these two terms to "phallogocentric," which we might roughly translate as "cocksure." It is through this cocksureness ... by which those who wield sexual and social power maintain their grip.[17]

Indeed, Van Halen represented a shift from "cock rock" to "*cocksure* rock" at a time when feminism became central to American politics and women were making unprecedented inroads as rock performers (e.g., Deborah Harry, Stevie Nicks, Patti Smith, Ann and Nancy Wilson). Or, as Robert Christgau pointed out in a highly mordant rhetorical question that ended his review of *Van Halen II* (*The Village Voice*, 1979), "So how come formalists don't love the shit out of these guys? Not because they're into dominating women, I'm sure."

The Flying Lizards: "Sex Machine" (Top Ten, 1984)

The Flying Lizards exemplify the extent to which punk and avant-garde/experimental music converged by the late 1970s. As discussed in chapter 2, post-punk moved punk away from strict rock formalism through incorporating popular black music genres (funk, disco, reggae, etc.) and avant-garde/experimental music (dissonance and noise). Many post-punk performers were young, relatively inexperienced, and often had little if any formal training;

they entered music through the DIY ethos of punk and ventured into avant-garde musical terrain. Conversely, the Flying Lizards were the brainchild of David Cunningham. A composer and musician who studied under Michael Nyman at the Maidstone College of Art, Cunningham was drawn to popular music and record production, serving as co-producer on the experimental rock band This Heat's eponymous debut album.[18] Cunningham was also an associate of David Toop and Steve Beresford, two key members of the London Musicians Collective (LMC), which formed in 1975 as a forum for musicians of varying technical proficiency working in various genres such as modern classical, experimental music, free jazz, and punk. In this environment, Cunningham conceived the Flying Lizards, although technically they were not a band but a "production company" under contract with Virgin Records.[19]

The Flying Lizards (1979) included contributions from Beresford, Toop, rock journalist-musician Vivien Goldman, avant-punk singer Patti Palladin, professional voice-over artist Deborah Evans-Stickland (a.k.a. Deborah Evans), and painter Michael Upton as part of the production company. In that anti-covers had become something of a vogue in the wake of Sid Vicious' "My Way" and Devo's "Satisfaction," the Flying Lizards' debut single was a bizarre but recognizable reworking of Barrett Strong's 1959 R&B hit "Money (That's What I Want)," although it is debatable whether the "standard version" is Strong's original version or the Beatles' relatively similar cover version, especially for British audiences.[20] "Money" became an unlikely UK Top 5 hit and narrowly missed the U.S. Top 40 (it peaked at number 50); however, it is debatable if the commercial success of "Money" owed to its reception as a New Wave novelty song or a joke record rather than a post-punk anti-cover. In the Flying Lizards' version of "Money," a heavily processed "trash can" drum machine sound acts as the rhythmic base, and the main riff, often but understandably mistaken for a banjo, is actually played on prepared piano. The soulful female R&B backup vocals in the chorus on both Strong's and the Beatles' versions are replaced by tuneless male doo-wop groans, a highly discordant noise guitar solo follows the second chorus, and the outro features what sounds like recurring sonar pings.

Lyrically, "Money" is not a criticism of excessive wealth and personal greed (e.g., Pink Floyd's "Money"), but the struggle to maintain any sort of economic security, a statement that took on political significance in that it was first sung by an African American in 1958 and portrayed the socioeconomic relationship between class and racial inequality. Comparing the Beatles to the Flying Lizards, Simon Reynolds noted, "Deborah Evans [*sic*] replaced Lennon's lusty working-class rap with icily enunciated aristocratic disdain."[21]

Indeed, Evans-Stickland's stiff monotone largely recites the lyrics as opposed to any attempt at singing, let alone providing a melodic hook. Moreover, the recitation does not necessarily work in accordance to the meter of the song. Lines are occasionally spoken too fast or too slow against the rhythm of the song, and at times it sounds like Evans-Stickland is not even listening to a backing track but being visually cued as to when to start and stop speaking. As a political song, one aspect of "Money" is the representation of class politics and the premium placed on working-class "authenticity" as far as being a credible rock musician, especially punk's contempt for suburban, middle-class "poseurs." Reynolds' critical gesture to establish the Beatles—specifically John Lennon—as having working-class "authenticity" aside, the Flying Lizards' version of "Money" becomes a sardonic representation of a jaded, idle-rich upper class whose concern is not making ends meet but always wanting more. Rather than lower-class alienation and frustration, the vocals project a "disconnected" and arrogant air of upper-class avarice and indifference.[22]

By the early 1980s, the experimentalism and leftism of post-punk had given way to New Pop and synthpop. This shift was exemplified by the band Scritti Politti. Formed in Leeds ca. 1977, the name was a pun on a book by Antonio Gramsci, the early ideological influence on Scritti Politti founder Green Gartsdale (better known as "Green"). Their first single, "Skank Bloc Bologna" (Rough Trade, 1978), was a post-punk assemblage of lurching reggae, hints of jazz, grating atonal guitar, political lyrics, and vocals highly influenced by Robert Wyatt. Indeed, Scritti Politti sounded like the Sex Pistols had they used Soft Machine rather than the New York Dolls as their musical template. Corresponding with the decline of post-punk, by 1981 Green abandoned much of the Marxist political sloganeering and avant-garde musical leanings in favor of a Scritti Politti "deconstructing" popular music in an attempt to be both musically accessible and culturally subversive. Incorporating R&B, Motown, funk, and lovers rock (a soul-influenced style of reggae especially popular in England), the rebranded Scritti Politti was eminently commercial dance-pop with erudite lyrics that worked as love songs as well as sly references to the critical theories of Jacques Derrida and Jacques Lacan. Green also renounced the "messthetics" of the post-punk era as bands "filled with irritating *noises* and failed attempts at *music*."[23] As much as Green consciously applied critical theory to popular music, Scritti Politti became the antithesis of Jacques Attali. The problem of noise was converted to the solution of music and, by extension, potential social disorder into established social order. Even ardent New Pop supporter Simon Reynolds conceded, "It's doubtful that the subtle subversion woven into Scritti's superslick sound was picked up on by most listeners.... It was hard to see how [it] could be read as anything other than straightforward upward mobility."[24]

Following a three-year hiatus, the Flying Lizards released their final album *Top Ten* in 1984 on the independent label Statik Records.[25] It amounted to a farewell album that consisted of anti-covers from various genres uniformly done in the "Money" format of mechanistic music and monotonal female recitation performed by Cunningham, Sally Peterson, and guest musicians ranging from ex–Henry Cow bassist John Greaves to pop-rock keyboardist Julian Marshall. Songs ranged from Little Richard's "Tutti Frutti," Larry Williams' "Dizzy Miss Lizzy," "Tom Jones' "What's New Pussycat?," and the Crystals' "Then He Kissed Me" to Leonard Cohen's "Suzanne," Jerry Lee Lewis' "Great Balls of Fire" and "Whole Lotta Shakin' Goin' On," and James Brown's "Sex Machine."

In order to analyze the Flying Lizards' anti-cover of "Sex Machine," it is necessary to assess James Brown's original/standard version. Officially titled "Get Up (I Feel Like Being a) Sex Machine," it is one of Brown's classic funk songs emphasizing the guitar-bass-drum trio with horn section punctuations.[26] After Brown counts off the song, the band plays eight quarter notes until the first rhythmic "shock" of the song occurs when the drums begin to play a half-time beat. Although the tempo conforms to Brown's count-off, the song sounds much slower than what was expected (here one could compare the Ramones where the fast count-off was effectively matched by a fast backbeat). Recalling Susan Fast's critique of "Whole Lotta Love" that contended "the riff might be experienced metaphorically as the body being jolted ... the body is kept in a fairly constant state of intensity or arousal," this is an apropos description of "Sex Machine" as well. In keeping with Brown's famous axiom "always on the one," the "release" is on a D♯ played on the one of the first bar, and the "jolt" in the riff is a syncopated F–D♯ progression one octave higher that starts on the one of the second bar. Also like "Whole Lotta Love," the riff is continually repeated throughout much of the song. In this way, a similar "state of intensity and arousal" is manifest in the main riff of "Sex Machine" and it can also be read as a musical representation of sexual intercourse.

In Brown's version of "Sex Machine," the male voice has a crucial presence. The first twelve seconds consists of Brown making an enthusiastic announcement he's ready for sex and wants to get the song started and asks if the band is ready as well; the "male chorus" of band member voices shouts affirmative responses. The main vocals are done in a call and response. Brown's patented lead vocals, replete with his array of shrieks and grunts, are augmented by organist Bobby Byrd chanting between Brown's vocals. More specifically, there is a lead male voice extolling his sexual arousal and prowess while another *male* voice interjects his support. In this respect, Eve Kosofsky Sedgwick suggested,

> "Homosocial" is a word occasionally used in history and social sciences, where it describes social bonds formed between persons of the same sex; it is a neologism, obviously formed by analogy with "homosexual," and just as obviously meant to be distinguished from "homosexual." In fact, it is applied to activities such as male bonding which may, in our society, be characterized by intense homophobia, fear, and hatred of homosexuality. To draw the "homosocial" back into the orbit of "desire," of the potentially erotic, then, is to hypothesize the potential unbroken continuum between homosocial and homosexual—a continuum whose visibility, for men, in our society is radically disrupted.[27]

The contradiction as far as masculinity in American society, particularly in the wake of the men's movement since the 1990s, is how the "continuum" between homosocial and homosexual is not so much "radically disrupted" but categorically denied. They become mutually exclusive domains where, as Sedgwick noted (writing in 1985), "male bonding" is consciously infused with "intense homophobia." While American sitcoms like *Home Improvement*, *The King of Queens*, *According to Jim*, and *Two and a Half Men* represent the more blatant examples, this becomes a problematic aspect of popular music as well. The morbid symptoms of counterculture sexism were defined (rightly or wrongly) in the 1970s as a decade of cock rock that began with Led Zeppelin and culminated with Van Halen. In the 1980s, glam aesthetics reemerged in both New Wave and heavy metal. British New Pop adopted androgyny, makeup, and upper-class fashion with Duran Duran's *Tiger Beat*-meets-*GQ* look becoming the rule and the bohemian gender-bending of Culture Club's Boy George serving as the exception. Concurrently, American metal "hair bands" like Cinderella, Poison, and Warrant adopted "feminine" makeup accoutrements like eye shadow, lipstick, nail polish, and well-coiffed permanents; Twisted Sister pushed glam into the realm of muscular drag queens in black and pink Spandex. On one hand, this can be read as an acknowledgment of the continuum between the homosocial and the homosexual where homoerotism and same-sex desire was, at the least, hinted at through androgyny and gender-bending.[28] On the other hand, it can be read as representing a further exclusion of "the woman" in the male-dominated world of rock where men could appropriate and colonize the "female image" in an all-male milieu and thereby consolidate the phallogocentricism of rock music.

In this context, Brown's version of "Sex Machine" can be further compared to Led Zeppelin's "Whole Lotta Love." While Waksman suggested the Page-Plant musical relationship sustained "the homosocial content of cock rock," Fast contended the same-sex relationship was symbolically gendered, with Page (the wielder of the guitar-technophallus) cast in the masculine role as giver and Plant (the moaning, screaming singer) assuming "the role of receiver of sexual pleasure during intercourse ... thus strengthening his role as feminine other to Page."[29] In Brown's "Sex Machine," the vocalists are all men and the lyrics make no mention of women specifically. Instead, the lyrics are almost stream of consciousness exaltations and ruminations by Brown that he is ready, willing, and able to have sex while Byrd staunchly urges on Brown's proclamations. This is not to say that "Sex Machine" is an implicit anthem to gay sex (although one could potentially read it that way). Rather, it is a song where the homosexual and homosocial continuum is not "radically disrupted" but "unbroken." The continual repetition of the main riff as the signifier of sexual intercourse represents *male desire* for sex, the *ideal* of heterosexual sex as the pervasive anchor for the male bonding ritual where men incessantly discuss sex among themselves in the absence of women—all set to a steamy, funky rhythmic groove.

If James Brown's version of "Sex Machine" can be read as a musical representation of the role of male homosocial desire in the discourse in male heterosexuality, then the Flying Lizards' cover of "Sex Machine" is translated into a sardonic critique of heterosexual intercourse that places the emphasis on "machine" rather than "sex." To contextualize, one topic explored by postpunk bands—specifically the Gang of Four—was the contradiction between sexual fantasy and sexual reality and how the latter often does not live up to the former. Not unrelated, they raised the issue of how popular music acts as an integral discourse maintaining an imaginary of sexuality over the real. Two songs by the Gang of Four from their debut album *Entertainment!* (1979) can be briefly analyzed in this respect.

"Damaged Goods" begins with drummer Hugo Burnham providing a persistent backbeat (the exception rather than the rule in Gang of Four songs). Guitarist Andy Gill juxtaposes a syncopated funk-reggae riff that, for lack of a better way to describe it, sounds like barbed wire. Dave Allen's bass supplies the steady rhythm as well as most of the melody with a funk-disco bass line that alternates between two measures in E and two measures in C throughout the song; it is modified only by slight rhythmic and melodic alternations (syncopated additions of seconds, fifths, sevenths, and octaves, and simple runs between chord shifts). This musical framework houses the song's lyrical topic as the frequent *letdown* of libidinal liberation during sex (so much for Wilhelm Reich). The drums maintain a backbeat as the rhythm of intercourse in a way that is not passionate or primal, but decidedly "mechanical." Gill's jagged atonal guitar with its staccato and disruptive start-stop syncopations is consistently "out of sync" with the backbeat. In the phallic symbolism coded into rock guitar, it provides highly uncomfortable musical friction with irregular poking and prodding throughout "Damaged Goods" and dropping out entirely twice in the course of the song for several seconds, presumably in order to "rest" before it resumes its abrasive thrusting attack *against* the beat. It is only at the "climax" of the song that the guitar gives the listener the "money shot" with a fairly traditional guitar solo. Amid it all, Allen's funky bass lines ironically provide the music of sweet lovemaking between Burnham's drums maintaining the unremitting beat of sex and Gill's guitar providing the jarring and dubious "technophallus."

"Anthrax" begins with a minute and a half of Gill coaxing feedback and other noises from his guitar (string scrapings, hitting the body of the guitar, etc.) without any sense of dynamics, no dramatic effect in building expectations, or any demonstration of technical virtuosity. It becomes the antithesis of "Eruption" as Eddie Van Halen's display of technical prowess and phallic power that serves as the prelude for "You Really Got Me." On "Anthrax" the guitar simply emits intermittent electronic crashes and hums until Gill plays a cliché, dissonant two-note guitar solo bend a few times, primarily to cue Burnham, who enters with a drum pattern of eighth notes on the floor tom and the snare on the one and upbeat between the two and three, which provides a persistent rhythmic pulse while negating the backbeat. Allen follows shortly thereafter with a syncopated bass line working both with and against the drums, and the rhythm section repeats the pattern for the duration of the song without change. As Gill described it, "There's this totally bizarre, robotic drumbeat matched with a weird two-bar-loop bass line, so the emphasis in both drums and bass falls entirely in the unexpected place ... and my guitar ... [is] random free-form noise."[30] At the two-minute mark in "Anthrax," the guitar feedback suddenly stops—leaving only the bass and drums. This was a common technique the Gang of Four referred to as "anti-solos," in which the presence of an instrument was established by its sudden and/or extended absence in a song and the silence it generated rather than sound. Instruments routinely paused for several beats, dropped out for several bars, rested for an entire section, or did not play for extended portions of the song. In this way, the Gang of Four used *silence* as a crucial compositional tool much like John Cage. Silence was not a momentary relief for the listener amid the onslaught of noise but a means to maintain and exacerbate tension by the startling absence of musical components that "should" be there (i.e., Cage's *4'33"* in which a performer sits at a piano without playing a note for four and a half minutes).[31] After the guitar drops out, two conflicting vocals begin simultaneously. Jon King sings the lyrics from the perspective of a horny, lovesick bachelor while Gill provides a deadpan recitation of a manifesto against rock bands and the clichés and conventions of rock songs which "mystify" interpersonal relationships, occasionally joining King in unison for select words of the verses.[32]

The Flying Lizards' anti-cover of "Sex Machine" addresses sex in a highly comparable way, albeit musically far different than the Gang of Four. As noted, "Sex Machine" sounds quite similar to "Money" and the whole of *Top Ten* as far as instrumentation and performance. A metronomic drum machine anchors the song's repetitive main riff played by Julian Marshall on a prepared piano with a highly mechanical-percussive sound. Sally Peterson delivers a stilted recitation of Brown's visceral exaltations while Michael Upton dispassionately intones Bobby Byrd's vocal encouragement. Unlike the homosocial celebration of male sexuality between Brown and Byrd, Peterson and Upton engage in a blasé exchange, the male and female voice impassively intoning the exact same words about sex over a musically comic-robotic setting, representing a disinterested heterosexual couple going through the motions of sexual intercourse that becomes increasingly unsatisfying and unproductive.

The main riff is repeated throughout the song's 5'11" duration, with the only variations being the intrusions of disconcerting noises and the use of then-cutting-edge sampling technology. The moaning and groaning sounds of sexual ecstasy are replaced by the noises of car accidents and other sounds of industrial mishaps: skidding tires, impacting metal, and machinery breaking down. Also sampled is Peterson's parody of James Brown's non-verbal vocal interjections that sounds like a strangled gasp, suggesting a non-verbal response of pain rather than pleasure. Midway through "Sex Machine" the samples appear with increased frequency to the point that sex is not only rendered mechanistic but unproductive to the point of a potential risk for injury. By the final minute, it becomes less of a song and more akin to listening to a remix experiment by a self-indulgent record producer, which is to say finishing off a few minutes of unsatisfying sex with some personal masturbation. In short, as the sex continues, the worse it gets, and the Flying Lizards effectively negate one of the central themes of popular music: the attainment of sexual pleasure.

Kim Wilde: "You Keep Me Hangin' On" *(Another Step, 1986)*

"You Keep Me Hangin' On" was written and produced by Holland-Dozier-Holland, first recorded by the Supremes and released on Motown

Records in 1966. Lyrically, the song is in the first person where the singer is being mistreated in a relationship and asking the partner to end the situation so the singer can attain personal freedom. Rather than a traditional verse-chorus-bridge arrangement, "You Keep Me Hangin' On" is structured around a repeated G♯–F♯–C♯–E–D♯ chorus section (four bars; last bar E and D♯ two beats each) with varying lyrics based around the title. A verse section appears three times over the course of the song. The first and third verses are A–A–E–B (four bars played twice)–F♯ (two bars)–D♯ (two bars) for twelve bars total. The second verse is modified into a shorter progression of A–A–E–B–A–A–E–G♯, with G♯ played three bars for ten bars total.

The song is in G♯-minor and there is a noticeable change between chorus and verses. The verses begin on an A as an accidental note (not A♯ per the G♯-minor scale). As much as the verse beginning with an unexpected note that is not in the key signature of the song, the chorus is almost entirely composed of sharp notes, which maintain a greater degree of musical tension as opposed to natural notes; in turn, the verses are in natural notes that act as a release of the tension that shifts to sharp notes at the end of the verse as a tension-producing transition back into the sharp-note-dominated chorus. Hence, the song's conflict of entrapment versus freedom is expressed musically as well as lyrically. Moreover, "You Keep Me Hangin' On" begins with the famous monotone "Morse code" electric guitar riff to replicate the sound of an SOS signal being sent by telegraph; it is underscored by brass playing the chorus note progressions on the one of each bar. The drums enter and the snare plays on every beat while a tambourine supplies the backbeat; in the verses, the guitar drops out and is replaced by deadened congas. In this way, there is additional tension established by the rhythmic drive that manifests oppression around aural signifiers of the unremitting snare beat, the tambourine as the sound of shackles, and the congas the sound of being "trampled on" overlaid with the guitar sending an SOS signal to the listener.[33]

This serves as the musical framework for the vocals. By 1966, Diana Ross had become the de facto lead vocalist of the Supremes and was already being positioned for a future solo career. Ross had a delicate soprano that was effective on pop-inclined songs like "Where Did Our Love Go?," "Baby Love," and "I Hear a Symphony" that contrasted with the more traditional soul style of backup vocalists Florence Ballard and Mary Wilson. However, for "You Keep Me Hangin' On," Ross sang two lead vocal tracks and Ballard also recorded a lead vocal track that was mixed lower alongside Ross' lead tracks; Ballard's lower, fuller voice is most pronounced in the chorus following the second verse when Ross briefly sings the background vocal part and Ballard sings the lead vocal.

This tactic to "strengthen" the lead vocal suggests the underlying problem of the Supremes' version. The singular voice is represented as unable to effectively carry the song, let alone adequately convey its message of liberation. Here one can compare Aretha Franklin's cover of "You Keep Me Hangin' On."[34] It recalls Franklin's signature song, her cover of Otis Redding's "Respect," which she converted from a song that could come off as chauvinistic when sung by a man into a feminist anthem where the woman is demanding that the man treat her with the respect she deserves. Franklin's southern soul version of "You Keep Me Hangin' On" contains strong gospel, R&B, and rock elements (Duane Allman reportedly played guitar on the track) while Franklin's powerful vocals deliver the lyrics as a direct challenge with a confidence that she can and will prevail. This is not to suggest that Franklin is a "better" singer than Ross or that southern soul was a "better" brand of soul than Motown. Rather, the issue is that Ross' voice is lilting, sweet, and even vulnerable. It captures powerless but does not convey empowerment, which becomes the central tension of the song between liberty and captivity within an inequitable relationship. Instead, the song becomes a desperate plea by the woman to the man to liberate her from the relationship rather than a defiant declaration that she is liberating herself.

Vanilla Fudge's overhaul of "You Keep Me Hangin' On" was done in a single take as a ponderous, psychedelic–hard rock workout that lasted seven-plus minutes on album; it was edited to a three-minute single that made the Top Ten in 1967 (the single is the version discussed).[35] Among the several alterations Vanilla Fudge made included changing the key to E-minor from G♯-minor, altering the chord progressions, and modifying the song structure. The chorus is a repeated four-bar E–D–B–C progression while the lone verse is F–F–C–G–F–F–C–E–E (nine bars). Furthermore, the ringing "Morse Code" guitar riff on the Supremes' version is converted into a leitmotif of a pounding "distress signal riff" played by the full band in stop-start unison on E. Vanilla Fudge also slowed down the song considerably, and the overdriven distortion on the electric guitar and especially Tim Bogart's bass combined with Carmine Appice's choppy backbeat punctuated with drum fills exacerbates the already leaden pace.

The song begins with Mark Stein's somber organ before the full band enters by crashing in on the one of each bar with the chorus chord progression and Appice's waves of drumrolls before the band erupts into the distress signal riff. This shifts into the chorus with Stein's overwrought lead vocal and the band supplying the background vocals. The verse of the song follows, and despite the many differences, what the Supremes' and Vanilla Fudge's versions share is that the verse begins on an accidental note (F as opposed to F♯) which is not in the key of the song, providing a sudden and surprising tonal change. Moreover, Stein sings lines from the first and second verses of the Supremes' version, one of the more empathic sets of lyrics asking for a definitive end to the relationship which would finally put a stop to the woman's ongoing manipulations and his tortured heartaches. Following the verse, there is a brief reprise of the distress signal riff before returning to the chorus where Stein continues to bemoan his fate with ad-lib vocals while the background vocals sing the chorus lyrics. This shifts to a brief, four-bar E–D–E–D variant, and the distress signal riff is played again until it momentarily halts while the forlorn organ plays an E–D progression before the full band explodes into the distress signal riff yet again until the song abruptly ceases with the scatter of tone clusters from the organ and the band ending the song in a unison E.

While the drive of the Supremes' version is persistent and infused with aural signifiers of recurring repression (tambourine as shackles, congas as "being tramped" in the verses), the drive of Vanilla Fudge's version is more "tidal," and to this extent the song can be read metaphorically around the mythical sirens.[36] The distress signal leitmotif begins just before the first chorus, reoccurs throughout, and concludes the song. Hence, the ship is already in distress when the melodramatic vocals describe the experience of being held hostage emotionally by a woman (trapped in the grip of the siren's allure) with the backing vocals serving as the homosocial "Greek chorus" sympathizing with the male singer's plight. The inevitable ending is the distress signal being continually and frantically sent out and suddenly halted at the moment the song ends with the man's life left in ruins due to the woman's irresistible and destructive machinations (the ship being catastrophically wrecked on the rocks by the sirens). In this way, if Vanilla Fudge can be read as translating "You Keep Me Hangin' On" into three-minute epic tragedy, it also becomes a pathos-drenched saga of the man being wronged and ultimately destroyed by the seductive and sadistic woman—a standard trope in rock music.

Part of a famous British pop music family, Kim Wilde's father Marty Wilde was a pop star during the 1950s and 1960s and her mother Joyce Baker was a member of the popular vocal group the Vernon Girls.[37] In the 1970s, her brother Ricky Wilde was marketed as a "teen idol" pop singer in the UK, garnering considerable name recognition if not overwhelming commercial success. In 1980, Ricky Wilde was recording demos with veteran record producer Mickie Most, who worked with 1960s rock legends the Animals, the Yardbirds, and Donovan. Kim Wilde recorded some background vocals for the sessions, and an impressed Most signed her to his RAK Records label. One also suspects Most saw commercial potential in Kim Wilde's "punk-meets-fashion-model" look as well as her singing at a time when an unprecedented number of women were becoming successful rock music performers, particularly in the burgeoning New Wave market. While Madonna became global capitalism's "Queen of Pop," Kim Wilde was one of the most commercially successful female pop music performers from Britain during the 1980s.

In 1981, Wilde's debut single "Kids in America" became a hit record across Europe. As with most of her 1980s musical output, it was written by Marty and Ricky Wilde, with the latter serving as her record producer, musical director, and backup musician (guitar, keyboards). In 1982, the song became a Top 30 hit in the U.S., in no small part due to the music video for the song being regularly aired on the fledgling MTV network. "Kids in America" can be described as hopelessly dated or emblematic of the 1980s' New Wave synthpop sound.[38] A reverb-drenched snare provides a metronomic backbeat, and a treble-biased bass guitar plays driving eighth-notes. Keyboards add clinking arpeggios whereas electric guitar is ostensibly absent save the conclusion of the song where distorted power chords can be faintly heard in the mix to reinforce the bursts of string synthesizer on the one of numerous bars (a tactic also used on "You Keep Me Hangin' On"). In fact, a dominant sound in the mix of "Kids in America" is actually a heavily flanged electric guitar that produces an eighth-note pulse of clicking, whooshing white noise in the verses and a sound like swooshing radio static in the chorus.

In this respect, "Kids in America" utilizes electronic noise as part of the song, albeit not to the extremes of the early recordings of Roxy Music or Pere Ubu as far as the synthesizer producing an array of electronic sounds as opposed to mimicking conventional instruments. The song begins with a sequenced, pulsating electronic tone augmented by ambient, dissonant noises resembling car horns and passing traffic over which Wilde begins the first verse and the full band does not enter until 0'28" into the song. In the finale, noises replicating the sirens of emergency vehicles can be heard. The aural signification suggests that what begins as an evening of hipster exploration of what Norman Mailer rhapsodized as "the Wild West of American night life" ultimately ends in a devastating crash.

As opposed to Night Ranger's Reagan-era, arena-rock anthem "You Can Still Rock in America" (1983), "Kids in America" is not a patriotic "feel-good" song that celebrates rock individualism and living in a liberal democracy as one and the same experience. The synthpop setting renders the song extremely cold, and Wilde's vocals project mixed emotions that veer between jaded boredom and desperate longing for some unattainable pleasure (in this way, similar yet different from the Flying Lizards' "Money"). There is little joy or revelry expressed in "Kids in America" where the pursuit of happiness becomes predatory rather than liberating.[39] By the time the song reaches its finale and the ending chant of the title—ironically sung by voices with distinct British accents—the song becomes a sardonic and sinister critique of American youth culture amid the Reagan Revolution.[40]

Wilde's most successful single was a cover of "You Keep Me Hangin' On" which topped the Billboard charts for one week in June of 1987. Wilde performed the song as a synthpop version highly influenced by Hi-NRG disco, a rock-orientated style of disco that was "slamming rather than swinging."[41] It is largely modeled on the Supremes' version with the exception of a key change—Wilde's version is in G♮-minor—and the utilization of Vanilla Fudge's altered chorus chord progression which is played as G–F–D–D♯. The first and third verses are A♯–A♯–D♯–A♯ (four bars, repeated twice)–F (two bars)–D (two bars) and the second verse A♯–A♯–D♯–A♯–A♯–A♯–D♯–G, with G played four bars for eleven bars total.

The song begins with synth arpeggios while a string synthesizer plays the chorus chord progression and is soon joined by a steady bass drum thump on each beat. Wilde begins singing, and unlike the Supremes' and Vanilla Fudge's versions which feature a lead vocalist and separate background vocalists, she sings lead as well as overdubbed backing vocals. As a solitary voice, it manifests a sense that Wilde is effectively "alone" and isolated as she describes the situation. A clean funk guitar riff also begins, referencing the "Morse code" guitar riff of the Supremes' version and the "distress signal" sections in the Vanilla Fudge version. However, the song abruptly shifts into the chorus at 0'31" with an almost overpowering snare backbeat (treated with gated reverb) and the guitar playing heavily distorted power chords on the one in tandem with the string synth. As discussed in chapter 6, the electric guitar coded as a signifier of masculinity is subverted in Britney Spears' version of "Satisfaction" where the power chords are briefly audible in the pre-chorus before being subsumed by the "feminine" synthesizer-dominated, dance-pop setting in the chorus. There is a similar yet different effect in Wilde's version of "You Keep Me Hangin' On." In the chorus, on the one of each bar there is a continual repetition of electric guitar power chords (masculine-coded) and string synths (feminine-coded) as a gendered musical relationship that is repeatedly "stressed"—in *both* senses of the word.

In the verses, the guitar is absent and instead the rhythm section dominates with the thick, treble-biased bass guitar playing eighth-note octaves and the bass drum a syncopated eighth-note rhythm with the omnipresent snare backbeat. To this extent, the most noticeable aspect in the transition from chorus and verse is an element of silence as far as the guitar/string synth "wall of sound" being momentarily absent. However, it does not necessarily allow a brief sense of relaxation in the song before it resumes in the chorus. The bass-drum rhythm maintains the thumping Hi-NRG disco drive with mechanistic, repetitive propulsion. The tonal transitions between verses and chorus are noticeable, but reversed from the sharp notes prevalent in the chorus and natural notes of the verses in the Supremes' version. In Wilde's version, natural notes dominate the chorus, with the crucial departure being the D♯ that ends the four-bar progression with an ascending half step that repeatedly establishes a "note" of escalating tension. The verses are primarily dominated by sharp notes (A♯ and D♯) juxtaposed against the chorus. Yet the chorus–verse transitions are not as musically dramatic in that *all* the changes remain within the tonal confines of the G♮-minor scale. This is unlike both the Supremes and Vanilla Fudge versions where the verses begin with an unanticipated accidental note. The absence of the accidental note in the verses acts to musically blur the lyrics' dichotomy between liberation and subjugation.

Also contrasting to the Supremes and especially Vanilla Fudge, Wilde's vocal is dissimilar from the disparate pleading of Diana Ross or the overwrought self-pity of Mark Stein. Instead, Wilde conveys a tense combination of distant indifference and intense distress chronicling a situation where the likelihood of any liberation is nullified. As touched on, the signature "Morse code" guitar riff of the Supremes' version and Vanilla Fudge's "distress signal" riff is briefly hinted at in the intro of Wilde's version and then abandoned for the rest of the song. Instead, the distress is manifest through the "slamming" repetition of the song itself: the strict adherence to key signature, the power struggle between the dense metal guitar/string synth blasts on the one of each bar in the chorus, the unrelenting backbeat, the mechanistic disco rhythm especially prevalent in the verses, and the dispassionate yet distraught vocals all converge in claustrophobic monotony. At one level, the reappearance of the synthpop arpeggios that begin the song after the second verse ostensibly provide a sudden musical "variation" and their return in the concluding fade-out brings a sense of "finality" in the conclusion; in another way, they act as a further aspect of the overall cyclical repetition and entrapment of the song. Rather, the most dramatic moments of change in Wilde's version are two points where the (masculine) guitar ruptures the song with "noise." Sustained lead guitar notes modulated with the tremolo bar give way to dissonant notes and feedback when the song transitions from the third verse to the chorus (2'56"–3'12") and during the chorus itself (3'36"–3'43"). They serve as disconcerting explosions of musical violence amid the unrelenting cycles of the song.

In this regard, another critical moment occurs near the end where Wilde adds a line that explicitly states she is being *abused* in the relationship. Here one can consider Wilde's promotional music video for "You Keep Me Hangin' On." Given the video was done in 1987, the overall look is somewhat dated and is replete with many of the overused video techniques of the era, but in terms of content, the video augments the ominous undercurrent of Wilde's cover. While in color, it is dominated by monochromatic hues and the environment is a claustrophobic, disheveled, expressionistic setting where the only furniture is a bed with black linen. A sense of disorientation is exacerbated by the handheld camera pans, the frequent jump-cut editing, backwards footage, and occasional freeze-frames. Throughout the video, a silhouette of a man blocks the only exit points—an open doorway and a gaping hole in the stone wall. In other scenes, male hands at the edge of the frame try to grope Wilde as she half staggers, half dances down a hallway. In a macabre parody of music video clichés, Wilde begins and ends the video lying in bed in a full-length black outfit. Almost inevitably, in music videos of the era a woman lying in bed would be dressed in sexy attire and strike numerous suggestive poses.[42] Instead, Wilde simply lies on the bed, immobile and even numbed in a dark, skewed world where any escape routes are continually blocked by a menacing male presence. In the end, Wilde's version of "You Keep Me Hangin' On" raises the disturbing issue of domestic abuse where the woman is trapped in a musical setting of continual intimidation and probable punishment in relationship to the man.

8

Black Musicians, White Songs: Race and Covers in the Late Counterculture Era

Rufus Harley: "Where Have All the Flowers Gone?" (Recorded in 1969; Released on Courage: The Atlantic Recordings, *2006)*

During the 1960s, contentious divisions emerged within jazz as well as between jazz and other popular music genres. Free jazz shook the jazz world, spearheaded by Ornette Coleman and his harmolodics theory of music. As Coleman put it, "Harmony, melody, speed, and rhythm, time and phrases all have equal position, in the results that come from the placing and spacing of ideas."[1] Coleman's harmolodic theory can also be described as constructing a horizontal structure of musical organization (melody = harmony = rhythm) rather than a vertical hierarchy (melody > harmony > rhythm) by which noise possibilities are extended by eliminating the constraints of tonality and time signatures. Coleman's harmolodic theory was inherently political, not only in challenging the formal tenets of Western music but representing a kind of collectivist anarchism. In discussing the Pop Group, a "free funk" post-punk band highly influenced by Coleman and James Brown, Rob Young suggested

> Harmolodics is a utopian system.... Everybody plays individually, and the whole finds its equilibrium between individual and collective playing. Like a vision of collectivity, the hierarchy of "lead" and "backing" instruments is broken down; music making becomes an endless succession of conversations, revised statements, and arguments.[2]

Coleman's longtime bassist Charlie Haden made free jazz explicitly political with Liberation Music Orchestra (LMO), a free jazz big band. Adapting traditional revolutionary songs from Central and South America as well as American folk and patriotic songs for the basis for free jazz improvisations, LMO also performed original compositions by Haden like "Song for Che" and "Circus '68 '69." The inspiration for the latter song occurred when Haden watched the 1968 Democratic National Convention on TV and, amid one of the many breakdowns in order, liberal factions sang "We Shall Overcome" while the orchestra played "You're a Grand Old Flag" in an attempt to drown the other out.

Archie Shepp was another stalwart of the free jazz movement, and his turbulent and often abrasive brand of free jazz was eminently political. As Shepp put it, "Art cannot be thought of as interchangeable with life on all levels.... IT IS LIFE.... Then music at times must terrify!"[3] On "Rufus (Swung, His Face at Last to the Wind, Then His Neck Snapped)," Shepp's coarse, fragmentary tenor saxophone blasts and gurgles in tandem with the furious bass-drum interplay effectively evoked images of a man strangling and twisting from a noose during a lynching. The Revolutionary Ensemble—a trio of Leroy Jenkins (violin), Sirone (bass), and Jerome Cooper (drums)—released *Vietnam* in 1972, an album consisting of two 20-plus-minute performances, "Vietnam 1" and "Vietnam 2." As a musical representation of the war, fragments of ragtime and blues were violently juxtaposed with allusions to Western music ranging from Sousa to Schoenberg along with utilization of drones and scales used in non–Western music to construct a musical battlefield.

What might be termed "transcendental free jazz" emerged with performers like John Coltrane, Albert Ayler, and Sun Ra. As Coltrane moved from bebop to free jazz on records like *Ascension* (1965) and *Meditations* (1966), he became increasingly drawn to African, Middle Eastern, and especially Indian music. As Joachim E. Berendt noted, "Considering that conventional tonality, stemming from European music, had meanwhile been stretched to the breaking point [Coltrane] was searching for a kind of substitute ... in the 'modes' of Indian and Arab music."[4] One of the more controversial free jazz saxophonists, Albert Ayler used almost rudimentary motifs drawn from New Orleans jazz funeral processions, circus music, marches, hymns, polka, and waltz as a basis for frenzied excursions that suggested an evangelical church service with the instruments replicating convulsing bodies and speaking in tongues. Using electronic as well as acoustic instrumentation, Sun Ra and his Arkestra big band engaged in lengthy musical explorations around Sun Ra's highly personal mythology that incorporated elements of Egyptology, the civil rights movement, and intergalactic travel—one might say the past, present, and future.

In sum, the politics of free jazz entailed adopting traditional American black music and non–Western music at a time when the American civil rights movement was raging and Third World national liberation movements and revolutions were proliferating. Equally important, free jazz represented a rejection of tonality as "the musical language of the bourgeois era" (Adorno). Berendt contended,

> The formal and harmonic emancipation from the music of the "white continent" was part of a greater racial, social, cultural, and political emancipation. "Black music," as it was interpreted by many of these musicians and by LeRoi Jones (Amiri Baraka), one of their more eloquent spokesmen, became "blacker" than ever before in this process by *breaking its strongest link with the European tradition, the harmonic laws.*[5]

While free jazz was a central point of contention, it was not the only one during the 1960s. "Third Stream" jazz posited intersections of classical music and jazz as mutually productive rather than mutually opposed to each other— be it the archaic (the Modern Jazz Quartet) or the avant-garde (Anthony Braxton). Samba and bossa nova became something of a musical vogue. Other black American popular music genres began to appear in jazz like blues, funk, gospel and soul (e.g., the work of keyboardist Les McCann). However, rock and pop proved less welcome. Drummer Shelly Manne bitterly complained, "I don't think one good think has come from rock and roll. Whatever good things you find in it were there long before, in rhythm and blues.... Rock has taken all those things and blown them out of proportion into a grotesque, crude way of playing."[6] Not all jazz musicians shared Manne's contempt for rock. Miles Davis began to incorporate rock into jazz in ways that were commercially and critically successful. In the process, Davis broke the unofficial taboo on electronic instrumentation save the clean-sounding electric guitar or electric organ (as noted, one exception was Sun Ra, who was using several electronic keyboards and even a Moog synthesizer by the end of the 1960s). Extended jazz improvisation combined with funk and rock on *Filles de Kilimanjaro* (1969), *In a Silent Way* (1969), and *Bitches Brew* (1970), the last of which proved especially popular with a younger generation attuned to the Jimi Hendrix Experience and Sly and the Family Stone.[7]

Another was Rufus Harley, who recorded four albums for Atlantic from 1965 to 1970. A trained saxophonist and flautist, Harley converted to Scottish Great Highland Bagpipes as his primary instrument, reportedly after watching John F. Kennedy's funeral on TV and hearing the bagpipe ensemble that participated in the memorial. To be sure, bagpipes are *not* standard instrumentation in jazz—let alone a bagpiper equally at home covering "A Love Supreme" or "Amazing Grace." This is not to say jazz musicians have shied away from incorporating unconventional instrumentation. As examples, Anthony Braxton utilized contrabass clarinet, Eric Dolphy the bass clarinet, and Yussef Lateef oboe and bassoon. Rahsaan Roland Kirk was, quite literally, a multi-instrumentalist. Through circular breathing, using false fingerings, and making alterations on his instruments, Kirk could play two and even three wind instruments simultaneously.[8] As well as saxophone, flute, and clarinet, Kirk played obscure variants in the saxophone family like the "manzello" (an altered soprano saxophone also known as a "saxello" with a curved neck and upturned bell) and the "stritch" (an alto saxophone which is straight rather than curved); he also used homemade instruments like the "trumpophone" (a trumpet with a soprano saxophone mouthpiece).

Harley compares to Kirk for three reasons. As noted, both employed instruments typical and atypical in jazz. On his third alum for Atlantic, *A Tribute to Courage* (1968), Harley used a jazz combo (piano, double bass, drums) and alternated between flute ("Ali"), soprano saxophone ("'X'"), tenor saxophone ("About Trane"), and bagpipes ("Sunny," "A Tribute to Courage (JFK)," and "Swing Low, Sweet Chariot"). Second, Harley and Kirk were formally unconventional enough to be considered avant-garde in comparison to mainstream jazz performers like Dave Brubeck or Maynard Ferguson but accessible as compared to the avant-garde of Anthony Braxton or the Revolutionary Ensemble. Third, Kirk and Harley routinely covered pop and rock hits. Covers are not uncommon in jazz but tend toward covers of other jazz compositions or popular standards (e.g., John Coltrane's cover of "My Favorite Things"). However, while jazz traditionalism was openly hostile to the extremes of free jazz, it was equally appalled with pop and rock's potential to "commercialize" jazz. In contrast, Kirk stated, "I just want to play. I think I could work opposite Sinatra, B.B. King, the Beatles, or a polka band, and people would dig it."[9] Indeed, Kirk's covers ranged from mainstream hits like "Alfie" and "I Say a Little Prayer" (both Bert Bacharach–Hal David songs) to soul classics ("Ain't No Sunshine," "What's Going On," "My Girl") and soft rock (Bread's "Make It with You").

Harley's final album for Atlantic, *King/Queens* (1970), began with covers of "Eight Miles High," "Moon River," "Love Is Blue," and "Windy" and closed with two original compositions, "King" and "Queens."[10] For the cover songs, Harley's band consisted of Eric Gale (electric guitar), Chuck Rainey (bass guitar), Richard Tee (piano), Jimmy Johnson (drums), and Montego Joe Sanders (congas, percussion). They performed songs in a fairly straightforward manner, much more along the lines of a rock or soul band than a jazz ensemble.[11] In this way, there is a highly incongruent yet intriguing collision, with bagpipes as the lead instrument playing covers of popular songs accompanied by a soul-rock band within the jazz genre. The immediate issue is that a "Scottish Highland Bagpipe is tuned to a scale that cannot be represented in orthodox notation. It is roughly that of the white notes of a piano with C and F about a quarter tone sharp [a tone between C and C♯ and between F and F♯, respectively]."[12] This makes it especially difficult, but not impossible, for bagpipes to play in tandem with instruments tuned to conventional Western chromatic scales, especially fretted instruments and keyboards which are scaled to play in half-step intervals only (i.e., each space on the fretboard or the white and black keys of a keyboard).[13] In that electric guitar, electric bass, and keyboards were the instruments utilized in Harley's backup band, the very conditions of musical production in the ensemble made moments of tonal dissonance almost inevitable.

Before analyzing Harley's version of "Where Have All the Flowers Gone?" (henceforth "Flowers"), it is necessary to discuss the song itself. "Flowers" was initially written by Pete Seeger in 1955, and in 1960 Joe Hickerson added two additional verses and a restatement of the first verse with Seeger's approval to express a stronger anti-war sentiment in the song.[14] As much as the specific political statement of the lyrics, one aspect of folk music as "populist music" is that songs are fairly simple as far as musical construction and performance demands; one does not have to be a virtuoso, let alone possess substantial technical skill. It can be played by a novice guitarist, the lyrics can be easily memorized, and the song does not require an extensive vocal range. The simple chord progression repeats G–Em–D–C for the first three lines of each verse and C–G–C–D–G for the fourth line. All chords are one bar in duration and the final G can be extended as many bars as desired until transition to the next verse (for instance, the performer can talk to the audience, recount experiences, make a political speech, etc.). Like many folk songs, "Flowers" is carried by the vocal melody and the message transmitted by lyrical content which forms a cyclical narrative: the flowers are picked by girls, the girls get married, their husbands join the military, the troops end up in cemeteries, and their graves are decorated with flowers. The song was recorded by numerous folk performers ranging from the apolitical (the Kingston Trio, the Brothers Four) to the highly political (Joan Baez) and became widely associated with the peace movement.

Harley's cover of "Flowers" was recorded in 1969 (during the *King/Queens* sessions) at the height of U.S. military involvement in Vietnam; however, it remained unreleased until 2006 when it was included on *Courage: The Atlantic Years*, a CD box-set reissue of his work for Atlantic Records.[15] In that Harley performs an instrumental version of "Flowers," there are no lyrics to convey the message although the listener knows it is an anti-war song; more correctly, the anti-war message is conveyed musically. Particularly in the first verse, "Flowers" is *extremely* atonal as the bagpipes and its microtonal notes struggle with the rest of the instruments, compounded by the fact that Harley seemingly plays numerous "sour notes" as far as the song melody as well. As much as the numerous ruptures of tonality in the song, the sound of the bagpipes can be analyzed in two ways. While the Scottish Great Highland Bagpipes are a Western instrument, bagpipes are not exclusive to Western Europe and are used in Eastern European, Middle Eastern, North African, and Indian music. Moreover, as a double-reed instrument, the bagpipe has a shrill, piercing, almost metallic tone that best compares to the oboe (the clarinet and saxophone are single-reed instruments). In certain respects, bagpipes have a kind of "Eastern" sound; the bagpipe drones recall Indian sitar and tamboura music or Mongolian throat-singing while the melody sound produced is not unlike a *shehnai* (Indian oboe), a *suona* (Chinese oboe), or in a more specific context, a *kèn đám ma*, a northern Vietnamese oboe used primarily in funerals (the literal translation of the instrument is "funeral oboe").

To be sure, there is a considerable problem with universalizing Eastern music at the expense of national and regional specificity, as well as instrumentation and genre. Rather, during the 1960s a generic idea of "Eastern music" largely based around Indian music was being circulated in popular music, especially rock and jazz—best expressed by the popularity of Ravi Shankar, whose sitar music greatly influenced musicians ranging from John Coltrane to George Harrison. This presence of "Eastern music" in American popular music corresponded with America's military operations in Vietnam, and Harley's bagpipes undercut the weepy folk melody of a song about dead soldiers with jarring atonality and Eastern musical qualities—a sound akin to a north Vietnamese funeral oboe—to represent the war dead while the steady beat of the funk-rock dirge represents the American war machine lumbering away in Vietnam.

However, there is a similar yet different way to read Harley's cover of "Flowers." Most versions of the song rely on the voice, lyrics, and melody to poignantly transmit the message of the song as a "humanistic" condemnation of war and the tragedy of lives lost on the battlefield, historically doomed to be repeated ad infinitum. Harley's instrumental cover manifests the same message in a way that is equally despairing but far more disturbing. The bagpipes border on sounding like a buzzing, penetrating, whirling noise being produced on a synthesizer as it wildly modulates across the tonal scale with atonal arpeggios and digressive runs rather than faithfully replicating the melody of the song. The dirge funk-rock rhythm produced by the electric instruments collides with Harley's extremely and, at times, excruciatingly dissonant bagpipes as they become a disconcerting and almost "inhuman" noise where the melody of "Flowers" is mutilated beyond recognition. As discussed in chapter 1, Jimi Hendrix's instrumental version of "The Star-Spangled Banner" utilized dissonance and noise to give the absent lyrics about bombs and rockets disconcerting new meaning amid the daily slaughter in Vietnam. Similarly, Harley's version of "Flowers" gave the absent lyrics about dead soldiers and cemeteries new meaning amid the images of flag-draped coffins being unloaded from cargo planes.

Moreover, like Hendrix's version of "The Star-Spangled Banner," Harley's cover of "Flowers" can be read as a commentary on the status of America as a liberal-democratic society. While Hendrix captured the volatility of the era, Harley provided something more disheartening. While bagpipes are not common in popular music, they have become a fixture of state funerals. In the end, Harley's version of "Flowers" is not so much a requiem for "the American Dinosaur" but quite the opposite: it was the elegy for traditional American liberalism. As Kevin Boyle noted, "The liberal coalition had collapsed on a Memphis hotel balcony and in a Los Angeles hotel kitchen, the White House and on Capitol Hill, in the streets of Chicago and Detroit, and the rice paddies of Vietnam."[16] Harley gave a resigned eulogy for a decade of intense turmoil where little had changed as far as social and political conditions. Langston Hughes famously asked, "What happens to a dream deferred?" Harley gave a cryptic answer: the dream was not deferred but dead.

The Isley Brothers: "Ohio/Machine Gun"
(Givin' It Back, 1971)

> It's still hard to believe I had to write ["Ohio"]. It's ironic I capitalized on the death of those American students. Probably the biggest lesson learned at an American place of learning. My best CNSY cut. Recorded totally live in Los Angeles. David Crosby cried after this take.[17]—Neil Young

On April 30, 1970, the U.S. invaded Cambodia under pretext of eliminating Viet Cong bases (none were ever found). A wave of anti-war protests erupted, and on May 4, 1970, four students were killed and nine wounded when the Ohio National Guard opened fire on demonstrators at Kent State

University; it remains unclear if the victims were involved in the protest or were bystanders caught in the hail of bullets. The outrage over Kent State galvanized the anti-war movement, produced a surge in protests, and strengthened anti-war sentiment across America.[18] In June of 1970, Crosby, Stills, Nash, and Young (CSNY) released "Ohio" in direct response to Kent State.

Before discussing CSNY's "Ohio," it is necessary to contextualize Neil Young and CNSY. Young's musical career has largely been defined around a nexus of hard rock, folk, and country that could veer into "avant-garde" territory. While Young's hits included the uncluttered ballads "Old Man" or "Heart of Gold," Young became a rock legend for cacophonous mid to slow-tempo epics favoring heavy distortion and lengthy guitar solos such as "Cowgirl in the Sand," "Cortez the Killer," and "Hey Hey, My My (Out of the Black)." In this respect, one can discuss the noise implications of Neil Young. Preferring a "live" approach over flawless recordings fixed by overdubbing, Young's recordings can contain audible mistakes like flubbed transitions, missed notes, and unsteady tempos. Young's vocal register was high, nasal, and at times shrill. His electric guitar was greatly and sometimes exceedingly distorted through overdriven amps and effects pedals (delay, echo, octave division, reverb, etc.). The guitar could also sound like it was simply out of tune. Young often used alternate tunings besides the standard EADGBE such as "standard dropped" (DGCFAD) or "double dropped D" (DADGBD)—the latter tuning used on "Ohio." His use of open chords over barre chords could produce dissonant "tone clusters," and his rhythm guitar playing could be choppy, erratic, and even sloppy, playing as much against the beat as with it. Likewise, Young's lead guitar could approach free soloing, disregarding tonality and meter in favor of unleashing volleys of guitar noise. "Southern Man" (*After the Gold Rush*, 1970) was a vehement commentary on racism in the American South, with lyrics addressing slavery, cross burnings, whippings, lynching, and fears of miscegenation.[19] In two long solo sections, one in the middle and the other serving as the outro, the piano provided a monotonal boogie-woogie line while the drums shifted from half-time to a stiff backbeat. Young's soloing veered from atonal bends and runs to fragments of leads that sounded like they were being physically hacked from the guitar to aurally represent the potential explosions of violence set up by the lyrics.

In a band setting, Young rarely if ever performed without a second guitarist (or in the case of CSNY, usually a third or even fourth guitarist on a given song). Young's atonal lead guitar tendencies were further exacerbated by their contrast to a tonal rhythm guitar, and Young's rhythm guitar could undercut a tonal lead with a background of dissonant chording. "Cortez the

Killer" (*Zuma*, 1975), a song about the Spanish conquest of Latin America, eschews verse–chorus structure and simply repeats an Em7–D–Am7sus4 four-bar riff utilizing double dropped D tuning. The already plodding tempo is exacerbated by half-time drumming where the syncopations and drumrolls sound clumsy rather than jazzy to the point the rhythmic drive is frequently interrupted. In a long instrumental intro, Frank "Poncho" Sampedro plays the four-bar riff on rhythm guitar while Young plays discordant, meandering lead guitar and sings a series of verses over the repeated riff until the song fades out (total time: 7'32"). While Young's lyrics are a bit too enamored with the noble savage myth, the music represents the conquest of the New World as a long, arduous, and violent process.

In 1968, Young's and Stephen Stills' band Buffalo Springfield had broken up, David Crosby was recently fired from the Byrds, and Graham Nash was unhappily a member of the Hollies. During an impromptu jam session at a party, they discovered their capacity for intricate three-part harmonies and decided to work together while not officially becoming a "band" (an issue returned to shortly). One of the early supergroups in rock, CSN's debut album was a commercial success and the vocal harmonies became their musical trademark. While they were effective when done in small doses and not overpowering the mix, vocal exercises like the seven-minute "Suite: Judy Blue Eyes" came off as interminable hippie doo-wop. In 1969, Neil Young joined CSN and they became Crosby, Stills, Nash, and Young; their second concert as a quartet was Woodstock. *Déjà vu*, the first CSNY record, was released in spring of 1970 and produced three Top 40 singles: "Teach Your Children, "Our House," and a cover of Joni Mitchell's song "Woodstock." While "Teach You Children" and "Our House" are addressed later, "Woodstock" was converted from an ethereal piano ballad to mid-tempo folk-rock with biting electric guitar riffing, typically discordant Young soloing, and the trademark vocal harmonies. "Woodstock" also glorified the festival to the point that Max Yagsur's mud-soaked farm was depicted as a primordial Garden of Eden, the attendees a mass of unwashed Adams and Eves, and the festival the Genesis of a new and better world.[20] Indeed, between the rhapsodic account of "Woodstock" and the righteous anger of "Ohio," CSNY was "near enough the official band of the hippie generation."[21]

"Ohio" is a compressed song lasting 2'58"—the optimum length for a single—with a verse–chorus–bridge–chorus–verse structure punctuated by Stills' recurring lead guitar breaks producing a truncated urgency. A sense of peril is established with Young's dissonant D5–F–C guitar riff, a half-time drum beat, and Young's plaintive lead vocals denouncing the State—specifically mentioning Richard Nixon—while calling for oppositional political action. The musical framework contains noise possibilities in the abrasive tangle of Young's choppy rhythm guitar and Stills' recurring twisting guitar leads as well as the Gm7–C chorus uncomfortably propelled by a reversed backbeat. The issue becomes how the noise potential of "Ohio" is undermined by tonality, specifically the vocal harmonies in the chorus and the wordless vocal harmonies that act as a short bridge. As noted, the multi-layered vocal harmony became the brand identity of CSNY. This also meant they were frequently overused and self-indulgent. Put more bluntly, they could sound cloying and even whiny. When "Ohio" was rush-recorded and released as a single, another CSNY song was also on the charts, Nash's "Teach Your Children." A country-pop ballad with syrupy harmonies, "Teach Your Children" self-righteously preached that the counterculture's responsibility was not only teaching the next generation hippie values but enlightening the older generation to the errors of their ways. The end result sounded like a song from a public service announcement encouraging membership in the local PTA. The first single off *Déjà vu*, Nash's "Our House," was a similar, saccharine folk-pop song about living with then-girlfriend Joni Mitchell that sounded like a valorization of domestic suburban life rather than a bohemian hippie lifestyle. For a band that seemingly represented the counterculture dissent of the era, CSNY could not only sound trite but, for lack of a better term, "counter-revolutionary."

To this extent, CSNY's "Ohio" raises the issue of making political music within the constructs of dominant liberal ideology. When CSN initially formed, it was not coincidental that they christened the project with their individual surnames. In an interview with *Hit Parader* (September 1969), Graham Nash insisted,

> It's important that you don't talk about us as a group, because we're not. We're three individuals making an album together ... I just left a group and I don't want to be part of another one ... I don't want to feel I have to be at a certain place at a certain time, to arrange my life to suit anyone else but me. If you're doing something groovy and something groovier comes along, well, you should just go and do that. I've always been kind of selfish that way.[22]

Here Nash expressed one of the counterculture's core dilemmas, the inability to resolve the contradiction of individuality and community. The "liberal freedom" celebrated by the counterculture was steeped in classical liberalism: individualism, social atomism, pursuit of self-interest (economic, sexual, etc.), and the belief that naturally cooperative individuals are the core of building a "great society" rather than a great society constructing better individuals—the mythic status of Woodstock as the highest stage of liberal democracy. The counterculture was unable or unwilling to view the relationship between the individual and society as inherently contradictory or to recognize that they shared a liberal ideology with the State they vociferously opposed. As Situationist International theorist Raoul Vaneigem put it, "In the liberal system, freedom is destroyed by mutual interference: one person's liberty begins when the other's ends. Those who reject this basic principle are destroyed by the sword; those who accept it are destroyed by justice. Nobody gets their hands dirty.... The State is the bad conscience of the liberal."[23]

This is not to say the counterculture in America was an abject failure, but it was inherently restricted as far as being "revolutionary." As Jean-Pierre Depétris suggested,

> If the student movement of 1968 provided the SI with a certain audience, this encounter was full of misreadings.... The SI did not succeed in breaking through the rigid frameworks of militarism or culture ... or in undermining the habits of consumerism. The counterculture in the United States had a far broader and more profound impact, spreading into every aspect of life—ghetto struggles, class relations, the freedom and dignity of minorities, artistic, literary, scientific, and technological invention. Even the most conservative of Americans could scarcely deny its stimulating and regenerative effects. It would be equally difficult to deny the fact that it ended up being absorbed into the commodity spectacle.[24]

As discussed in previous chapters, the fundamental problem for oppositional culture is the extent to which it can be eventually implemented and negated by the economic-political system in which it operates, here noting Young's own candid self-assessment that he "capitalized" on the Kent State tragedy and "Ohio" became a song-commodity for CSNY and Atlantic Records as much as an emphatic anti–Establishment political statement.[25]

In this context, the ideological relationship between the counterculture and the State also needs to be considered around the question of violence. In Jean-Luc Godard's avant-garde documentary *British Sounds* (1968), one of the narrator's polemical statements is "This is the moment when despair ends and tactics begin." This line was taken from Vaneigem's *The Revolution of Everyday Life* (1967): "No murderers—and no humanists either! The first accepts death, the second imposes it. Let ten people meet who are resolved to the lightning of violence rather than the agony of survival; from this moment, despair ends and tactics begin. Despair is the infantile disorder of the revolutionaries of everyday life."[26] *Individual* liberation could only be achieved by *collective* action that manifested "violence" but categorically rejected murder, bombings, or robbery—vandalism, property damage, and self-defense against police brutality were another matter—in favor of spontaneous student and worker strikes, mass demonstrations, and the widespread graffiti campaigns that nearly toppled the French government in May of 1968.

Particularly in America, the counterculture ultimately could not conceive of "violent revolution" without applying the traditional definition of violence as terrorism and non-violence as pacifism. While the counterculture branded itself as the "peace and love" radical alternative to the State, violence was increasingly becoming counterculture modus operandi (see also chapter 3). From January 1969 to April 1970, there were 4,330 bomb attacks across America with approximately 1,560 of the perpetrators identified: 56 percent were tied to student unrest, 33 percent came from racial extremists (white as well as black), 8 percent were crime related, 2 percent stemmed from labor conflicts, and 1 percent targeted religious institutions.[27] The "Days of Rage" instigated by the Weather Underground (WU) in Chicago from October 8 to 11, 1969, left dozens of demonstrators, police, and bystanders injured in three days of sporadic rioting. While the underground press largely denounced the Days of Rage and Altamont, Charles Manson soon after became the poster boy for a disillusioned counterculture following the Manson Family's indictment for the Tate-LaBianca murders. In early 1970, the underground newspaper *Tuesday's Child* ran a cover photo of Charles Manson with the headline "Man of the Year" while WU leader Bernadine Dohrn hailed the Manson Family's killing of the LaBiancas by proclaiming, "Offing those rich pigs with their own forks and knives, and then eating a meal in the same room—far out!"[28] The WU subsequently proclaimed 1970 "the Year of the Fork."

On March 6, 1970—less than two months before Kent State—three WU members were killed when a nail bomb they were constructing accidentally detonated in a Greenwich Village townhouse. The intended target was a couple's dance at Fort Dix. Between the designated target and the nature of the weapon, it is difficult to argue the intent was anything other than inflicting human casualties. By April of 1970, the Berkeley underground newspaper *Tribe* ran an editorial defending the bombings of banks, police stations, government buildings, campuses, and other institutions—with the disclaimer that attacks needed to be well planned as to not injure anyone—under the title "Responsible Terrorism," and five days later California governor Ronald Reagan responded, "If it takes a bloodbath, let's get it over with."[29] In short, the counterculture could champion violence when it was directed at the system and condemn it once the State directed violence at them.[30]

While Vaneigem dismissed despair as "an infantile disorder" that had no place in revolution, it bears mentioning that despair permeates Neil Young's songs, be it denouncing the era of Reaganism in "Rockin' in the Free World" or describing the abyss of drug addiction in "No More" (both from 1989's *Freedom*). Indeed, it is this pervasive sense of despair that makes Young's music compelling. However, as a CSNY song, "Ohio" ultimately suggests that "when despair ends, martyrdom begins," precisely at a time when the counterculture was turning to violent solutions while denouncing State violence. The vocal harmonies blanket the simmering rage hinted at by the music with a pious indignation expressing aversion and sorrow as to what occurred at Kent State. In short, "Ohio" allowed the counterculture to maintain its double standard on violence and retain the moral high ground against the State.

The Isley Brothers were formed by Roland, Rudolph, and O'Kelly Isley as an R&B band. Their first hit songs were "Shout" (1959) and "Twist and Shout" (1962), although later cover versions of the songs are the best known. "Shout" was immortalized in the film *Animal House* (1978) as performed by "Otis Day and the Knights," while "Twist and Shout" was a Top Five hit single for the Beatles in 1964. By the turn of the decade, the Isleys added younger brothers Ernie (guitar) and Marvin (bass), formed their own independent label T-Neck Records, and began crossover efforts into the pop/rock market. In 1971, the Isley Brothers released *Givin' It Back* which included covers of James Taylor's "Fire and Rain," Bob Dylan's "Lay Lady Lay," Stephen Stills' "Love the One You're With," and CSNY's "Ohio" done in a medley with Jimi Hendrix's "Machine Gun," a song which appeared on *Band of Gypsys* (1970; Band of Gypsys was also one of rock's first all-black lineups comprised of Hendrix, bassist Billy Cox, and drummer Buddy Miles).

The Isley Brothers' version of "Ohio/Machine Gun" has a much looser or "disorganized" feel than the condensed structure of the CSNY version. It begins with a snare drum martial beat and a somber organ playing the D5–F–G riff. Lead vocalist Ronald Isley ad-libs variations of the verse lyrics anxiously detailing the arrival of soldiers while a wah-wah rhythm guitar plays a variation of the vocal melody and an ominous fuzz lead guitar alternates with the vocals in the verse as a kind of "call and response" (the specific mention of Richard Nixon in the CSNY version is omitted). The lead guitar line from "Ohio" is briefly played before the song returns to the intro section and more vocal ad-libs describing the approaching soldiers until the verse is reiterated followed by the chorus sung collectively by the Isleys with a sense of soul anguish rather than folk piety. A crucial difference is a driving, tumultuous, syncopated break punctuated by lead vocal ad-libs—a musical signifier of the moment of massacre and ensuing chaos—until the song returns to the main riff and the lead guitar line. The band then sings the wordless melody of the bridge immediately followed by the lead vocal singing the verse and then the chorus sung collectively. Again, it ends with the syncopated break followed by a restatement of the "Ohio" lead guitar riff. A lengthy group chant of the chorus lyrics denouncing the killings ensues, punctuated by more distressed vocal ad-libs, as the music builds in intensity until the chant ends and "Ohio" transitions to "Machine Gun." More specifically, the stuttering main guitar riff of the song is utilized whereas the lyrics in Hendrix's version are replaced by a tortured, improvised lead vocal describing hails of bullets and people being killed as well as referencing lines from "Swing Low, Sweet Chariot." A second voice provides a solemn recitation of various biblical passages (Luke 23:34—"Bless them father, for they know not what they do"; Mathew 5:5—"Blessed are the meek for they shall inherit the earth"). As a pained voice recounting the carnage and misery of war and a somber voice pleading for compassion and guidance collide, the guitar and drums play the sputtering "machine gun" rhythm—at times in unison, at times in call and response, at times independently, and at times in arrhythmic conflict. In conjunction with the vocals and rhythm section, the lead guitar solo emits sporadic high bends to suggest cries and screams. As the climatic fury of "Machine Gun" dissipates, the song returns to the chorus of "Ohio" for a brief coda and fades out.

As discussed in chapter 1, Paul Hegarty suggested Hendrix's version of "The Star-Spangled Banner" represents a point where Hendrix and the State "drift" between each other amid the nascent Woodstock Nation. Similarly, the Isley Brothers' juxtaposition of "Ohio" and "Machine Gun" represents a drifting between the domestic front of America where students were being killed demonstrating for peace and the overseas front of Vietnam where soldiers and civilians were being killed in an untenable war. As far as racial politics, CSNY's "Ohio" was a folk-rock song performed by white musicians about the killing of white anti-war protestors in the Midwest. Hendrix's "Machine Gun" was a hard rock song performed by black musicians about Vietnam where, between 1965 and 1969, African Americans comprised 11 percent of the national population, 13 percent of the soldiers in Vietnam, and 15 percent of the casualties.[31] In his controversial "Beyond Vietnam" speech (April 4, 1967), Martin Luther King, Jr., stated,

> We were taking the young black men who had been crippled by our society and sending them eight thousand miles away to guarantee liberties in Southeast Asia which they had not found in southwest Georgia and East Harlem. So we have been repeatedly faced with the cruel irony of watching Negro and white boys on TV screens as they kill and die together for a nation that has been unable to seat them together in the same schools. So we watch them in brutal solidarity burning the huts of poor villages, but we realize they would hardly live on the same block in Chicago.[32]

The Isley Brothers' version of "Ohio" juxtaposed with "Machine Gun" represents a multiplicity of political driftings: between America and Vietnam, between white and black, between demonstrators and soldiers, between peace and war, between racism and nationalism, between campuses and rice fields, between ghettos and villages. Within these drifts, the commonality was death.

The Four Tops: "A Simple Game" (Single, 1972)

In 1956, Chuck Berry's hit song "Roll Over Beethoven" categorically pronounced high culture, specifically classical music, as antithetical to rock and roll.[33] However, by the early 1970s, progressive rock emerged as a commercially successful subgenre. Bands like Emerson, Lake, and Palmer (ELP), Yes, Jethro Tull, Genesis, King Crimson, Gentle Giant, and Van der Graaf Generator specialized in combining classical, jazz, English folk, and rock music into lengthy, highly complex compositions marked by virtuoso musicianship and verbose lyrics.[34] Progressive rock was almost unanimously crucified by American rock critics, and Lester Bangs summarized the view when he called ELP "the insidious befoulment of all that was gutter pure in rock.... It's worse than eclecticism, its eugenic entropy by design."[35] Jacques Attali made progressive rock his musical and political scapegoat as well: "Popular music and rock have become recuperated, colonized, sanitized ... by an implacable ideological and technical recuperation: Jimi Hendrix was replaced by Steve Howe, Eric Clapton was replaced by Keith Emerson."[36] As Attali would have it, the *noise* and *social disorder* that erupted in 1960s rock was subdued into *music* and *social order* in the 1970s with the advent of progressive rock. While ELP may have been unfairly singled out for vilification, their attachment to the bourgeois high culture of classical music, their array of expensive musical equipment, and the audacious concert spectacles such as spinning grand pianos, rotating drum platforms, and an attempt to tour with a personal orchestra in 1977 could only have one inevitable effect. As Keith Emerson put it, "We were seen as rock's ultimate capitalists."[37]

An ardent defender of progressive rock, Edward Macan claimed it "represents an Apollonian extension of countercultural values, emphasizing an inner spiritual quest and the search for some sort of deeper metaphysical truth."[38] As a "hybrid" of classical music and rock music, Macan contended "the raw, admittedly artless music of Chuck Berry, Jerry Lee Lewis, and Little Richard was transformed into the complex, monumental, multidimensional progressive rock style."[39] Yet this hybrid form was ideologically antithetical to "hybrid music" as Adorno used the term to describe the operas of Weil/Brecht, where there is a tense juxtaposition that both uses and abuses the classical canon and popular music to expose the cracks and flaws in capitalist society.[40] Rather, Macan claimed progressive rock "*reconciled cultural opposites* ... high and low culture, European and African American creative ideas. In the best progressive rock, one senses the tension that results from *attempting to balance these values*."[41]

The Moody Blues were among the more popular progressive rock bands during the late 1960s and early 1970s. In fact, this was the second incarnation of the Moody Blues, who originated as an R&B-influenced rock band consisting of Mike Pinder (keyboards, vocal), Roy Thomas (flute, harmonica, vocals), Graham Edge (drums), Denny Laine (guitar, vocals), and Clint Warwick (bass). They had a hit single with "Go Now" (1964) and were fairly well known when Laine and Warwick left the band ca. 1967. They were eventually replaced by Justin Hayward (guitar, vocals) and John Lodge (bass, vocals) and their arrival coincided with the advent of the Beatles' *Sgt. Pepper's Lonely Hearts Club Band* as well as emerging synthesizer technology. The Moody Blues pioneered use of the Mellotron, a polyphonic keyboard that could replicate strings, brass, woodwinds, choir, and other sounds through prerecorded tape strips triggered by the keys.[42]

With *Days of Future Passed* (1967, which also featured backing from the London Festival Orchestra), the Moody Blues moved in a psychedelic "symphonic rock" direction, with English folk and classical influences largely replacing R&B. While they favored "concept albums," the Moody Blues did not specialize in lengthy songs with complex, sectional arrangements (e.g., ELP's 20-minute "Tarkus" or Jethro Tull's 40-plus-minute "Thick as a Brick"). Instead, albums were more akin to suites composed of independent songs, frequently linked by instrumental passages and sometimes unintentionally hilarious recitations, with the advantage that a song could easily be edited for radio play as a potential hit single (e.g., "Nights in White Satin" and "Tuesday Afternoon" from *Days of Future Passed*). Lyrically, the Moody Blues exemplified progressive rock's emphasis on individual liberation through personal illumination. As Macan described their 1968 release *In Search of the Lost Chord*,

> [It] opens by depicting the materialism of modern industrial society, exemplified by the nine-to-five lifestyle ("Ride My See-Saw") as the root of spiritual impoverishment. As the album progresses, music ("House of Four Doors"), hallucinogens ("Legend of a Mind," a veritable paean to Timothy Leary), and transcendental meditation ("The Actor") are shown as steps on the road to cosmic consciousness, which is depicted by the album's final song "Om."[43]

"A Simple Game" was written by Mike Pinder and released as the B-side of "Ride My See-Saw," the first single off *In Search of the Lost Chord*. It begins with a kind of dreariness and Pinder's fairly monotone lead vocal set to a sparse musical accompaniment of acoustic guitar, Mellotron, and relaxed drumming. Lyrically, the song expresses a utopian promise of a better tomorrow and the formation of an egalitarian community where each individual's potential is fully realized. In this way, the verses convey the present and a longing for community expressed by a single or individual voice (Pinder). While the choruses convey the impending utopia in the future as the rest of the band contributes choir backup vocals in multi-tracked layers. The main musical variations in the chorus are the snare switching from the relaxed backbeat in the verses to a steady quarter-note beat and the addition of a churning, fuzz-distorted guitar. They signify an underlying, building "force" as multiple voices join with a common goal of togetherness. However, in the extended chorus finale, individual voices begin to stand out or "rise above" the group harmonies (the collective), with Pinder's moans and Hayward's soaring wordless vocals especially audible as the song fades out. In the end, the cycle is complete where achieving utopian community allows *individual* voices to reemerge with even greater strength.

As touched on in chapter 4, Simon Frith suggested that as rock became the dominant genre in popular music, R&B became viewed as "essentially a collective form that was thought not to allow for genuine individual artistic expression."[44] This becomes crucial in discussing the Four Tops' version of "A Simple Game." Levi Stubbs, Renaldo "Obie" Benson, Abdul "Duke" Fakir, and Lawrence Payton were Detroit inner-city high school students and members of different amateur singing groups when they were asked by mutual friends to perform together at a graduation party in 1954. They stayed together for 43 years until Payton died in 1997. After a decade of working nightclubs and supper clubs across America, the Four Tops signed to Motown Records in 1963 and quickly joined the upper echelon of the Motown roster of performers like the Miracles, the Supremes, the Temptations, Martha and the Vandellas, Marvin Gaye, and Stevie Wonder with a string of hit songs over the course of the 1960s. Like several other Motown acts, the Four Tops worked extensively with the H-D-H songwriting/production team. While Payton was the unofficial musical director as far as arranging the four-part harmonies (Payton and Fakir were tenors, Benson a baritone), Stubbs became the primary lead vocalist. Stu Hackel noted,

> Stubbs' trombone baritone soon became H-D-H's favorite vehicle. Writing up-tempo songs at his upper register, forcing him to reach for notes, they

could make him sound happy and bold while nearly in tears. When his commanding timbre rubbed against their clever stories of longing and loss, the tension yielded drama, urgency, and even quaver. Heartbreak had never seemed so irresistible, or so danceable, raising masculine vulnerability to a new level of pop acceptance.[45]

In 1967, Motown Records underwent considerable changes. As noted, one factor was H-D-H leaving Motown in an acrimonious royalty dispute with Berry Gordy, Jr. Another was the Detroit riots in the summer of 1967. A police raid on an after-hours bar ignited three days of what became one of the largest outbreaks of mass civil disorder in American history until the Michigan National Guard and the U.S. Army occupied the city to restore order. Forty-three people were killed, over 1,000 injured, at least 5,000 rendered homeless, and several thousand arrested. Property damage exceeded $100 million. Kevin Boyle suggested that

> the Detroit riot was inevitable. Despite the Great Society's expansive promises, many of the city's African-Americans remained locked in poverty. Detroit's largely white police force had earned a reputation for brutality in the ghetto, and the city's vocal black power advocates had fueled the flames of discontent. At the time though, many of the nation's liberals were stunned that Detroit, the center for Great Society activism, could fall victim to such devastation.[46]

Between the aftermath of the Detroit riot and new songwriters and producers entering the Motown fold, the label rebranded itself as a more socially conscious and more rock-orientated soul music. In 1970, Motown released the Temptations' "Ball of Confusion" and Edwin Starr's "War," two songs that exemplified Motown's rebranding from the H-D-H "symphonic soul" sound to the "psychedelic soul" sound pioneered by producer Norman Whitfield and characterized by heavy funk drumming, blasting horns, copious electric guitar, studio effects, and polemical political lyrics.[47] The same year, Motown singed Rare Earth, an all-white rock band who had hits with covers of the Temptations' "Get Ready" and "(I Know) I'm Losing You."[48]

The Four Tops took a different route. Their last record with H-D-H, *Reach Out* (1967), included cover versions of Tim Hardin's folk song "If I Were a Carpenter" as well as recent pop-rock hits such as the Left Banke's "Walk Away Renèe," the Association's "Cherish," and the Monkees' "Last Train to Clarksville" and "I'm a Believer" (keeping in mind the Monkees were, at the time, widely denigrated as being an ersatz Beatles' consciously manufactured by the culture industry to be TV and pop-music stars). "Walk Away Renèe" was notable as it typified the H-D-H Motown symphonic soul formula and the Four Tops' ability to project "masculine vulnerably" in an era where sexism and overblown machismo were increasingly defining the counterculture and rock music. "Walk Away Renée" is a song is about a man mourning the loss of his significant other, and it is clear in the lyrics that he is the one responsible for the relationship's failure, not her. The Four Tops' version of the song is a mid-tempo soul ballad featuring a piano, a string section, a harp, muted trumpets, and the toms on the drum kit mixed loudly so as to resemble timpani rolls. Stubbs sings the song replete with the occasional cracks and strains in his powerful baritone as he struggles to hit the higher notes—not struggling in the sense of lacking talent, but struggling in the sense he is singing in an uncomfortable key for his voice. In contrast, the background vocals are smooth and stable (wordless accompaniment in the verses, lyrics in the chorus) whereas Stubbs' pained voice occasionally falters as if he is having difficulty expressing himself and his situation, or that he "can't go on" and needs a moment to compose himself before he can continue the song (again, possibly a performance tactic owing to the musical conditions of production that H-D-H placed on Stubbs). In the bridge featuring the muted trumpets, one of them plays an audibly noticeable "muffed note" in a way that suggests the trumpet got momentarily "choked up" as well. As far as gender politics, "Walk Away Renée" serves as a counter-discourse to the cavalier misogyny of the Stones' "Under My Thumb" or the self-pitying "victimized" man in Vanilla Fudge's cover of "You Keep Me Hangin' On." The message is that the man ruined a good thing, and the listener can empathize with the intense emotional loss and pain he feels.

Following H-D-H's departure, the Four Tops worked with several outside producers and songwriters. One was Frank Wilson, whom Payton described as an "experimental cat."[49] Wilson encouraged the Four Tops to pursue their own musical interests, and one was a cover of "A Simple Game." In fact, Moody Blues producer Tony Clarke produced the Four Tops' version while the Moody Blues served as the backing musicians and vocalists along with session musicians providing orchestral strings and brass.[50] While it might be more correct to term the end result collaboration rather than a cover per se, there are marked differences between the two versions. The Four Tops' version is slightly faster and shorter by truncating the extended chorus finale (total time of 2'56"—optimal single length—as opposed to the 3'45" Moody Blues version). As important, the Four Tops grew up in the North End area of Detroit, and Stubbs recounted, "If you didn't live in that area, you didn't go to that area."[51] Given that the Four Tops grew up in a rough environment of urban poverty and their hometown was engulfed in a catastrophic riot a few years earlier, the Four Tops' version of "A Simple Game" is much more strident and aggressive–in short, angrier—than the mellow idealism of the Moody Blues. The song begins with an eerie brass note before the band starts, and rather than one person assigned the lead vocals in the verses (i.e., Mike Pinder), there is an alternation of voices. Payton sings the first two lines of the verses, Stubbs sings the next two lines, and all of the Four Tops collectively sing in the chorus and bridge. In this way, the contrast between the calm rhythmic flow of the verses and the steady quarter-note snare beat in the choruses and bridge is also much more pronounced in the Four Tops' version. Whereas the Moody Blues construct a binary around individuality seeking community (verses) and collectivity (chorus), in the Four Tops' version there is a "collation building" in the verses with one voice followed by a second voice expressing the lyrics' sentiments, and then all the voices joining the chorus as it explodes into a musically intense announcement of collective self-determination.

Moreover, there are two aspects of the Four Tops' version of "A Simple Game" that make it much more reminiscent of classic Motown symphonic soul rather than contemporary Motown psychedelic soul—let alone English progressive rock. One was the quarter-note snare beat that dominates the chorus and bridge of "A Simple Game." H-D-H frequently used this drum pattern instead of a backbeat rhythm, specifically on the Supremes' "You Keep Me Hangin' On" and Four Tops hits like "It's the Same Old Song," "Standing in the Shadows of Love," and "Bernadette." The other is the prominent, quasi-classical strings and brass in "A Simple Game," particularly in the bridge. H-D-H commonly used such horn and string section arrangements, so their presence in a Four Tops song is not incongruous but almost typical. To this extent, there are limitations in Macan's suggestion that progressive rock "reconciled cultural opposites." This process was better manifest in "A Simple Game" through the coalition formed by the Four Tops (soul music, black Americans) and the Moody Blues (progressive rock, white Europeans). "A Simple Game" integrates progressive rock and soul music—genres usually categorized as mutually exclusive white music and black music—into a potent assemblage. The difference was in the message. The Moody Blues offered a future promise of liberal-democratic utopia whereas the Four Tops demanded an end to the discrimination, poverty, and repression of the many in the now.

9

Dance with Laibach: Covers and the Critique of the Nation-State

The Laibach Project

> As for the degenerate artists, I forbid them to force their so-called experiences on the public.... I will purge the nation of them.—Adolf Hitler
>
> We are fascists as much as Hitler was a painter.[1]—Laibach

In order to analyze the Slovenian industrial band Laibach as what Glenn Gosling termed "more an ideological offensive than a rock band"[2] and the crucial role of anti-covers, it is necessary to provide a historical context. The collapse of the Soviet Union arguably began in 1979 with the invasion of Afghanistan, which reignited the Cold War after several years of détente. By the 1980s, Western politics markedly shifted to the Right, with Thatcherism in the UK and Reaganism in the U.S.; Ronald Reagan was a staunch anti-communist intent on winning the Cold War once and for all through economic rather than military force. The success of the Solidarity movement in Poland posed an immense contradiction as far as worker revolution. On one hand, it was a populist movement led by labor unions against a repressive state; on the other, it was an anti–Marxist labor movement that embraced capitalist and liberal-democratic ideology. The hypocrisy of Reagan and Margaret Thatcher supporting Solidarity was more than evident in that they were all but exterminating organized labor in the United States and the UK during the 1980s (i.e., Reagan's mass firing of air traffic controllers in the PATCO strike in 1981 and Thatcher's government crushing the British miners' strike in 1984–85). Conversely, as far as orthodox Marxism, the Left was placed in the uncomfortable position of siding with the State against a workers' uprising.

In 1989, a wave of revolutionary movements swept Eastern Europe.

Poland, East Germany, Czechoslovakia, Bulgaria, Hungary, and Romania abandoned communism in favor of capitalism and liberal democracy. East and West Germany reunified into the nation-state of Germany in 1990. In 1991, the official dissolution of the Soviet Union ended the Warsaw Pact, liberating former Soviet satellite nation-states. The European Union (EU) was officially established in 1993, and in the same year Czechoslovakia separated into the nation-states of the Czech Republic and Slovakia. While the transition to a post–Soviet Europe was largely peaceful, the two exceptions were Romania, where over 1,000 people were killed in the uprisings, and Yugoslavia, where an estimated 150,000 to 250,000 were killed in the Yugoslav Wars of 1991 to 1995.

In the aftermath of World War I, Croats, Slovenes, and Serbs, three nations with divergent cultures, languages, religions, and politics, coalesced into one state. Robert O. Paxton noted,

> After the defeat of the common Habsburg enemy, the Serbs (Orthodox religion, Serbo-Croatian language, Cyrillic alphabet), the Croats (Catholic religion, Serbo-Croatian language, Roman alphabet), and Slovenes (Catholic religion, Slovenian language, Roman alphabet) found little to unite them. The new kingdom's decentralized federal districts exaggerated the divisions. Since the Croatian leader Stepan Radič had turned to the Third International, separatism was overlaid with a Bolshevik threat. King Alexander abolished the constitution in January 1929, replaced the ethnically based federal districts with a centralized authority, and renamed the kingdom Yugoslavia, thereby "solving" in one blow the problems of revolution, local separatism, and governmental instability.[3]

During World War II, Yugoslavia was conquered by Nazi Germany but mounted a resistance movement headed by Marshal Tito (Josip Broz), a Croatian communist who became Yugoslavia's post–World War II head of state until his death in 1980, unifying the country around a Yugoslavian nationalism instilled by fighting Nazism and the establishment of a post–World War II communist state. In 1948, Tito broke with Stalin over the role of Soviet influence in Yugoslavian internal politics. As Yugoslavia did not share any geographic borders with the USSR, it was less susceptible to Soviet intervention and largely remained outside the Soviet Union's sphere of influence. The USSR invaded border nation-states Hungary in 1956 and Czechoslovakia in 1968 to suppress national and liberal reform movements

While the violent separation of Yugoslavia into smaller nation-states in the 1990s is addressed shortly, it can be traced to Tito's death in 1980 and a reemergence of national independence movements. The same year, Laibach—the old German name of Ljubljana, the capital of Slovenia—was formed. As

Gregor Tomc noted, "The two events were interlinked. The marshal's demise triggered social and political instability in Yugoslavia which, in turn, produced an ideal climate for Laibach's political aesthetics."[4] In 1984, Laibach became co-founders and the musical production branch of the radical art collective *Neue Slowenische Kunst* (New Slovenian Art, henceforth NSK), dedicated to a purposely contradictory aesthetic of "retro avant-garde" and treating cultural production as collectivist labor.[5] As Laibach stated, "A collective principle is a collective principal and one can only practice it if he leaves a big part of himself outside it."[6]

As an industrial band, Laibach shared as well as departed from the strategies and tactics of the pioneering industrial band Throbbing Gristle. TG assembled incongruent elements of avant-garde and experimental music (electronic music, musique concrète, minimalism, noise) alongside popular music genres such as disco, Europop, exotica, psychedelia, and synthesizer-based Krautrock bands like Kraftwerk and Tangerine Dream. The lyrical and visual imagery of TG emphasized graphic sex and violence and an obsession with the Third Reich that veered perilously close to being as enamored with fascism as repelled by it.[7] Paul Hegarty argued,

> The initial subversion of industrial music is a total refusal of values and morally induced fear of phenomena and imagery. Ideology comes in, either as musicians clarify their perspective or as a tool for further confusion (Laibach).... What would briefly be known as "electronic body music" did seem to be a fascistic mobilization of a newly ultra-disciplined body.... Laibach joined in with this style, creating pulverizing versions of major hits ... exposing the previously unnoticed totalitarian moments of songs.... The use of fascistic and Communist imagery, combined with a heroic agrarian aesthetic, made them seem to valorize a Volk-based "renewal," but what they managed ... to do was subvert the still extant Communist regimes of Eastern Europe, liberals in the west, and presumably fascists, who would tire of their frivolity.[8]

Like the Sex Pistols, Laibach can be interpreted as a situationist use of music, and some critical caution need be exercised. As Andrew Hussey pointed out, "Since the 1970s, few bands who call themselves radical have been unable to resist the glamour associated with the term 'Situationist'.... The term 'Situationist' has come to stand for an artistic subversion of style or technique, rather than, as the Situationists originally intended, a subversive use of art."[9] To this extent, a situationist use of music entails *détournement*, defined in *Situationist International 1* (1958) as an "integration of past or present artistic productions into a superior construction of a milieu. In this sense, there can be no situationist painting or music, but only a situationist use of those means ... détournement is a method of propaganda, a method which reveals the wearing out and loss of importance of those spheres."[10] There is also a crucial difference between postmodern quotation and situationist *détournement*. As Guy Debord, a founder of the Situationist International, emphatically put it in *The Society of the Spectacle*, "*Détournement* is the ANTITHEISIS of quotation."[11] *Détournement* entails a "serious parody" that appropriates, distorts, and desecrates the original forms into new and potentially subversive products. In "A User's Guide to Détournement" (1956), Debord and Gil J. Wolman contended, "Any elements, no matter where they are taken from, can be used in making new combinations.... The mutual interference of two worlds of feeling, or the juxtaposition of two independent expressions, supersedes the original elements and produces a synthetic organization of greater efficacy. Anything can be used."[12]

As a "synthetic organization of greater efficacy," Laibach's détournement of divergent musical genres encompassed popular music (disco, hard rock, punk, techno, etc.), industrial and noise music, military marches and military drill chanting, national anthems, folk songs, and classical music (specifically Richard Wagner and Carl Orff—the former's music adopted by the Third Reich and the latter widely perceived as a Nazi sympathizer). Some songs were performed in English and some in German. However, songs across the spectrum of popular music genres as "anti-covered" by Laibach end up sounding almost identical in their uniform redundancy, a comical yet grim classical-industrial-martial music which questioned the ideologies that musical genres are culturally and historically constructed to represent (i.e., marches and Wagner as "fascist" versus rock and industrial as "radical" musical statements). The imagery of Laibach was a similar incongruent assemblage drawn from European mythology, Orthodox Catholicism, Slovenian culture, Socialist Realism, and the Third Reich: the Laibach logo is a Greek cross (*crux immissa quadrata*) inside a cog. Likewise, Laibach's live performances parodied the rock concert spectacle into what Robert Christgau suggested about Kiss in his review of *Dressed to Kill* (*The Village Voice*, 1975) as "the liberal fantasy of rock concert as Nuremberg rally." Indeed, Laibach concerts functioned as multimedia assault bordering on a ludicrous yet terrifying political event replete with searchlights, strobe lights, a highly regimented stage presentation, and paramilitary stage attire. An onslaught of tightly synchronized, rapid-fire back projections of video images was also utilized, drawing from commercial advertising and political propaganda, with Laibach occasionally performing in tandem with the promotional videos for given songs.[13]

Laibach deliberately dismantled the aesthetic distinctions of avant-garde vs. commercial, oppositional culture vs. affirmative culture, and highbrow vs.

middlebrow vs. lowbrow. Not unrelated, Laibach ruptured the comfortable political separations of left vs. right, liberal vs. conservative, and ultimately the competing ideologies of capitalism, communism, and fascism. Alexei Monroe observed,

> Laibach's methodology is based upon the amplification of "rendering audible" of the hidden codes and internal contradictions of a series of artistic, musical, political, linguistic, and historical "regimes" ... Laibach interrogate regimes by rendering audible/visible a series of contradictions that "common sense" ideology has to keep concealed in order to maintain the ideological self-reproduction of "the system." For instance, connections between rock and Fascistic mobilization, or between scientific industrialism and mystic nationalism, become apparent, destabilizing the order of things.[14]

As Laibach put it, "In principle we are not trying to criticize or praise, but first of all analyze the relation between art and politics, culture and ideology. But if you find a relevant critique in our work which can serve your understanding of things, then that was definitely our intention."[15]

Given NSK's support of Slovenian independence and the disparity of the aesthetic-ideological collisions, it was difficult to assess whether Laibach was on the extreme Left or Right of the political spectrum. Not surprisingly, the Yugoslavian government viewed Laibach with a great deal of suspicion and effectively banned them, although Laibach generated a fan base and critical interest across Europe during the 1980s. Signing to Mute Records, one of the leading independent labels in the UK, Laibach released *Opus Dei* in 1987. As a means to reveal the underlying elements of totalitarianism in rock songs and rock spectacle, the album included a grinding industrial/martial anti-cover of "Life Is Life," an innocuous worldwide hit song by the Austrian arena-rock band Opus, and an anti-cover version of Queen's "One Vision" titled "Geburt Einer Nation" ("Birth of a Nation," which inevitably referenced D.W. Griffith's film of the same name and its glorification of the Ku Klux Klan).[16] Subsequent Laibach releases were *Let It Be* (1988), a deconstruction of the Beatles' entire final album, and a 12" EP anti-cover of the Rolling Stones' "Sympathy for the Devil" (1988) that included several alternate versions of the song. Along with the recurring critique of rock totalitarianism, Laibach's industrial reconfiguration of songs by the two most important rock bands of the 1960s offered a demystification of the counterculture "peace and love" dream that collapsed by the end of the decade: *Let It Be* as the product of the acrimonious breakup of the Beatles and "Sympathy for the Devil" a grisly reminder of Altamont.

A related issue is "world music." The common view of world music is that it acts as a *synthesis* of Western and non–Western music—more specifically, Western pop, rock, and dance genres merged with a variety of non-Western music (African, Asian, Caribbean, Indian, Latin American, Middle Eastern, etc.). In the 1950s and 1960s, the "exotica music" of Les Baxter and Martin Denny combined pop, jazz, and easy listening with Pacific Island and Latin American music (it would make a comeback in the 1990s, as discussed next chapter). The Beatles' and other musicians' flirtations with Indian music in the 1960s also constituted an early attempt at world music. Post-punk bands incorporated black music like disco, funk, reggae, and African music with avant-garde/experimental music in a punk framework (Talking Heads, Gang of Four, Pop Group, etc.). However, Paul Gilroy argued that bands such as the Police "inverted the preconceptions of Rasta by calling themselves the Police and armed with 'Aryan' good looks and dedication to 'Regatta de Blanc' served, within pop culture at least, to detach reggae from its historic association with the Africans of the Caribbean and their descendants."[17] In short, the Police did not so much appropriate reggae but colonized it into considerable commercial success.

World music is predicated on a worldview that music is a "universal" language despite its cultural, historical, and national specificity. By extension, world music is frequently hailed as politically progressive, with music the stuff of a multi-cultural, multi-national melting pot. What is less discussed is the extent to which world music acts as the soundtrack for global capitalism. Timothy D. Taylor noted, "'World music' is caught up in a complexly intertwined phenomena of travel, tourism, globalization, and new consumption patterns, and justified with the veneer of discourses of collaboration."[18] Laibach recognized the national character of music as something both potentially productive and destructive: on one hand, an expression of a *collective* identity of a people; one the other, sentiment ripe to be exploited by the State for purposes of patriotism, xenophobia, war, and genocide. Indeed, "world music" in relation to nationalism and global capitalism underwent a radical critique by Laibach on *Volk* (2006), a collection of songs deconstructing the national anthems of numerous countries, each titled with the name of the country: among others, "Germania," "America," "Francia," "Rossiya," "Zhonghuà" "Nippon," "Slovania," and the NSK national anthem (since 1991, NSK defines itself as a "micronation" of Slovenia known as "NSK State").[19] "Volk" is German for "nation" or "people," and "volk" is Slovenian for "wolf"—the record cover of *Volk* was a kitsch watercolor painting of sheep in a pasture.

Laibach's "synthetic organization" is anything but a synthesis of musical styles (e.g., jazz-rock fusion or world music) but functions as a kind of negative dialect where the musical parts do not blend but internally collide in montages.[20] On *NATO*, Laibach's "world music" was not a blending of First

World and Third World musical genres and, by extension, a blending of cultural, ideological, and national differences into the global harmony of "one world"—a term frequently used by Laibach not to signify the "global village" but a global totalitarian order in the era of multi-national capitalism, neoliberalism, and postindustrial society. Instead, *NATO* was a collision of the First World and Second World through a *détournement* of American and European musical genres recorded and released during the height of the Yugoslav Wars.

NATO *(1994)*

> If there is ever another war in Europe, it will come out of some damn silly thing in the Balkans.—Winston Churchill quoting Otto von Bismarck, speech in the House of Commons (August 16, 1945)

> During the war, nations in the Balkans were victims and prisoners of EU segregation and the conflict in ex–Yugoslavia gave a dear lecture to Europe of what can happen if the differences are not respected and problems not resolved in time and if the smallest in the community are not taken seriously.... The whole of Europe has the blood of the Balkans on their hands.[21]—Laibach

The dissolution of Yugoslavia began when Croatia, Macedonia, and Slovenia established independent nation-states in 1991. Slovenia's secession resulted in the Ten Day War with what remained of Yugoslavia, leaving approximately 60 people dead and 330 wounded. The Croatian War of Independence between separatist and loyalist Croat factions also begin in 1991, and intermittent civil warfare lasted until 1995, with approximately 20,000 people killed over its duration. The Bosnian War started in 1992 as a civil war between the newly established nation-state of Bosnia and Herzegovina against dissident Bosnian Serb and Bosnian Croat factions; it effectively escalated into a war between Bosnia and Herzegovina versus Croatia and Serbia (the latter then still part of Yugoslavia).[22] Over the course of three years of war and genocide, the nation-state of Srpska was established in 1992 and NATO air and naval forces engaged in "police actions" including air strikes against Serbian targets until a peace treaty recognized Bosnia and Herzegovina as a nation-state in late 1995. Part of the agreement entailed 60,000 NATO soldiers dispatched to the war-torn regions to serve as a peacekeeping force. The Bosnian War ended with a *minimum* of 150,000 people killed and 175,000 wounded. Over 25,000 deaths were the direct result of genocide, and 20,000 to 50,000 women were sexually assaulted in mass rape campaigns.

In this context, *NATO* was a "concept album" consisting of anti-covers of songs relating to war and conquest.[23] While the Yugoslav Wars were central to *NATO*, an underlying theme is Western domination of Eastern Europe and the proliferation of global capitalism following the collapse of Soviet communism. With the exception of "Mars on River Drina" all the songs on *NATO* are drawn from various Western (First World) musical genres. Not unrelated, *NATO* is a somewhat more "commercial" album than its more leaden, industrial predecessors. In particular, there was pronounced use of percolating drum machines and electronically sequenced techno rhythms juxtaposed with dense choir vocals, synthesizers, and orchestral percussion instruments with particular emphasis on clash cymbals and timpani.[24] Moreover, given the mass rape campaigns that occurred during the Bosnian War, *NATO* prominently features women as lead and background vocalists within the choir setting.[25] The songs also run in a deliberately organized thematic order:

> Classical music
> Gustav Holst—"Mars, the Bringer of War" from *The Planets*
> [retitled "NATO"]
> Soul music
> Edwin Starr—"War"
> [heavily altered lyrics]
> 1980s rock music
> Europe—"The Final Countdown"
> Status Quo—"In the Army Now"
> Pink Floyd—"The Dogs of War"
> Punk/Industrial music
> D.A.F.—"Alle gegen Alle" ("All against All")
> Counterculture-era rock music
> The Raiders—"Indian Reservation"
> Zager and Evans—"In the Year 2525"
> [retitled "National Reservation" and "2525" with altered lyrics]
> Serbian patriotic music
> "March on the Drina"
> [retitled "Mars on River Drina"]

The opening track "NATO" is an adaptation of Holst's "Mars." Here the immediate connection is established between NATO as "the bringer of war," and more specifically the renewal of the Cold War that ended with the downfall of the Soviet Union, the economic and political reorganization of Eastern Europe along Western European economic-political lines, and the resulting wars and genocide in the former Yugoslavia. "NATO" begins with a repetitive disco/techno drum machine, although the snare sound occurs intermittently on various beats rather than providing a stable pattern (backbeat, half-time, every beat, etc.) while the rhythm track is accompanied by a modulating synthesizer noise somewhere between a shortwave radio and turntable scratching. Over the mechanical, synthetic beat and the high-pitched pulsating noise, string and brass synths play the main orchestral parts of "Mars" accompanied by clash cymbals and rumbling timpani.

As much as "NATO" serves as a kind of "overture" establishing the specter of war, the utilization of "Mars" serves another purpose. Popular music has a long history of adapting or, more pejoratively, "appropriating" classical music. Some of these could be turned "subversive" such as the Shangri-las' "Past, Present, and Future" (1966) utilizing Beethoven's "Moonlight Sonata" for the piano part over which a woman's faltering recitation can be heard as a veiled account of being raped rather than a failed romantic relationship. However, most "covers" of classical music in popular songs came in two forms.[26] One was progressive rock bands that adapted classical music in order to, as Robert Walser suggested, "refer to a prestigious discourse and thus bask in reflected glory."[27] The famous organ riff from Procol Harum's "A Whiter Shade of Pale" was a pastiche of Bach's "Air (on a G string)" and "Sleepers Wake," while Jethro Tull's "Bourée" was a jazz-rock cover of Bach's "Bourrée in E minor." Emerson, Lake, and Palmer covered works by classical composers (Aaron Copland, Modest Mussorgsky, and Alberto Ginestara) while Emerson, Lake, and Powell as well as King Crimson performed cover versions of "Mars." While Laibach also references a past "prestigious discourse," they do so to explicitly connect Western classical music to war, domination, and imperialism.

The second use of classical music was done for more crassly commercial purposes, to manufacture pop instrumental hits. In 1972, hit songs included Deodato's jazz-funk cover of Strauss' *Also Sprach Zarathustra*, while Apollo 100's "Joy" was a bouncy dance-pop cover of Bach's "Jesu, Joy of Man's Desiring." Walter Murphy had a hit with a disco arrangement of Beethoven's Fifth Symphony titled "A Fifth of Beethoven," and David Shire did a disco cover of Mussorgsky's *Night on Bald Mountain* titled "Night on Disco Mountain"—both songs appeared on the soundtrack of the film *Saturday Night Fever* (1977). This is not so much suggesting that classical music as "high art" is co-opted into "mass culture," but music or any other form of cultural production can be implemented to serve the purposes of any economic-political system—be it generating capital or ideology—and Laibach's *détournement* of incongruent aesthetics, ideologies, imagery, and musical genres as a "synthetic organization of greater efficacy" exposes their myriad and contradictory relationships.

"NATO" is followed by a version of Edwin Starr's 1970 psychedelic soul anthem "War." It begins with a symphonic version of the stop-start intro riff with string synths, brass synths, and timpani while a choir sings the opening lines of the song asking what value war has. However, the next line that adamantly proclaims war has no value is conspicuously omitted, along with the rest of the lyrics denouncing war in Starr's version. Instead, the answer to the opening rhetorical question in Laibach's version features an almost ethereal female choir listing the names of various Western multi-national corporations over a techno rhythm sequence that could be described as "generic."[28] While Starr's tumultuous psychedelic soul version emphatically proclaims that war does nothing but exacerbate human suffering, Laibach's linear classical-techno version points out that what war accomplishes is furthering the financial interests of global capitalism.

"The Final Countdown" is the first of three consecutive 1980s rock songs on *NATO*, the original version an international hit song by the Swedish arena-rock band Europe—an apropos choice given that a central theme of *NATO* is the economic and political reconfiguration of Europe in the 1990s. Laibach utilizes the main electronic keyboard riff of the original version but eliminates the guitars, bass, and drums in favor of the disco drum machine and electronically sequenced techno beat accompanied by choir backing vocals, string and brass synths, clash cymbals, and timpani. In this way, while the first three songs on *NATO* are taken from three vastly different genres (classical, soul, and arena rock), they end up sounding almost identical in Laibach's *détourned* versions, although "The Final Countdown" is also the first song on *NATO* to prominently feature the guttural lead vocals of Milan Fras. Lyrically, the song is about an intergalactic journey, and the "final countdown" is the moments before the spacecraft is launched from what seems to be a dying Earth. However, there is a key modification from Europe's version where Laibach substitutes the planet Mars (war) for Venus (love) as the destination. Moreover, in the Cold War era of the 1980s, "The Final Countdown" was sometimes interpreted as a song about the threat of World War III and "the final countdown" the launch of nuclear weapons, manifest in Laibach's music video for "The Final Countdown," entirely done in computer animation where the members of Laibach are show at a chessboard moving ICBMs as chess pieces.

"The Final Countdown" is followed by "You're in the Army Now," a midtempo, arena-rock song originally recorded by Boland in 1981 and covered by Status Quo, who had a European hit single with their version in 1986.[29] Laibach's version begins with cymbal crashes, snare rolls, choral vocals, and string synths before a drum machine with a pronounced snare sound begins a half-time rolling gait to suggest marching soldiers. The gruff, spoken lead vocals are punctuated by timpani rolls, a percussive piano, string synths, and various electronic noises while a choir repetitively intones the song's title. At approximately the two-minute mark, the drum machine is joined by effects-treated snare rolls and a harrowing scream. As the song progresses toward its finale, the choir voices become increasingly dissonant, which bears directly on the lyrics. "In the Army Now" was written in the second person and directed at an individual convinced by a recruiter that a stint in the military amounts to an overseas vacation and making them the community idol. However, as the song continues, the newly enlisted soldier is quickly sent to the battlefield where the options are killing or getting killed. The soldier is duped by the imaginary of army life only to experience the real of war, signified by the increasing dissonance of the choir voices underscored by mechanistic, martial rhythms.

"The Dogs of War" was originally recorded by Pink Floyd and released on *A Momentary Lapse of Reason* (1987).[30] The structure is slow 12-bar blues in 12/8 with a repeated chord progression of Cm (4 bars)–D♯m (2 bars)–Cm (2 bars)–G♯7 (1 bar)–Fm (1 bar)–Cm (2 bars). It begins with a effects-treated panting that sounds equal part animal and mechanical followed by an ominous three-note pattern played by a string section (or string synths) with a timpani on the one of every other 12/8 measure. A swelling organ enters and follows the same pattern as the timpani, and David Gilmour sings in a bluesy shout, the lyrics condemning war as the machinations of the wealthy power elite; in the chorus section, Gilmour is joined by soul-gospel female background vocals. It is not until almost three minutes into the song that the rhythm section enters and Gilmour plays a guitar solo underscored by the backing vocals. At roughly four minutes, "The Dogs of War" changes to a 4/4 half-time beat and a saxophone solo until at 4'35" when the time signature returns to 12/8 for a final verse and chorus.

Laibach's version of "The Dogs of War" begins with a timpani thump followed by a churning, mechanistic rhythm sequence. A drum machine enters playing a 4/4 up-tempo disco beat with a hollow bass drum sound on every beat and an eighth-note, open-closed hi-hat sound; however, the drum machine and sequencer interact in an out-of-sync polyrhythm. The lead vocals harshly recite the explicitly political lyrics backed by layers of choir voices and the conspicuous absence of other musical instruments. Hence, the changes and variations primarily occur at the rhythmic level. At 0'43" a sound resembling an echoed gunshot begins to accent the two of each bar; at 2'45" the gunshot sound begins playing a backbeat. "The Dogs of War" becomes a representation of the military-industrial "war machine" as it is not only activated but accelerated in the drive toward war where the human costs pale in relation to the economic and political benefits for a power elite. It is only at 3'57" that the rhythmic drive of the song momentarily halts in favor of a brief orchestral bridge of choir, clash cymbals, string synth and timpani. It serves as a parodic fanfare for the war machine as it "gears up" and the electronic rhythms begin anew as the song fades out.

"The Dogs of War" is followed by a version of "Alle gegen Alle" ("All against All") originally by the German punk-industrial band D.A.F. and released on *Alles ist gut* (*All Is Well*, 1981).[31] D.A.F.'s version of "Alle gegen Alle" is a minimalist song with a motorik backbeat, a repetitive riff somewhere between boogie-woogie and 12-tone music played by percussive electric keyboard, and shuddering vocals shouted in German.[32] The only other sounds are sporadic whooshes of electronic noise and occasional punctuations by background vocalists shouting "Hey!" In contrast to the more polemical "In the Army Now" and "The Dogs of War," the lyrics of "Alle gegan Alle" are vague descriptions of actions and attire that could refer to the military, paramilitary organizations, or even street gangs. Each time the verse is sung, it ends with a chorus as a repeated restatement of the title, recalling Thomas Hobbes' maxim, "Out of civil states, there is always war of every one against every one ... and the life of man [is] solitary poor, nasty, brutish, and short."[33]

Rather than anti-cover per se, Laibach's version of "Alle gegen Alle" it is largely faithful to the original—it is the only song on *NATO* sung in German—and based more on addition and less on deconstruction in that Laibach embellishes the stark minimalism of the D.A.F. version. The percussive keyboard is replaced by a more lugubrious and distinctly "electronic" synthesizer riff, and the motorik backbeat is punctuated by two syncopated gunshot sounds that occasionally appear over the course of the song. Like the rest of the songs on *NATO*, overlapping choir vocals accompany the menacing lead vocals; what might be termed a bridge that appears in the middle and just before the end of "Alle gegen Alle" is dominated by a symphonic, almost bombastic brass and string synth bursts along with the choir. Here the "contradiction" is manifest by infusing what can be heard as an anti-fascist punk/industrial song with elements of Wagner and Orff—two composers (rightly or wrongly) associated with the Third Reich. Moreover, in the historical context and the trajectory of *NATO*, "Alle gegen Alle" represents the onset of the Yugoslav Wars as "war of everyone against everyone."

"National Reservation" is an anti-cover of the Raider's 1970 hit "Indian Reservation." The Raiders came to prominence as Paul Revere and the Raiders in the mid–1960s as a garage rock band whose gimmick was dressing in matching Revolutionary War uniforms and playing in front of a colonial American flag (a fact that one suspects was not lost on Laibach). By the end of the decade and Vietnam making any association with the military and warfare eminently unattractive, the band name was shortened to the Raiders, and the colonial army uniforms were ditched in favor of contemporary hippie fashion. Ironically, the rechristened band's first hit was "Indian Reservation," a protest song about the internment of Native Americans on federal reservations. It begins with a bluesy, descending organ line before the rhythm section begins a swing-martial "one-two-three-and-four-and" beat. The organ punctuates the four of each bar, at 0'28" a ratchet adds a rattling sound on the two, and at 0'50" horns punctuate the two as well. At 1'00" the drums shift to backbeat, and a two-note ascending line from a string section accents the one of each bar until the song reaches the chorus. Using a call-and-response, stop-start structure, tom-tom rolls suggesting "war drums" accompanied by strings alternate with a cappella group vocals proclaiming the dignity of the Native Americans. The second verse largely matches the arrangement of the first verse with the exception being the somber, symphonic counter-melodies provided by the horns and strings which goes into a second chorus. The song then closes with a brief, building variation of the opening martial rhythm and a group chant that offers the hope that the Native American nation will rise again.

In contrast, "National Reservation" begins with an electric guitar playing the opening and the drums and male choir combining on the "one-two-three-and-four-and" rhythm while a female choir sings the melody line in tandem with string synths. A timpani roll ends the intro and a drum machine provides a slow backbeat with a ratcheting sound slightly audible at the beginning of each bar while choir and synths provide the musical backing for the ominous growled lead vocals, with brass synth blasts occasionally punctuating the two of a given bar. The chorus of Laibach's version substitutes the toms, strings, and group vocals for timpani, string synths, and choir. A parodic 1960s-style organ solo follows the chorus which leads into a second verse. However, the second chorus is omitted; the second verse goes directly into the ending chant of the song. As much as the musical reconfiguration, "National Reservation" alters the lyrics so the song is not about Native Americans but Eastern Europeans and how their culture, language, and lands of the indigenous population have been colonized. More specifically, while "Indian Reservation" depicts

Native Americans as the casualties of Manifest Destiny, "National Reservation" represents Eastern Europeans undergoing economic and political "territorialization" by the West in the form of NATO and the European Union (as of 2013, Croatia, the Czech Republic, Estonia, Latvia, Lithuania, Romania, Slovakia, and Slovenia are members of the EU). Indeed, the lyrical references to the native who still remains "red" underneath his suit is translated from the "redskin" colonized by westward national expansion across America into the communist "red" colonized by Western capitalism expanding across the former Iron Curtain. In turn, the ending chant is reconfigured to express the hope that a future civilization will emerge out of the present conditions of barbarism.

NATO continues with an anti-cover of Zager and Evans' "In the Year 2525" retitled "2525" that also radically alters the music and lyrics of the original. The Zager and Evans version is a folk-rock song that opens with the first verse and a trumpet fanfare. It is propelled by strummed acoustic guitars and a snare on every beat while strings and brass provide an orchestral accompaniment. Like "Where Have All the Flowers Gone?," the structure of "In the Year 2525" features a series of verses constructing a cyclical narrative where the lyrics recount the history of Earth in the distant future over a span of around 1,000-year increments as an increasingly technocratic dystopia until natural resources are exhausted and human life becomes extinct. A short bridge section describes a new planet being born elsewhere in the universe at the same time the Earth dies, and the song begins anew with a reprise of the first verse and into the second verse as the song fades outs, signifying a cosmic, synchronic cycle of death and rebirth.

Musically, Laibach's version of "2525" dispenses with the drum machines and sequenced electronic rhythms that are otherwise central to *NATO* in favor of a dirge featuring choir and an orchestral backing provided by brass and string synths as well as the ubiquitous timpani. Lyrically, the song is not set in the distant future but begins in 1994, and each verse progresses year by year to 1999. The lead vocals forgo their usual barked harshness in favor of a more operatic yet severe singing style describing a decade of ongoing war, destruction, and suffering. To this extent, Laibach's "2525" converts "science fiction" into a contemporary commentary on the present and potential future carnage of the Yugoslav Wars.

In this setting, *NATO* closes with "Mars on River Drina," an anti-cover of the Serbian patriotic song "March on the Drina" (a.k.a. "March on River Drina") written to commemorate a Serbian victory over Austria-Hungary at the Battle of Cer in 1914 and the first Allied victory in World War I. In that *NATO* begins with Holst's "Mars, the Bringer of War" as the overture, the finale "Mars on River Drina" becomes the point where the virtual war has been actualized in then–Yugoslavia with an ambiguous message. By 1994, NATO was conducting air strikes on Serbia and in this way "Mars on River Drina" can be read as a song of Balkan resistance against Western military intervention. At the same time, Serbian forces were accused of being responsible for the vast majority of acts of genocide during the Bosnian War, and this song can be heard as a final commentary on the atrocities of war.

"Mars on River Drina" begins with an eerie electronic noise. Timpani and martial snare drums provide the rhythmic foundation for a choir singing the melody, string synths, and brass synths that play along with the snare patterns. Male non-verbal interjections suggest the vocal sounds made by marching soldiers. At 1'55" the song drastically changes. Deadened toms begin a syncopated "war drum" pattern, a drum machine is used to manufacture synthetic snare rolls suggesting distant machine-gun fire, and an intermittent electronic sound resembles helicopters. Low brass synths provide a kind of bass line, a synthesizer mimic bugles, and the choir sings the melody amid dissonant organ tone clusters. As important, the choir makes a variety of non-verbal interjections like shouts and whoops along the lines of Stockhausen's *Mikrophone II* as much as recalling the choir of Benjamin Britton's somber *War Requiem* or Orff's stirring *Carmina Burana*. "Mars on River Drina" suggests a representation of not only war but genocide, a chaotic slaughter in which the vocal sounds are ambiguous as to whether they are the screams of the victims or the cheers of the victimizers.

Ultimately, *NATO* is not so much a "rock opera" but an "industrial rock opera" chronicling the collapse of Soviet communism, the triumph of Western capitalism in Europe, and how the price was paid by the former Yugoslavia in the early 1990s. The historical/narrative arch of *NATO* can be divided into three acts:

Act I: Instigation
    "NATO"—threat of war
    "War"—motives for war
Act II: Mobilization
    "The Final Countdown"—approaching war
    "In the Army Now"—recruitment for war
    "The Dogs of War"—escalation toward war
Act III: Annihilation
    "Alle gegen Alle"—outbreak of war
    "National Reservation"—subjection in war
    "2525"—decimation of war
    "Mars on River Drina"—total war

The Dilemmas of Laibach

> For once ... let's put our heads down and have an informative popular music-based quiz without resorting to jokes: the coward's way out.—Richard Ayoade, *Never Mind the Buzzcocks*
>
> Our humor is a deadly serious one.[34]—Laibach

Laibach's musical-political project is deliberately problematic and even perplexing. Perhaps it is best to situate the ways that are more unproductive in reading Laibach. First, to merely focus on ideology and whether Laibach is communist of fascist is an oversimplification. As Paul Hegarty noted, ideology is used by Laibach to perpetuate misconceptions and misperceptions rather than offer a precise position on where they stand politically. Rather, Laibach quite uncomfortably assembles the imagery of the totalitarian Left (Soviet Union and Stalinism) and totalitarian Right (Fascist Italy and the Third Reich) to turn totalitarian ideology on its head. However, Laibach equally represents a rejection of liberal democracy and global capitalism as another form of totalitarianism, in particular the critique of post–Soviet Europe on *NATO*.

Raoul Vaneigem characterized the situationist movement as a "revolution of daily life." Laibach can be described as a situationist use of music to expose the "totalitarianism of everyday life." In this way, Laibach is not a Dadaist mauling of rock to ostensibly satirize pop totalitarianism like the Residents' *The Third Reich and Roll*. In "A User's Guide to Détournement," Debord and Wolman argued that Marcel Duchamp drawing a moustache on the *Mona Lisa* merely scandalized bourgeois art and not bourgeois society, while Bertolt Brecht, whose tactics were closer to the situationists than Duchamp (i.e., Dada), was ultimately constrained by Brecht's limiting himself to the theatrical stage and not the theater of real life.[35] The Residents' "noise" was ultimately confined to an anti-art assault on rock, with the commentary on pop totalitarianism a surface oppositional addendum. Nor is it sufficient to classify Laibach as "a postmodern protest band," like Devo's "noise" as a satire of rock ideology. Along with the issue of assessing where cultural opposition ended and cultural opportunism began with Devo, by making rock ideology's tenets of individualism and rebellion principal objects of mockery, the "noise" of Devo invited a simplistic binary criticism from rock critics aligned to rock ideology: Devo endorsed conformity and obedience (read: fascism). The Sex Pistols' "noise" was manifest in the performance of punk onstage and offstage as a situationist use of music against the condition of rock in the mid–1970s, while the failure was the reliance on strict rock formalism and traditionalism rather than a détournement of incongruent and even conflicting musical genres.

The Residents, Devo, and the Sex Pistols represented a negation to the status quo of mainstream culture and politics and were thereby "subversive." As Debord and Wolman put it, "We must now push this process of *negating the negation*."[36] In negating the negation, Laibach adopts all the trappings of totalitarianism as "serious parody" to analyze the degree to which popular music becomes a central, ideological organizing force of society and, by extension, a mechanism of nation-states to maintain their cultural-economic-political existence. Here Slavoj Žižek best expressed the oppositional potentials of Laibach:

> Cynicism, as today's prevailing mode of ideology, means that it is the positive condition of the functioning of the system, [and] that its own ideology, by its own subject, must not be taken seriously. An ideal subject, today, is the one who has ironic distance toward the system.... The reversal of this ... the only way to be really subversive is not to develop critical potentials, ironic distance, but precisely to take the system more seriously than it takes itself seriously, and I think that this is maybe one of the keys to Laibach's strategy.[37]

10

In with the Old: Covers and Generational Politics

The Midlife Crisis of Rock and Roll

Along with James Dean's last angry teenager in *Rebel without a Cause* (1955), rock music emerged in the 1950s as a generational signifier of an alienated young population in the Cold War era. However, the contemporary status of rock music can be analyzed around Raymond Williams' critique of dominant, residual, and emergent culture. As Williams described it, *emergent culture* consists of

> new meanings and values, new practices, new relationships and kinds of relationships are continually being created. But it is exceptionally difficult to distinguish between those which are really elements of some new phase of dominant culture ... and those which are substantially alternative or oppositional it: emergent in the strict sense,rather than merely novel.[1]

The case can be made that rock music was a form of emergent culture, not simply a hybrid of R&B and country, but a hybrid of black and white culture. As Simon Frith suggested, "The shock was not musical ... but ideological: it was the overt, assertive, *social* intermingling that was threatening."[2] While Frith is correct on this point, rock was not only ideological in its assemblage of black and white music but a new kind of "noise" that rejected bourgeois ideas of music (hence, Jacques Attali's particular contempt for progressive rock, discussed in chapter 8). Rock rejected civility, constraint, and virtuosity (i.e., "talent"); it also became a genre defined by electric instrumentation, amplification, and studio composition that upped the ante as far as the noise possibilities of music.

Over the course of decades, rock has undergone a number of permutations that often comment on the previous generation's preferred brand of rock as much as commenting on the current state of rock music in society and social issues at large. The origins of 1950s rock as an expression of youth rebellion escalated into the 1960s counterculture movement with rock a primary expression of political discontent. Early punk's "back to basics" approach in the 1970s was also an *ideological* rejection of what rock had become amid in the counterculture and post-counterculture era ca. 1966 to 1976; in turn, the musical and political limitations of punk gave way to post-punk. Likewise, hardcore emerged as a reaction to 1970s punk and post-punk as much as rock music and experienced its own crisis by splitting into hardcore traditionalism and post-hardcore. The 1990s "slackers" and their generational signifier of grunge music—specifically Nirvana's *Nevermind*—adopted a guitar-driven sound that not only drew from (post-)hardcore and (post-)punk but pre-punk genres like 1960s psychedelic rock and 1970s hard rock as a reaction to the 1980s dominated by British New Pop, synthpop, and metal "hair bands."

Rock is made up of competing and complementary subgenres and, as a cultural discourse, "sub-discourses." It is not a historically unified whole of cultural rebellion as mythologized in the film *School of Rock* (2003).[3] Yet rock continually self-defines itself as a continually emergent, oppositional culture the more it becomes dominant culture and increasingly tied to *residual culture* as posited by Williams:

> The residual, by definition, has been effectively formed in the past, but it is still active not only and often not at all as an element of the past, but as an effective element of the present.... A residual cultural element is usually at some distance from the effective dominant culture, but some part of it, some version of it—especially if the residue is from some major area of the past—will in most cases have had to be incorporated if the dominant culture is to make sense in these areas.... It is in the incorporation of the actively residual—by reinterpretation, dilution, projection, discriminating inclusion and exclusion—that the work of the selective tradition is especially evident.[4]

In this context, the focus of this chapter is how rock's relationship with residual culture manufactures a "selective tradition" through "interpretation, dilution, projection, discriminating inclusion and exclusion." More specifically, it examines pop and rock cover songs by older mainstream musical performers and, in particular, American cultural icons Frank Sinatra, Pat Boone, and Johnny Cash. While the songs themselves may not be "political," the act of the older performers covering rock songs becomes a negotiation of generational differences and a "political process."

Frank Sinatra: "Something" (Single, 1970)

The Beatles' protracted breakup arguably began after *Sgt. Pepper* and became inevitable in early 1969 with the disastrous *Get Back* sessions. Rather than peter out in rancorous ennui, the Beatles reconvened to record *Abbey Road*, all but officially designed as the Beatles' final album (the decision to salvage the scrapped *Get Back* recordings into what became *Let It Be* after *Abbey Road*'s release drastically changed that plan). Nonetheless, *Abbey Road* was not an entirely conflict-free affair. Lennon despised McCartney's music-hall-inspired song "Maxwell's Silver Hammer" and refused to participate on its recording. Moreover, the 16-minute "Medley" that closed the album was assembled from several shorter finished and unfinished songs by Lennon and McCartney that George Martin and McCartney combined through studio editing; it began with McCartney's song "You Never Give Me Your Money," and there was little doubt it was directed at Allen Klein, then-CEO of Apple Records.

George Harrison was arguably the Beatle who benefited most from *Abbey Road*, contributing two of his best-known songs, "Something" and "Here Comes the Sun."[5] Indeed, given that John Lennon and Paul McCartney were the primary songwriters, "Something" provided a cogent summary of the post–*Sgt. Pepper* Beatles sound. The A–C–A–A♯–B–C melody hook begins the song and operates as a transitional phrase between verse–chorus–bridge sections. Verses are dominated by phase-shifted guitars, half-time drumming, and Harrison's lead vocals. The chorus adds quarter-note organ punctuations, and the first chorus introduces a string section that continues throughout the song. While the verse and chorus are fairly leisurely, the bridge takes on a more urgent quality, with Ringo Starr shifting to a slightly jarring drum pattern with snare rolls on three and syncopated full-band rhythmic shifts between vocal lines. The strings become prominent and the group harmonies more dynamic and expressive. Following the bridge, the band returns to a more relaxed rendition of the verse–chorus section featuring a Harrison guitar solo (1'44"–2'14") after which a third verse and chorus concludes the song.

With the exception of McCartney's "Yesterday," "Something" is the most-covered Beatles song in their catalog.[6] Frank Sinatra covered both songs. Originally recorded and released on *Help!* (1965), "Yesterday" is a melancholy but brisk ballad lasting 2'06" sung by McCartney, who also played acoustic guitar backed by a string quartet. On *My Way* (1969), Sinatra's rendition of "Yesterday" lasted almost four minutes, the extended length owing to the song being played at a *much* slower tempo and Sinatra's much more spacious phrasing of the lyrics. As well as orchestral backing and a pronounced harp part, Sinatra's cover incorporated jazz elements like slow swing drumming and a vibraphone. However, Sinatra covering a Beatles' song was notable but not particularly groundbreaking. By 1968, "Yesterday" had already become something of a popular music staple and was covered by performers across musical genres ranging from the Brothers Four (folk) and Ray Charles (R&B) to Willie Nelson (country), the Supremes (Motown), and Perry Como (MOR).[7]

In 1970, Sinatra covered "Something" as a single release in a highly complex arrangement combining big band and orchestra. It lasts some 30 seconds longer than the Beatles' version, with the guitar solo omitted and the song extended by adding a second bridge and a fourth verse–chorus to conclude the song; there are also some brief instrumental embellishments and the song is done at a slightly slower tempo. However, the main difference is that the Beatles' version has an understated elegance whereas Sinatra's version has an overstated bluster. It begins with an intro of flute, strings, and muted trumpets that settles into a slow, jazzy, half-time rhythm for the first verse. For the chorus, the drum shifts to a swing backbeat, a harpsichord enters, and muted trumpets play the hook line into the second verse which returns to a half-time beat underscored by the harpsichord with wisps of flute and brass. In the second chorus, the drums again shift to swing backbeat while bustling saxophones join in and play the second hook line into a short break of swirling strings and a two-note brass blast that announces the bridge. Amid a hectic interplay of blaring brass, spiraling saxophones, and syncopated jazz drumming, Sinatra sings the first bridge lyrics before the song ebbs for the third verse and a return to a half-time swing beat and a musical backing of harpsichord and smoky French horns. This goes into the third chorus and the inevitable swing backbeat rhythm where the strings play the hook line which erupts into a full-scale, big-band rave-up that continues unabated throughout the second bridge along with soaring strings. It culminates with a spinning arpeggio of descending strings and a fourth verse (technically, a reprise of the third verse). The less-stressed half-time beat resumes, the strings are the dominant instrumentation, and the harpsichord is now absent. Reentering the chorus, the backbeat swing drumming begins anew along with saxophones and muted trumpets until the song gradually winds down into its ending.

The problem with Sinatra's cover of "Something" is, to use the title of another Harrison song, "it's all too much." Sinatra's orchestral version of "Yesterday" can be faulted as overlong and even a bit slushy, but it effectively conveys the downhearted mood of the song and Sinatra's vocals are resonant and, as important, restrained in his somber delivery of the lyrics. "Something" becomes a triumph of technique over feeling. The frantic complexity of the shifting parts underneath Sinatra's assured crooning converts "Something" into a showcase rather than a song, a musical experience that impresses and overpowers the listener into a sense of being "moved." Moreover, the *assumption* of "Something" is that the song is directed at a significant other in a relationship that provides happiness rather than the song being directed at an object of unrequited love, and Harrison's lyrics are highly ambiguous in this regard, especially in the bridge of the song.[8] In Sinatra's version, the "uncertainty" of love is generated by the continuous rhythmic and harmonic shifts in the arrangement yet negated by Sinatra singing with his characteristic bravado, manufacturing a sense of confidence and security that he is the one in charge of the course of the relationship. Ideologically, it is the same message transmitted in Van Halen's cover of the Kinks' "You Really Got Me."

Ultimately, the importance of Sinatra covering the Beatles was historical as much as musical as it represented a moment of cultural, generational, and political détente in the turmoil of the era. Sinatra covering the Beatles was a cultural concession by the Establishment that "rock and roll is here to stay," and the Beatles being covered by Sinatra signified that rock and roll was becoming culturally respectable. Indeed, by the end of the 1960s numerous older mainstream performers, much like soul and jazz musicians, began to enter into musical negotiations with pop and rock music.

"So Bad It's Good": Covers and Camp

> There is no such thing as bad music. Music only becomes bad in an evaluative context, as part of an argument.[9]—Simon Frith, "What is Bad Music?"

While famous for being the longtime bandleader and one of Johnny Carson's comedic sidekicks on *The Tonight Show*, Doc Severinsen was a virtuoso trumpet player who recorded numerous albums dating back to the early 1960s. In 1970, *Doc Severinsen's Closet* consisted of jazz covers of rock songs such as the Beach Boys' "Surfer Girl," a truncated version of "Medley" from *Abbey Road*, and King Crimson's "In the Court of the Crimson King"—the last of which sounded somewhere between Maynard Ferguson and Ennio Morricone. In 1969, jazz singer Mel Tormé did two albums covering pop and rock hits, *A Time for Us (Love Theme from Romeo and Juliet)* and *Raindrops Keep Fallin' on My Head*. One was the Turtles' "Happy Together" (*A Time for Us*), a psychedelic-pop hit highly reminiscent of *Sgt. Pepper*-era Beatles that Tormé covered as a big band number showcasing his signature "Velvet Fog" vocal style with scat vocal improvisations. Another was a reworking of Donovan's lurching psychedelic-rock hit "Sunshine Superman" (*Raindrops*) where the big band horn interplay was propelled by a frenetic, funky backing of wah-

wah guitar, electric piano, bass and drums while Tormé nonchalantly crooned the surreal lyrics.

Hugo Montenegro was an orchestra leader, arranger, and soundtrack composer whose credits included TV western shows–the comedy *Here Come the Brides* and the drama *The Outcasts*—as well as Dean Martin's "Matt Helm" films *The Ambushers* (1967) and *The Wrecking Crew* (1968) and Frank Sinatra's "Tony Rome" film *Lady in Cement* (1968). In 1968, Montenegro also had a hit song with his cover of the main theme of *The Good, the Bad, and the Ugly*. On *Moog Power* (1969) and *Good Vibrations* (1969), Montenegro covered pop and rock covers considerably rearranged around Montenegro's interest and work in spaghetti western and espionage/crime film soundtrack music. His cover of "Happy Together" (*Good Vibrations*) offers a convenient comparison to Tormé's version. Rather than a big-band arrangement, Montenegro's lounge version assembled ensemble vocals, syncopated rhythms, harpsichord, flute, spaghetti western–style strings and brass, and a Moog synthesizer providing a forlorn whistling sound. Montenegro's version of Jimmy Webb's "MacArthur Park (Allegro Part III)" (*Moog Power*), a hit song recorded by actor-singer Richard Harris in 1968, jettisoned the slow balladry of the verses and chorus in favor of the fast instrumental bridge that appears at approximately 4'53"–6'19" in Harris' version. Montenegro's version consists of a rock band backbeat and rapidly shifting interactions of wordless vocal interjections, strings and brass, timpani, electric organ, and Moog synthesizer replicating harpsichord, trumpet, and other instruments. It best compared to theme songs for TV detective dramas or action sequences from crime films.

While Montenegro flirted with the Moog synthesizer, Dick Hyman became one of its chief proponents at a time when the instrument was in its infancy.[10] While best known for his association with Mitch Miller, Hyman was a respected jazz pianist and session musician. In 1969, Hyman's *MOOG: The Eclectic Electrics of Dick Hyman* included the Top 40 hit "The Minotaur," essentially a long Moog solo using the "trumpet sound" propelled by a 3/4 drum-machine beat. Also released in 1969, *The Age of Electronicus* featured Hyman covering an array of pop, rock, and soul hits using Moog synthesizer, electric organ, and drum accompaniment. Booker T. and the M.G.'s "Time Is Tight" was leisurely driven by percussive electronic sequencing and jazzy rock drumming with the melody played on Moog using both a chiming electrical sound and the trumpet sound; it suggested a livelier—or at least less mechanistic—version of Kraftwerk's "Autobahn." In contrast, James Brown's "Give It Up or Turn It Loose" became positively jarring. The funk drum beat was accompanied by an intermittent pulse of buzzing noise mimicking the guitar riff, the intermittent horns became almost random glissando pings and sizzles, and the vocal melody was played with a dense Moog setting that sounded like a distorted cross between a trumpet and hissing steam engine.

As briefly discussed last chapter, exotica music pioneer Martin Denny gained fame for his brand of "world music" (before the term existed) by combining pop, jazz, and easy listening with pronounced Latin American and Pacific Island musical influences. His debut album *Exotica* (1957) reached the top of the Billboard album charts, and his cover of Les Baxter's "Quiet Village" peaked at number four on the singles chart.[11] On his 1968 albums *A Taste of India* and *Exotic Love*, Denny did exotica covers of pop and rock hits. The Strawberry Alarm Clock's psychedelic-rock hit "Incense and Peppermints" (*A Taste of India*) featured Denny's international genre mixing incorporating sitar and flutes into a Latin-tinged rock backbeat, whereas the Rascals' "A Beautiful Morning" (*Exotic Love*) was done as a cocktail jazz piano number with extensive flute soloing interrupted by brief but highly disorientating breaks of tom-toms, marimbas, and flute excursions reminiscent of Frank Zappa.

While performers like Severinsen, Tormé, Montenegro, Hyman, and Denny sought to interpret contemporary pop and rock songs within their own respective genres (jazz, big band vocal, soundtrack music, electronic music, exotica), numerous mainstream performers of varying musical skills have recorded countless albums of pop and rock cover songs.[12] Though the efforts were sincere for the most part, the end results were unintentionally humorous failures subsequently chronicled on anthologies like the Rhino Records *Golden Throats* series, Capitol's *Ultra-Lounge: On the Rocks* series, and *Spy Magazine Presents: Soft, Safe, and Sanitized, Vol. 3*.[13] A case in point is *Golden Throats 4: Celebrities Butcher the Beatles* with a self-explanatory title as to how the listener should "properly" react to the covers of Beatles' songs (one could say the same about *Soft, Safe, and Sanitized* as a direct message that the listener can fully expect neutered mainstream versions of "oppositional" rock songs). To be sure, some of the covers included on *Celebrities Butcher the Beatles* are laughably dreadful.[14] The Brothers Four covered the Beatles' "Revolution" as a leisurely, jazz-inflected folk ballad with bluesy guitar lines and a Dixieland horn section (*Let's Get Together*, 1969). If the underground press could flay the Beatles' "Revolution" for being counter-revolutionary based on some select lyrics while ignoring the harsh dissonance generated by the electric guitars, then the Brothers Four's vapid version and the seemingly non-ironic musical references to "the Old South" amounted to an utterly reactionary gesture. Bing Crosby warbled his way through "Hey Jude" as if he were wearily working his way through yet another 1930s Tin Pan Alley tune (*Hey Jude/Hey Bing!*,

1969).¹⁵ Despite the compilation's title, other songs on *Celebrities Butcher the Beatles* fared better. Surf-rock duo Jan and Dean's cover of "Norwegian Wood" (*Popsicle*, 1966) was an adequate version similar to the Beatles' original, save the Beach Boys–style background vocals and the awkward use of a distorted 12-string electric guitar to mimic the sitar. Actor Telly Savalas' version of "Something" (*Telly*, 1974) was a lackluster MOR version of the song, but ultimately more innocuous than inexcusable. Tennessee Ernie Ford covered "Let It Be" as a country-gospel ballad (*Everything Is Beautiful*, 1970), and the shock was not Ford covering the Beatles, but how little it deviated from the Beatles' original arrangement and managed to be as "effective" as the Beatles in its own way.

Much stranger but no less intriguing, Mitch Miller and the Gang covered John Lennon's "Give Peace a Chance" along with several popular folk-protest songs on *Peace Sing-Along* (1970; it appeared on *Golden Throats 2: More Celebrity Rock Oddities!* but was omitted from *Celebrities Butcher the Beatles* although later included on *Soft, Safe, and Sanitized*). Mitch Miller was a veteran record industry arranger, producer, and performer best known for his TV show *Sing Along with Mitch* (NBC, 1961–64); Miller headed an all-male choir singing popular songs like "Five Foot Two (Has Anyone Seen My Gal?)" or "My Wonderful One" while he directly addressed the camera to encourage the viewer to sing along with the subtitled lyrics. "Give Peace a Chance" is set to a jazzy, soft rock groove (with Dick Hyman on piano), a male choir sings the chorus, and Miller recites Lennon's almost stream-of-consciousness rhymes nearly verbatim. It is quite hilarious to hear Miller, a personification of the Establishment, name-drop Bob Dylan and Norman Mailer as well as exclaim agitprop like "Hassle the Congress!"

There is a dual message offered by *Golden Throats, Ultra-Lounge: On the Rocks*, and *Soft, Safe, and Sanitized* in terms of the older "square" generation wrestling with the music of the younger "hip" generation. On one hand, these covers are assumed a priori to be uniformly abysmal, which itself is highly debatable. On the other, they have the luxury of being redeemed around what Susan Sontag termed "the ultimate Camp statement: it's good because it's awful.... Of course, one can't always say that."¹⁶ Hence, Phyllis Diller caterwauling her way through "Satisfaction" can be hilarious Camp rather than simply horrendous, or actor David McCallum playing the oboe on an MOR-rock instrumental version of "Satisfaction" can be amusing Camp rather than so much easy-listening fare. Generally the older generation is afforded more tolerance—or at least given more leeway—from the younger audience as far as their transgressions into rock music. Put differently, the greatest crime is not older performers covering classic rock songs and converting them to comical Camp artifacts but younger performers "desecrating" them into "inauthentic" pop product. The very act of Britney Spears covering "Satisfaction" amounts to popular music blasphemy until Spears is bestowed "credibility" as a popular music performer through the consensus of critics and consumers and it no longer becomes an act of personal debasement to purchase one of her CDs or DVDs.

Sontag observed, "Many examples of Camp are things which, from a 'serious' point of view, are either bad art or kitsch. Not all, though. Not only is Camp not necessarily bad art, but some art can be approached as Camp."[17] Once Mel Tormé's cover of "Sunshine Superman" was included on *More Celebrity Rock Oddities!, Soft, Safe, and Sanitized,* and *On the Rocks, Vol.1,* it was effectively and permanently consigned to the status of Camp. However, even suggesting that Frank Sinatra's cover of "Something" could bear inclusion on *Celebrities Butcher the Beatles* would be an unmitigated insult to Sinatra, the Beatles, and the popular music audience with "good taste," even though a case could be made that Sinatra's version of "Something" is an example of Camp if not "bad art." Sinatra is one of the select performers in popular music that becomes virtually immune to criticism, with Barbara Streisand, Tony Bennett, Johnny Cash, and Whitney Houston having attained similar status. However, in 1970 Bennett released *Tony Sings the Great Hits of Today!* The album was roundly panned by critics at the time and Bennett candidly recounted, "I actually regurgitated making that awful album."[18] One of the lowest points was a half-sung/half recited version of "Eleanor Rigby" that if done by any other performer would have screamed inclusion on *Celebrities Butcher the Beatles*. Nonetheless, because Bennett attained the status of "iconic" residual culture, any of his work that is fully conceded to be "bad art" is bypassed rather than stain Bennett with the designation of Camp.[19] As suggested in chapter 6, rock needs to designate the "inauthentic"—be it Pat Boone, the Partridge Family, the Spice Girls, or Hannah Montana—in order to construct a selective tradition of what constitutes "authentic rock," be it the Beatles, the Rolling Stones, the Who, Led Zeppelin, the Ramones, or Nirvana. Likewise rock "needs" Mel Tormé, the Brothers Four, Bing Crosby, Mitch Miller, and so on to provide the evidence of what constitutes "bad music" in order to define the selective tradition of residual culture that "stands the test of time" as great art (Sinatra, Streisand, etc.).

A related issue is the crucial difference between "authentic" Camp and "inauthentic" Camp. Sontag contended, "One must distinguish between naïve and deliberate Camp. Pure Camp is always naïve. Camp which knows itself to be Camp ("camping") is usually less satisfying. The pure examples of Camp are unintentional, they are dead serious.... Intending to be campy is ... forced and heavy-handed, rarely Camp."[20] As far as a concept album of cover songs, one notorious example of naïve Camp or "pure Camp" is William Shatner's *The Transformed Man* (1968), a laughably pretentious yet completely serious album featuring Shatner's histrionic recitations of poems, Shakespeare extracts, and popular songs like Bob Dylan's "Mr. Tambourine Man," the Beatles' "Lucy in the Sky with Diamonds," and Frank Sinatra's "It Was a Very Good Year," all set to musical accompaniment that might be charitably described as pretentious schmaltz.[21] The issue with Pat Boone's *In a Metal Mood* as a concept album of cover album—big band versions of heavy metal songs—is the degree to which Boone's project was deliberate Camp and an exercise in camping.

Pat Boone: "Smoke on the Water" (In a Metal Mood: No More Mr. Nice Guy, *1997)*

As far as rock history, Pat Boone's status could be termed "war criminal." In the 1950s, Boone recorded covers of R&B and rock songs that turned "black music" into "blanched music," targeting an assumed audience of white, middle-class teenagers. It was not coincidental that Boone's tepid cover of Little Richard's "Long Tall Sally" was included on *Soft, Safe, and Sanitized*. Moreover, at a time when rock was emerging as potential oppositional culture, Boone was a clean-cut, sweater-clad, outspoken religious conservative who epitomized the American Square in an era where being Hip was essential to cultural rebellion. By the 1970s, Boone moved into contemporary Christian music and TV programming while vociferously supporting right-wing political candidates and causes.

In 1997, Boone made a brief return to rock and roll (sort of) with the release of *In a Metal Mood: No More Mr. Nice Guy* (1997, henceforth *Metal Mood*). Given Boone's Christian conservatism and heavy metal being a musical genre stereotyped around debauchery and devil worship, finding a middle ground in big band music inevitably screamed that *Metal Mood* was "ironic" if not a flat-out joke record despite Boone's claims he was sincerely motivated by the "spirituality" of heavy metal music. In fairness, the concept did not seem as far-fetched at the time as it does now—Boone's execution of said concept being another matter. In the 1990s, there was a resurgent interest in lounge music and its overlapping subgenres like cocktail jazz, exotica, space-age pop, bachelor pad music, and swing revivalism. There were numerous CD reissues of records by Les Baxter, Martin Denny, and Juan García Esquivel along with various anthologies (Capitol Records' *Ultra-Lounge* series inaugurated in 1996). Alternative bands like Combustible Edison, Stereolab, and Squirrel Nut Zippers were strongly informed by lounge music. Released the same year as *Metal Mood*, the compilation album *Lounge-A-Palloza* included Combustible Edison and Esquivel performing "Mini Skirt" as well as the Japanese pop band Pizzicato Five covering "The Girl from Ipanema." However, the album's biggest surprise was MOR-singing duo Steve Lawrence and Eydie Gormé performing a macabre lounge cover of Soundgarden's "Black Hole Sun."[22] In this context, "lounge rock" was very much in vogue, and *Metal Mood* was part of this trend. Indeed, the cynic could claim *Metal Mood* was a calculated effort to capitalize on it.

Among the covers on *Metal Mood* was Deep Purple's "Smoke on the Water" (*Machine Head*, 1972). "Smoke on the Water" became a Top 5 single in the U.S. and one of the apocryphal heavy metal anthems of the 1970s; the opening riff remains one of the most immediately recognizable in rock. Lyrically, the song is a straightforward account of events that occurred in late 1971. Deep Purple embarked to Switzerland to record an album at the Montreux Casino with a mobile studio rented from the Rolling Stones. Unfortunately, just before the recording sessions were scheduled to begin, an audience member shot a flare gun during a Frank Zappa and the Mothers of Invention concert in the casino theater, resulting in a fire that destroyed the entire building (the title refers to the dense clouds of smoke that hovered over Lake Geneva). Now in the unenviable position of having invested a considerable amount of money in equipment and nowhere to record, Deep Purple scrambled to find a locale before renting the Montreux Grand Hotel. Using hallways and other parts of the hotel as makeshift recording booths, they managed to record much of what was eventually released on *Machine Head*. As a rock song about rock music, "Smoke on the Water" was not about rock's liberating pleasures, but its financial pressures.

Boone's version of "Smoke on the Water" was arraigned by Tom Scott, a jazz saxophonist and band leader with an impressive list of appearances on records ranging from Joni Mitchell, George Harrison, Paul McCartney, Steely Dan, Blondie, Whitney Houston, and Pink Floyd (among many others). Running approximately four minutes, Scott's arrangement uses a standard intro–verse–chorus–verse–chorus–bridge (guitar solo)–verse–chorus–outro structure with former Deep Purple guitarist Ritchie Blackmore supplying the solo and second guitar by Dweezil Zappa (Frank Zappa's son). Instead of the thundering bass-drum backbeat of the Deep Purple version, there is a Latin rhythm ensemble of drum kit, congas, shaker, tambourine, cowbell, and another well-known guest musician leading the charge on timbales, Sheila E. The verses are dominated by horns, keyboards, percussive Latin rhythms, and the occasional guitar lick inserted by Zappa; the choruses have a more pronounced rock snare backbeat as opposed the quarter-note drive of the verses (snare rimshots) but retain the Latin rhythmic syncopations and variations. For added measure, backup singers join in during the chorus to provide a "gospel music" element. After the second chorus, Blackmore's guitar solo serves as the bridge amid the lounge music backdrop before the song ends after a third verse and chorus.

The conversion of "Smoke on the Water" from heavy metal to lounge becomes a pastiche of big band horn riffing, exotica rhythms, and musical in-jokes. Moreover, throughout "Smoke on the Water" (and, for that matter, *Metal Mood* as a whole), Boone sings in a decidedly tongue-in-cheek "hepcat" lounge style. Not unrelated, "Smoke on the Water" is essentially a Deep Purple song about the difficulties of Deep Purple. The subject matter is not particularly relatable to Boone in giving a "sincere" performance as opposed to Johnny Cash's cover of "Hurt" where the song's lyrical themes of physical decay bear directly on Cash's severely declining health. Instead, Boone assumes a parodic "persona" of Pat Boone reimagined as a lounge-meets-metal singing star. Given the slick big band/exotica arrangement, the guest star presence, and the overall self-consciousness of the performance, it becomes difficult to view *Metal Mood* as naïve Camp as opposed to deliberate Camp. Moreover, as much as Boone was camping on heavy metal, *Metal Mood* was also Boone camping on his own wholesome public image.

From the prospective of the metal community, no one—including Boone himself—appeared to take *Metal Mood* seriously. Amid a mixture of cheers and boos, Boone appeared in wraparound sunglasses, a black leather outfit, fake tattoos, and a studded collar alongside Alice Cooper to present Metallica with the heavy metal artist of the year award at the 1997 American Music Awards—and to blatantly promote the following day's official release of *Metal Mood*. Boone and Cooper exchanged some good-natured ribbing, and when Metallica came onstage to accept the award, drummer Lars Ulrich proudly announced that Pat Boone was joining Metallica as the new lead vocalist. However, Boone's conservative Christian audience had a much more serious and highly negative reaction. Within a month after Boone's AMA appearance, the Trinity Broadcast Network (TBN) dropped Boone's show *Gospel Now* amid a wave of viewer protest—presumably for Boone's conduct unbecoming to a Christian. Boone subsequently appeared on a special telecast of TBN's

Praise the Lord along with TBN president Paul Crouch, Rev. Jeff Haycock, actor-minister Leon Isaac Kennedy, and evangelical Christian–heavy metal singer Jeff Fenholt.[23] In what largely amounted to two hours of damage control, the panel discussed whether or not Christianity and heavy metal were mutually opposed. Boone alternately justified *Metal Mood* as an attempt to spread the gospel to a wider audience base, chastised his critics for not getting the joke, encouraged TBN viewers to consider heavy metal beyond the stereotypes of satanic Neanderthals, and issued the requisite apology to anyone he may have unintentionally offended. Boone's explanation (read: contrition) was considered satisfactory, and *Gospel Now* returned to the TBN schedule.

While Boone's camping generated laughs, publicity, and an unwanted backlash, *Metal Mood* ultimately maintained the perception that Boone was a perennial joke to rock fans and ensured Boone remained a personification of "cheese" in American popular music. In the 1990s, a decade when genres like lounge music and trash cinema were a cultural vogue, cheese was considered a potential *subversive* mode of cultural production and consumption. Writing in 2000, Annalee Newitz contented,

> like camp, cheese is both a parodic practice and a parodic form of textual production ... and like camp, cheese describes a way of remembering history, a kind of snide nostalgia, for serious cultures of the past which now seem so alien and bizarre as to be funny.... The point of cheese, whether deliberate or "read in" by the audience, is to offer criticism of social norms, to regulate their power to the ash can of history through the use of "productive" derisive laughter.[24]

Newitz's assessment can be read in relation to *how* residual culture as an element of the past is represented in the present and the consequences to "tradition." The potential problem is that history becomes "snide nostalgia," residual culture is "alien and bizarre as to be funny," and the past is incorporated into the present through "derisive laughter." Again, this is precisely the issue with anthologies like the *Golden Throats* series. The negotiation between generational music is constructed so the older performers deemed *unworthy* of inclusion in the selective tradition of canonical performers become uniform objects of mockery, not just "archaic" but anachronisms to be *laughed at* by the present. Cheese is not "ignorant of the past"; it becomes contemptuous of the past. The camping and intentional self-parody of Boone can be read as subversive, but only to the extent Boone willingly satisfies his end as the butt of the cultural joke, the corny curio of residual culture desperately trying to fit in with the dominant culture of rock.

More recently, the connotations of "cheese" and "cheesy" have considerably changed in certain critical quarters and are now much more disparaging in terms of artistic value and subversive culture. Erik Anderson argued, "Cheese, like camp, is bad. But unlike camp, cheese is inauthentic and manipulative, in that it attempts to pass off its badness as something good, which it is not.... Thus some cheese can be seen as failed camp."[25] As discussed in chapter 6, Rob Sheffield contended that Spears' rebellious demands for individual freedom and self-determination made her "a true child of the rock and roll tradition ... *underneath the cheese surface*" (emphasis added). Sheffield's emphasis on content over form set aside, the redemption of Spears is based around her affinity to rock tradition and an ideology that bestows an authenticity that transcends the cheesiness of the music. In the case of Boone, the failure of *Metal Mood* as calculated camping can be expressed as a rhetorical question: "Who cut the cheese?"

*Johnny Cash: "Hurt" (*American IV: The Man Comes Around*, 2002)*

Rock music originated as a nexus of "black music" and "white music," specifically R&B and country as the initial assemblage in the 1950s. In becoming an "art form" in the 1960s, white music and culture became a more crucial component in rock, whether through Bob Dylan's folk Americana or the Beatles' modernist Continentalism. Simon Frith contended that country music contained an inherent conservatism as far as themes of family, religion, and sexual morality along with its highly traditionalist musical form; folk music was musically similar but expressed politically progressive views that overtly addressed issues of equality, freedom, and social change which thereby became a more "natural" ally with black music in the 1960s.[26] However, folk could easily be as conservative as country as far as musical traditionalism, as evidenced by the outrage of the folk community over Dylan going electric and his scathing response with the song "Positively 4th Street."

The political conservatism of country music is often framed around Merle Haggard and his songs "Okie from Muskogee" (1969) and "The Fightin' Side of Me" (1970). While conservatives embraced the songs as "tell it like it is" anti-hippie, anti-leftist anthems, the counterculture appreciated the potential irony of Haggard. Left-wing folk singer Phil Ochs covered "Okie from Muskogee" (*Gunfight at Carnegie Hall*, 1970), and hippie icons Grateful Dead were joined by the decidedly more conservative Beach Boys in a live version of "Okie from Muskogee" recorded live at the Fillmore East (April 27, 1971). Both cover versions were done in a straightforward manner as opposed to "anti-covers," although they could certainly be received as highly satirical cover versions by the counterculture audience.

In fact, there was a considerable *increase* of country music influence in rock by the late 1960s. The Grateful Dead routinely covered Haggard's "Mama Tried" in concert, with one version released on the live double album *Grateful Dead* (1971). Bob Dylan moved into a more overt country music direction on *John Wesley Harding* (1967) and *Nashville Skyline* (1969). A key band in the folk-rock movement, the Byrds released the country-influenced *Sweethearts of the Rodeo* (1968); Gram Parsons was a member of the Byrds at the time and later formed one of the first country-rock bands, the Flying Burrito Brothers. While the classical-jazz-folk hybrids of progressive rock were emerging from England (e.g., the Moody Blues, King Crimson), the Rolling Stones steadfastly retained their "R&B + country" roots as evidenced on their hit "Honky Tonk Woman" (1969).

The issue for the counterculture was not so much country music as a genre but the perceptions of country music's assumed audience as being lower class, rural, older, Southern/Middle American, and conservative. Conversely, folk has an assumed audience that was bohemian, urban, younger, Coastal American, and liberal. As rock ideology was consolidated in the 1960s, folk music represented the counterculture's activism and idealism, whereas country represented the counterculture's alienation and individualism. The allure of country music was that it harkened back to the Wild West and the romantic myths of "the outlaw" as the unrepentant rugged individual outside the confines of civil society. In fact, Haggard entered the country music market in the 1960s with bona-fide outlaw credentials: he served two years in San Quentin federal prison for armed robbery in the late 1950s. Moreover, the outlaw mystique in country music is very much tied to masculinity. Aaron A. Fox argued, "The fundamental opposition between law-and-order authoritarianism and 'outlaw' authenticity ... structured country's discourse of masculinity since the days of Jimmie Rodgers."[27] The outlaw mythos of country legends such as Hank Williams, Johnny Cash, Merle Haggard, and Willie Nelson resonated with the revolutionary machismo that fueled the counterculture. William L. O'Neill noted that "Che Guevara had more political sex appeal than Gandhi or Martin Luther King."[28] As far as rock ideology, country music had a certain political sex appeal lacking in folk music.

In this context, Johnny Cash eventually became one of the more important historical figures in American popular music. Cash began his career in the 1950s recording for Sun Records alongside Elvis Presley, Jerry Lee Lewis,

Carl Perkins, and Roy Orbison; among his early hits were "Folsom Prison Blues" and "I Walk the Line." Signing to Columbia Records in 1958, Cash became one of the biggest stars in the country-western genre as well as an early popular music "outlaw" with several brushes with the law and a well-documented battle with drug addiction. During the 1960s, Cash cultivated friendships with Bob Dylan and other anti–Establishment rock stars and, much to Columbia's trepidation, recorded live albums at federal penitentiaries to audiences of convicted felons, *Johnny Cash at Folsom Prison* (1968) and *Johnny Cash at San Quentin* (1969). The latter album produced a hit single with a cover of Shel Silverstein's novelty song "A Boy Named Sue"—the hilarity of which was not lost on an audience of inmates familiar with the sexual politics of prison life.

With his musical career at an apex, Cash moved to television for *The Johnny Cash Show* (ABC, 1969–71).[29] A comedy-variety show, it featured guests from across the musical, generational, and political spectrum including Bob Dylan, Pete Seeger, Merle Haggard, George Jones, Neil Young, Creedence Clearwater Revival, and Derek and the Dominos. Indeed, Cash's ability to "walk the line" between mainstream culture and counterculture was a key factor as to why Cash became a cultural icon for the post–Alternative generation with his *American Recordings* series. However, when the first volume of *American Recordings* was released in 1994, Cash's status was much closer to being a footnote in popular music history. Over the course of the 1970s, Cash's record sales drastically declined. From 1980 to 1991, only one album made the Billboard charts (1981's *The Baron* peaked at a meager #201), and Cash was dropped by his longtime label Columbia. His acting career was mostly limited to some made-for-TV westerns and a few appearances on the family drama *Dr. Quinn, Medicine Woman*. Moreover, the *American Recordings* were initially not overwhelming commercial successes, and the critical reception was largely positive but not unanimously favorable. Rather, Johnny Cash's cultural iconography was constructed—or at least solidified—around the eventual canonization of the *American Recordings*, and in particular Cash's celebrated cover of Nine Inch Nails' "Hurt" and the accompanying music video.[30]

Throughout his career, Cash's style and subject matter was decidedly darker than a contemporary like Willie Nelson. For example, both Nelson and Cash covered Beatles' songs. Nelson's country cover of "Yesterday" (1966) was a live acoustic guitar-bass-drum version and effectively poignant due to Nelson's thin, nasal, plaintive tenor.[31] In contrast, Cash's acoustic guitar/piano dominated country cover of "In My Life," a fairly upbeat pop-rock song as done by the Beatles, was delivered by Cash like a man on his death bed. In fact, "In My Life" was released on *American IV: The Man Comes Around* which also included "Hurt." Cash's musical trademark was a deep baritone that sounded both sinister and exhausted while his "Man in Black" image suggested a Wild West undertaker as opposed to Nelson's "hippie-meets-cowboy" image. Indeed, Cash's repertoire was an "American Gothic" brand of country-western informed by gospel, folk, rockabilly, and early rock and roll. There were recurring themes of failed relationships ("Jackson," "It Ain't Me, Babe"), sexual obsession ("Ring of Fire"), and situations ending in violent resolutions ("Don't Take Your Guns to Town," "Folsom Prison Blues," "Long Black Veil").

In short, Cash's work was fraught with elements of death, desolation, and despair—the same themes particularly favored by 1990s alternative bands, especially the "industrial" bands like Marilyn Manson, Ministry, and Nine Inch Nails (NIN). However, industrial music as an Alternative subgenre was markedly different than the 1970s–1980s industrial music typified by Einstürzende Neubaten, Cabaret Voltaire, Throbbing Gristle, or Test Department.[32] Early industrial music emphasized extensive dissonance and noise, monotony, musique concrète, percussive rhythmic and polyrhythmic drive over melodic and harmonic structures, unconventional use of standard rock instrumentation, and non-musical objects used as musical instruments. As an example, one can consider Cabaret Voltaire's cover of the Seeds' "No Escape." Released in 1966 on their eponymous debut album, the Seeds' original version was guitar-driven, two-chord garage rock with a driving snare quarter-note beat while the vocals described a man's all-consuming love for a woman in the first person. Cabaret Voltaire's version (*Mix-Up*, 1979) begins with disembodied, electronically altered screams before a drum machine provides an unremitting, hollow quarter-note thump. A retrograde, 1960s-sounding electric organ plays the main riff, and the electric guitar produces an overpowering wash of atonal noise with surplus distortion and phase-shifting. Electronic synthesizer noises and overdubbed screams—heavily processed with echo and other electronic effects—continually punctuate the song, and the snarled lead vocals are also treated with electronic effects. The theme of obsessive desire is translated into an aural nightmare of agonized, inexorable, and suffocating repetition.

Industrial music in the 1990s was characterized by an abrasive but relatively accessible assemblage of pounding dance beats, metal guitar riffs, synthesizer overlays, and vocals that were screamed and moaned rather than sung and frequently treated with electronic effects. The "artier" aspects of NIN owed to Trent Reznor being highly influenced by David Bowie, Joy Division, and Bauhaus as opposed to the more cartoonish Marilyn Manson drawing from Alice Cooper, Alien Sex Fiend, and 1980s synthpop.[33] In this context, NIN's version of "Hurt" (*The Downward Spiral*, 1994) begins with an electronic droning noise recalling wind blowing across a barren desert that underscores the song throughout its duration (6'16"). The main riff progression has a high degree of 12-tone dissonance over which Reznor sings the first verse describing the self-harm of drug addiction. This shifts to a chorus where a steady quarter note stream of dissonant guitar chords acts as the framework for Reznor mourning his self-inflicted putrefaction. Midway through the chorus a piano pattern and pounding floor tom enters before the song repeats the verse–chorus cycle, signifying that the process of self-destruction and self-deterioration is unchanging and even worsening as Reznor's vocals alternate between whispering and screaming. From the second chorus, the outro verse features more quarter notes of distorted and dissonant guitar chords and fuzz bass until the final lines (barely audible) are overwhelmed by three extremely distorted and dissonant guitar chords at the 4'30" mark of the song. The remaining 1'46" of the song consists of droning feedback and the eerie, electronic wind noise, signifying the cycle of self-ruin has not so much culminated but reached an unending nadir of disturbing stasis.

There is a crucial distinction between NIN's and Johnny Cash's versions of "Hurt." The NIN version is the journey into self-inflicted physical and mental decay through drug addiction (cf. the Velvet Underground's "Heroin," the Rolling Stone's "Sister Morphine," or Black Sabbath's "Hand of Doom"). Cash's version is reframed around his struggle with diabetic neuropathy and numerous other health problems that were effectively terminal by the time he recorded "Hurt." Hence, the crucial difference is that NIN's version depicts someone realizing the immense self-harm they are causing but unwilling or unable to prevent self-destruction. Cash's version is a lament of someone whose body is withering away and who is powerless to stop it. An acoustic guitar plays a C–D–Am verse riff much more tonally and in a more conventional country-blues mode while Cash sings the lyrics of the first verse in his emblematic weary baritone; midway through a piano chord plays on the two of every other bar. Entering the chorus, the acoustic guitar begins an Am–F–C–G quarter-note strumming pattern joined by piano playing a repeated treble G quarter note with sustained bass piano chords on the one on each bar. Returning to the second verse, the song resumes the C–D–Am acoustic guitar with the piano chord on two of every other bar; halfway through it is underscored by understated electric guitar feedback in the background. The second chorus adds a monotone organ drone to the Am–F–G–D acoustic guitar and treble G piano quarter-note drive as the song increasingly loses any tonal variation; the outro verse becomes a relentless quarter-note G monotone sustained by the drones of organ and low, rumbling, pedaled piano chords. It becomes oddly reminiscent of the early Velvet Underground in its use of minimalism and monotony for a highly compelling dramatic effect, rather than multiple instruments and complex arrangements exaggerating "drama" (e.g., Frank Sinatra's cover of "Something").[34] Moreover, the static quality of the music as a metaphor of impending death calls further attention to Cash's drained yet demanding vocals as they simultaneously express resentment and regret at the transpiring situation until the song abruptly stops or just "gives out."

Cash's musical rendition of "Hurt" cannot be separated from the music video for the song, directed by Mark Romanek.[35] The director of the controversial video for NIN's "Closer" (a sexually explicit song to begin with, the video included S&M imagery and a crucified monkey), Romanek was a long-time Cash fan and friend of Rick Rubin, the head of American Recordings. He offered to do the video at no charge and whatever budget the record label would provide. After securing the Cash family's trust, Romanek was given access to their home as well as the House of Cash museum in Henderson, Tennessee—closed in 1999 after flood damage and in a state of considerable disrepair. They served as the primary locales, and the principal shooting was done in two days. The initial visual shock was the degree to which Cash was visibly ill when the video was filmed. He is variously seen seated in a chair playing guitar and singing, at a piano playing it with one finger, and at a banquet table at the dilapidated House of Cash museum surrounded by Cash memorabilia as a representation of Cash's life and his deteriorating health. As the chorus begins, these scenes are intercut with film footage from the Cashes personal archives, ranging from home movies, the Folsom Prison concert, TV appearances, and film roles (following the first chorus, a clip culled from the 1971 western *A Shooting* depicts Cash growling, "You stay the hell away from me, ya hear?"). As the song builds in intensity, the editing rhythm of the montages of old and new footage begins to loosely correspond to the quarter-note drive that dominates the second chorus and outro verse. One of the more moving images is June Carter Cash looking at her offscreen husband with love, concern, and a kind of sadness; this cuts to old home-movie footage of the couple happily driving and playing with their children. In other scenes, Cash shakily pours a goblet of wine over the banquet table and seems on the verge of tears. Near the end, rather graphic images of the crucifixion become part of the montage with a close-up of nails being hammered into Christ's hands. This is not to suggest that an aggrandizing equation between Johnny Cash and Jesus Christ as "icons" is being made. Rather, the imagery refers to Cash's devout

Christianity and Cash's own bodily "crucifixion" from his failing health and the solace of peace found in death and the possibility of an afterlife. "Hurt" became a retroactive eulogy delivered by Cash himself.

From a perspective of traditionalist rock criticism, Cash's *American Recording* series embodied authenticity and sincerity whereas Pat Boone personified inauthenticity and camping. The importance of *American Recordings* is the extent to which Johnny Cash represented a negotiation of traditional country and Alternative rock in way that avoided the pitfalls of Camp or cheese. Cash took the songs seriously, and covered them just as seriously in a stark and unflinching way. As noted, part of the success of Cash's *American Recordings* owed to the correlation between Cash's music and "Man in Black" public persona and the imagery and themes of the 1990s industrial bands like NIN. "Hurt" provided an uncompromising glimpse into Cash's life and his impending death: June Carter Cash died three months after filming "Hurt," and four months later Cash followed. While "Hurt" was a musical and visual representation of imminent death, Cash made it as "real" as it could get.

Conclusion

The Politics of Listening

Without music, life would be an error.[1]—Friedrich Nietzsche

As competing cultural discourses, songs circulate throughout society and function as a product and producer of ideology within and across historical and national contexts. This raises the question of "political music," which is far too often judged by the genre presuppositions and lyrical content. For example, one can compare Green Day's "American Idiot" and Toby Keith's "Courtesy of the Red, White, and Blue (the Angry American)." Green Day guitarist/vocalist Billie Joe Armstrong recounted that "American Idiot" was written in direct response to hearing a Lynard Skynard song: "It was like, I'm proud to be a redneck and I was like, 'Oh my God, why would you be proud of that?' This is exactly what I'm *against*."[2] While ostensibly political polar opposites, what Green Day and Toby Keith share is that the former is standardized liberal punk and the latter is standardized conservative country, and neither offers anything musically or politically to offend their respective assumed audiences. Perhaps the more political gesture would be Green Day doing a punk anti-cover of Toby Keith or Toby Keith doing a country anti-cover of Green Day.

Jean Luc-Godard once remarked, "The problem is not to make *political* films but to make films *politically*."[3] Rather than making political music, the issue is "making music politically." As a cultural text, a song can be adapted, reconfigured, and translated in a multiplicity of ways within shifting cultural and subcultural parameters, economic and monetary exchanges, national and ethnic identities, communal and societal norms, and the political frameworks of the State. In this context, cover songs inhabit a crucial space in popular music. Part One considered how a cover song can undergo formal alterations ranging from minimal variations, considerable modifications, or radical deconstructions as anti-covers. As important, they can be read as affirmative, oppositional, or even reactionary political statements—intended or not. Part Two examined the historical trajectory of the Rolling Stones' "Satisfaction" and three cover versions across different decades, genres, historical conditions, and political pressures in order to ascertain the ways that "Satisfaction" was not only changed at the level of music but meaning. In turn, Part Three analyzed cover songs in terms of how they comment on and even confront the politics of gender, sexuality, race, nation-states, and generations within their historical context.

As social practice, the consumption of popular music is as important as the production of music. The moment someone begins listening to music, the listener necessarily becomes a critic. Indeed, a listener develops a relationship to music that becomes "individual" and even "personal," and the reaction to a musical performance can be positive, indifferent, or negative—and adamantly so—for any number of reasons. To use an example selected at random (i.e., opening to a page in a rock encyclopedia), one can consider Free's "All Right Now" (1970). Even if simply listening for "enjoyment," there are numerous and sometimes conflicting critical assessments that become part of the experience and frame an overall judgment of the song. The listener may like or not like the song structure (the key signature, time signature, main riff, chord progressions, and/or arrangement of "All Right Now"), specific aspects of the performance (Paul Rodger's vocals, Paul Kossoff's guitar playing, the Andy Fraser-Simon Kirkie rhythm section), or the performers themselves (the listener's reaction to the band members and what qualities they "project" within or outside the performance). Other factors can include the production (the recorded sounds and mix of various instruments on "All Right Now"), the genre of music (rock, more specifically hard rock, more pejoratively, "cock rock"), the lyrical message of the song (the view of masculinity and attitudes toward women expressed by "All Right Now"), and the ideological underpinnings (how "All Right Now" is indicative of the sexism of rock music, particularly in the 1970s, and sexism in society at large).

Cover songs suggest the issue of "listening to music politically" and thereby "*reading* music politically." The challenge, as Louis Althusser and Étienne Balibar suggested, is that "as there are no such thing as innocent readings, we must say what reading we are guilty of."[4] If listening is an act of reading music, the political decision made by the listener is not simply *what* they listen to, but *how* music is listened to and what is avoided as much as what becomes the focus of the listening experience. Lawrence Grossberg noted, "Culture works, not only in an economy of commodities, but an economy of meanings.... How we interpret the music, what meanings we give to it, and the relations between those meanings and our world, is never totally isolated from social and political struggles."⁵ Ultimately, songs express explicit or implicit "social and political struggles," whether it is "The Star-Spangled Banner" as covered by Jimi Hendrix or Whitney Houston, "Satisfaction" as covered by Otis Redding or Britney Spears, or "You Keep Me Hangin' On" as covered by Vanilla Fudge or Kim Wilde. As much as works of art, cover songs are historical documents and political editorials by which the listener can recall the past, examine the present, and consider the future.

Chapter Notes

Introduction

1. As a personal experience, in a high school speech class one assignment was poetry reading. I read Jethro Tull's "Thick as a Brick" in its entirety (in retrospect, I would have opted for something more "literary" off Van der Graaf Generator's *Godbluff*). Unfortunately, I was badly upstaged the next day when another student recited Deep Purple's "Space Truckin'" as if he were performing a monologue from *Hamlet* while on LSD.
2. Robert Christgau, "Rock Lyrics Are Poetry (Maybe)," originally published in *Cheetah*, December 1967. Archived at http://www.robertchristgau.com/xg/music/lyrics-che.php (accessed February 6, 2013).
3. Simon Frith, *Sound Effects: Youth, Leisure, and the Politics of Rock 'n' Roll* (New York: Pantheon, 1981), 35.
4. As quoted in Legs McNeil and Gillian McCain, *Please Kill Me: An Uncensored Oral History of Punk* (New York: Penguin, 1996), 161.
5. This is not always a reliable approach. In the early 1980s, I was playing bass in a post-punk band and practicing regularly to improve my skills. One method was learning a number of songs out of a Black Sabbath songbook. However, when I began to play along to the songs on the album, I had to relearn all the songs one fret lower, as Black Sabbath detuned the guitar and bass a half step (i.e., instead of the standard E-A-D-G tuning, using E-flat, A-flat, D-flat, and G-flat). In retrospect, simply retuning my own bass would have been the easier option.
6. Both quoted from Susan Fast, *In the Houses of the Holy: Led Zeppelin and the Power of Rock Music* (London: Oxford University Press, 2001), 165.
7. The exception would be musicians who compose their own material, perform solo, and release it through self-run distribution (i.e., an independent record or the Internet).
8. To elaborate, "authorship" in popular music is based around the performer and not the songwriters. As discussed, many of Motown's biggest hits in the sixties were written and produced by the team of Holland-Dozier-Holland. However, "Bernadette" is considered a Four Tops song and "You Keep Me Hangin' On" a Supremes song, even though both the songs were written by H-D-H. Authorship in popular music also entails that many rock performers (as well as performers in other genres) often write or co-write the songs they record (e.g., Bob Dylan, Neil Young, Joni Mitchell, Bruce Springsteen, Tom Petty, Madonna, etc.). Composition and performance become much more entwined in the "original version." Consequently, performers who rely on outside songwriters such as Britney Spears are considered less "authentic" than performers who write their own songs.
9. In fact, *Third Reich and Roll* coincided with the release of a Residents single covering "Satisfaction." Rather than discuss two avant-garde/punk anti-covers of "Satisfaction," I elected to discuss the Residents' broader assault on rock music with *The Third Reich and Roll*.

Chapter 1

1. This refers to the first verse only. Both songs have additional verses that can be sung, but they are often omitted in popular renditions. In the wake of 9/11, Major League Baseball substituted "God Bless America" for the traditional seventh-inning stretch song "Take Me Out to the Ballgame" for the remainder of

172 Notes—Chapter 1

the 2001 season. The change proved so popular that MLB allowed home teams to decide if they wanted to use "Take Me Out to the Ballgame" or "God Bless America" as their regular seventh-inning stretch song.

2. Playing the melody on a musical instrument tends to be much easier, in that it does not require a great deal of virtuosity, and musicians with a modest degree of training can play the instrumental versions of the national anthem with relative ease (e.g., a high school marching band).

3. William L. O'Neill, *Coming Apart: An Informal History of America in the 1960s* (New York: Times Books, 1971), 260.

4. Steve Waksman, *Instruments of Desire: The Electric Guitar and the Shaping of Musical Experience* (Cambridge, MA: Harvard University Press, 2004), 188.

5. For instance, anyone could simply record themselves bashing away on an electric guitar for a couple of minutes while stomping on assorted effects pedals and generating guitar feedback and title the performance "The Star-Spangled Banner" as a "subversive deconstruction" of the national anthem. The limitation of this tactic is that the "musical essence" of the national anthem is lost (read: the performer does not know how to play it), and the strength of Hendrix's version is that he uses the recognizable framework of the national anthem, both musically and politically, and both are radically altered as far as performance and message.

6. Paul Hegarty, *Noise/Music: A History* (New York: Continuum, 2007), 64; emphasis added.

7. Hegarty, 64.

8. As quoted in Abe Peck, *Uncovering the Sixties: The Life and Times of the Underground Press* (New York: Pantheon, 1985), 185. In fact, Hoffman was also involved in a minor outbreak of violence at Woodstock. During the Who's set, an LSD-addled Hoffman took the stage, commandeered Pete Townshend's microphone, and began a rant against the imprisonment of John Sinclair. Townshend, who had a reputation for onstage temper flare-ups when things were not going as he wanted (yelling, cursing, or spitting at other band members as well as smashing equipment), did not appreciate Hoffman's impromptu contribution. Townshend wacked Hoffman with his guitar and knocked him offstage into the security pit. The moment signified the real insolubility in the imaginary relationship between radical politics and rock music (see also Peck, 180)

9. As quoted in Irwin Stambler, *Encyclopedia of Pop, Rock and Soul* (New York: St. Martin's), 242.

10. Jacques Attali, *Noise: The Political Economy of Music*, trans. Brain Massumi (Minneapolis: University of Minnesota Press, 1985), 6.

11. Attali, "Afterword," *Noise*, 149.

12. Attali, *Noise*, 137.

13. The Fender Stratocaster Hendrix played at Woodstock was purchased in the 1990s by Microsoft co-founder Paul Allen for an estimated price somewhere between $1.5 and $2 million dollars. It is in the permanent collection of Seattle's EMP museum, a venture founded by Allen specializing in popular music and science fiction.

14. Peck, *Uncovering the Sixties*, 180; see also 177–80.

15. J. Hoberman and Jonathan Rosenbaum, *Midnight Movies* (New York: Da Capo, 1991), 99.

16. Houston later covered "I'm Every Woman" as part of the soundtrack to her film debut *The Bodyguard*. It became a hit single.

17. While Soft Machine was considered part of the English progressive rock music movement of the 1970s, Edward Macan argued that progressive rock was divided into distinct strains rather than a monolithic whole. One was the various classical-jazz-English folk-rock hybrids of the Moody Blues; Emerson, Lake, and Palmer (ELP); Yes; Jethro Tull; Genesis; and King Crimson. Another was the "glam art rock" of David Bowie and early Roxy Music, two performers that have become veritable institutions in English popular music. Yet another was the "Canterbury Sound" spearheaded by Soft Machine and bands like Caravan, Gong, Hatfield and the North, Quiet Sun, Henry Cow, Matching Mole, and Robert Wyatt's post–Soft Machine solo albums. The Canterbury Sound was much more influenced by modern jazz (Mingus, Coltrane, Coleman) and modern classical (Messiaen, Cage, Stockhausen, etc.) while far less informed by canonical classical music (Bach, Beethoven, etc.), more conventional jazz (big band, bebop, etc.), and English folk. Instead of progressive rock's often portentous tone and lyrics, the Canterbury sound was defined around a more absurdist sense of humor. See Edward Macan, *Rocking the Classics: English Progressive Rock and the Counterculture* (New York: Oxford University Press, 1997), chap. 6, esp. 127–29.

18. Versions of "Memories" were originally

recorded by the Wilde Flowers and Soft Machine in the 1960s, but unreleased at the time. It first appeared on Daevid Allen's album *Banana Moon* (1971), with Wyatt playing drums and handling lead vocals. Wyatt's version was best known prior to Material's cover version and can be considered the standard version.

19. More correctly, Houston performed the song live, but a previously recorded studio version was played on the TV broadcast in case of unforeseen technical problems.

20. *Rolling Stone*, September 4, 2003.

21. Jon Pareles, "Caution: Now Entering the War Zone," *New York Times*, February 24, 1991.

22. Theodor W. Adorno, *Essays on Music*, ed. Richard Leppert, trans. Susan H. Gillespie (Berkeley: University of California Press, 2002), 669; emphasis added.

23. In this context, both Hendrix and Houston were African American performers covering "The Star-Spangled Banner" in two decidedly different historical contexts: Hendrix when race was a highly divisive issue in American politics in the late 1960s; Houston when America was ostensibly a "post-racial" nation by the 1990s.

Chapter 2

1. As quoted in McNeil and McCain, *Please Kill Me*, 191.

2. As quoted in McNeil and McCain, *Please Kill Me*, 260.

3. Dick Hebdige, *Subcultures* (London: Routledge, 1978), 63. The class issue proves tenuous as far the British punk movement being uniformly comprised of disenfranchised white, working-class young people on the dole (see Hegarty, *Noise/Music*, 85). In fact, a core part of the Sex Pistols' early following was known as the "Bromley Contingent" (which included Siouxsie Sioux and Billy Idol), so named became they hailed from the London suburb of Bromley.

4. *Subcultures*, 25–26.

5. As quoted in Wilson Neate, *Pink Flag*, no. 62 in the 33 1/3 series (New York: Continuum, 2008), 26; emphasis original.

6. Theodor W. Adorno, "On Tradition," *Telos* 94 (1993–94): 78.

7. As quoted in Simon Reynolds, *Rip It Up and Start Again: Postpunk, 1978–1984* (New York: Penguin, 2005), 68; emphasis original.

8. "Definitions," *Situationist International 1* (1958). Reprinted in *Situationist International Anthology*, ed. and trans. Ken Knapp (Berkeley: Bureau of Public Secrets. 2006), 51.

9. *Situationist International Anthology*, 51–52.

10. See also Hegarty, *Noise/Music*, 95.

11. Andrew Hussey, "Requiem pour un con: Subversive Pop and the Society of the Spectacle," *Cercles* 3 (2001): 57.

12. Chris Thomas, best known as for producing Roxy Music, was contracted by McLaren to produce the Sex Pistols. Thomas considered Vicious' bass playing insufficient and Jones played bass on *Never Mind the Bollocks*, with the possible exception of "Bodies" on which Vicious may have played a bass track.

13. Virgin Records was founded by Richard Branson, who owned a successful chain of record stores and mail-order businesses specializing in import records. After numerous labels passed on Mike Oldfield's *Tubular Bells* (1973), Branson decided to release it himself on an independent label he christened Virgin Records. *Tubular Bells* sold millions of copies worldwide, and excerpts were used in the film *The Exorcist*. Virgin expanded its roster to the more avant-garde strains of rock like Robert Wyatt, Gong, and Henry Cow. By singing the Sex Pistols, Branson rebranded Virgin away from the declining genre of progressive rock and toward the ascending genre of punk. In this way, Virgin was in an ideal position as post-punk emerged as a kind of "progressive punk" and could parlay its brand identity for avant-garde rock into avant-garde punk.

14. As far as the British punk scene, the Damned's debut *Dammed Dammed Dammed* was released in early 1977, and the Clash's eponymous debut in spring of 1977. However, *The Clash* was not released in the United States until 1979, well after the Clash's *Give 'Em Enough Rope* (1978) which had a more hard rock sound supplied by producer Sandy Perlman (best known for his work with Blue Öyster Cult) and served as the first "official" American release. Moreover, the U.S. version of *The Clash* replaced some songs with later Clash singles.

15. *Bollocks* did not achieve U.S. Gold Record status (500,000 units sold) until 1987 and Platinum Record status (one million units sold) until 1992.

16. Jim Mendiola, "Anarchy in S.A.," *San Antonio Current*, January 2, 2003. Archived at www.randysrodeo.com/features/pistols/08.php (accessed May 19, 2008).

17. Like McLaren, Virgin capitalized on the Sex Pistols project long after it came to a screeching halt. In late 1979, Virgin released *Sid Sings*, a compilation mainly consisting of a poorly recorded concert done shortly before Spungen's murder with Vicious backed by guitarist Steve Dior and former New York Dolls rhythm section Arthur Kane and Jerry Nolan. In early 1980, Virgin released the aptly titled *Flogging a Dead Horse*, a compilation mostly made up of the A-side singles off *Bollocks* and *Swindle*.

18. "My Way" was recorded in Paris with session musicians Claude Engle (guitar), Sauveur Mallin (bass), and Pierre-Alain Dehan (drums). The *Swindle* version was remixed with a different vocal take and an overdubbed guitar solo by Steve Jones. The string section was also overdubbed and arranged by Simon Jeffes, best known as the leader of the Penguin Café Orchestra, a band that combined elements of avant-garde, MOR, and world music. *Sid Sings* included the unmodified version of "My Way."

19. Sheldon Schiffer, "The Cover Song as Historiography, Marker of Ideological Transformation," in *Play It Again: Cover Songs and Popular Music*, ed. George Plasketes (Burlington, VT: Ashgate, 2010), 87.

20. Raoul Vaneigem, *The Revolution of Everyday Life*, trans. Donald Nicholson-Smith (London: Rebel Books, 2006), 176.

21. Frith, *Sound Effects*, 266.

22. The confirmation of the Sex Pistols' assimilation into the spectacle occurred with the 1996 "Filthy Lucre" reunion concert tour.

23. Reynolds, *Rip It Up*, 16. Reynolds also suggested that the Capitol Radio interview was a key factor in the highly acrimonious relationship that developed between Lydon and McLaren.

24. Al Spicer, "Alternative TV (ATV)," *Rock: The Rough Guide*, 2nd edition, ed. Jonathan Buckley, Orla Duane, Mark Ellingham, and Al Spicer (London: The Rough Guide, 1999), 21.

25. The "Fuck Art, Let's Dance" maxim that ostensibly defined the early British punk movement ethos became widespread through its use as the advertising slogan of Stiff Records, which had a roster made up of veteran pub rockers like Nick Lowe and Ian Dury. When punk exploded ca. 1976, Stiff made opportune signings of Elvis Costello and the Damned to rebrand itself as a punk/New Wave label.

26. Colin Newman, liner notes to *Rough Trade Shops: Post Punk, Vol. 1*, Mute Records CD STUMM 224, 2003.

27. Frith, *Sound Effects*, 160; emphasis added.

28. While the punk movement is commonly associated with New York City (the proto-punk of the Velvet Underground and the New York Dolls, the early punk of the Ramones, the post-punk of the No Wave bands), the Midwest and the Rust Belt has been somewhat marginalized as far as its contributions to proto-punk (the MC5 and the Stooges from Michigan) and post-punk (Pere Ubu and Devo from Ohio; MX-80 Sound from Indiana).

29. Cryptic Corporation is largely assumed to be a front for the Residents, which entails that information and disinformation about the band could be circulated. Hence, background on the band can be suspect. What is known is that the Cryptic Corporation was founded by Hardy Fox, Homer Flynn, Jay Clem, and John Kennedy. Clem and Kennedy left Cryptic in 1982, and it is believed that since then the Residents have effectively been a duo of Fox providing the music and Flynn lyrics and vocals. When I saw the Residents live in 1986 on the "13th Anniversary Tour," the Residents added longtime collaborator Phillip "Snakefinger" Latham to the lineup on guitar (billed as "the Residents featuring Snakefinger"). Two of the Residents danced onstage in various costumes, and it was apparent they were women, while a third Resident played keyboard synthesizer (presumably Fox) and the fourth was lead vocalist and front man (presumably Flynn). In this way, the costumes and masks allow for outside performers to appear onstage as "Residents." In 2010, the Residents announced through Facebook that the Residents were officially a trio of "Randy, Chuck, and Bob." Cryptic neither confirmed nor denied the announcement.

30. The Residents made a short experimental music video for *The Third Reich and Roll* using excerpts of "Swastikas on Parade." Archived at http://www.youtube.com/watch?v=NRweyGHJ3bc (accessed January 11, 2013). Shot in black and white, the intro is stop-motion animation of men in huge iron masks driving shopping carts with large drills attached to the front. This is followed by a rendition of "Land of a Thousand Dances" performed by the Residents identically dressed in large sunglasses and wearing quasi–Ku Klux Klan outfits made of newspapers (the walls, mike stand, and percussion objects are covered in newspaper as well). The performance

abruptly ends when a soldier covered in aluminum foil raids the Residents' performance and kills them, which is set to the free jazz saxophone-gunfire duet. This cuts to a stop-motion animated conclusion set to "Wipeout," which includes two raw steaks pummeling a dancing swastika and objects ranging from the shopping cart tank, skulls, and a TV mechanically dancing about while an image of Adolf Hitler watches from a balcony.

31. Reynolds, *Rip It Up*, 201.

32. Lester Bangs, *Mainlines, Bloodfeasts, and Bad Taste: A Lester Bangs Reader*, ed. Jim Morthland (New York: Anchor Books, 2003), 228.

33. As quoted in Steve Waksman, *This Ain't the Summer of Love: Conflict and Crossover in Heavy Metal and Punk* (Berkeley: University of California, 2009), 264–65.

34. The Dead Kennedys were at the forefront of thrash music and hardcore populism in part because the DKs' lead vocalist and lyricist Jello Biafra consciously established himself and the DKs as national leaders of the movement. In 1981, the DKs' independently owned label Alternative Tentacles issued *Let Them Eat Jelly Beans!*, a 17-track compilation album with side 1 the upper-tier hardcore bands (D.O.A., Black Flag, Bad Brains, Circle Jerks, and the DKs) and side 2 devoted to "artier" and more avant-garde punk (Geza X, BPeople, Half Japanese, and Voice Farm). In 1982, Alternative Tentacles issued *Not So Quiet on the Western Front*, a double album compilation of almost 50 largely unknown hardcore/thrash bands, most of whom were indistinguishable from each other and many sounding similar if not identical to the DKs. Writing in 1981, Lester Bangs sardonically suggested that "[in 1977] every band in the world is the Stooges.... Obviously every band in the world is not the Stooges—every band in the world is the Dead Kennedys" (*Mainlines*, 122).

35. "I Fought the Law" has become a staple cover of punk bands ranging from the Clash, Green Day, Stiff Little Fingers, Social Distortion, and Anti-Flag.

36. Here one can recall Biafra's "free speech" activism which ultimately led to an appearance on *Oprah* debating censorship with PMRC co-founder Tipper Gore.

37. See also Waksman, *This Ain't the Summer of Love*, chap. 7, for an informative account of the question of aesthetic strategies pursued by metal and hardcore bands.

38. Gilles Deleuze, *Negotiations: 1972–1990*, trans. Martin Joughin (New York: Columbia University Press, 1995), 144.

39. Lester Bangs, *Psychotic Reactions and Carburetor Dung*, ed. Greil Marcus (New York: Anchor Books, 2003), 112.

Chapter 3

1. Attali, *Noise*, 137; emphasis added.

2. John Cage, *John Cage: An Anthology*, ed. Richard Kostelentz (New York: Da Capo, 1991), 55; emphasis added.

3. This became apparent in *The T.A.M.I. Show* concert film (1964). Chuck Berry opened the show and the Rolling Stones closed it, but had the unenviable spot of following James Brown. Richards' debt to Berry both musically and visually was overt, and Jagger came off as a pale imitation (pun intended) of James Brown.

4. Stambler, *Encyclopedia of Pop, Rock, and Soul*, 443.

5. Norman Mailer, "The White Negro," in *Advertisements for Myself* (Cambridge, MA: Harvard University Press, 1992), 339.

6. Mailer, *Advertisements for Myself*, 349–50.

7. The New York Dolls, one of the primary proto-punk bands of the 1970s, were influenced by the Stones to the point singer David Johansson and guitarist Johnny Thunders consciously mimicked Mick Jagger and Keith Richards.

8. Peter Shapiro, "The Rolling Stones," in *Rock: The Rough Guides*, 2nd ed., 832.

9. As quoted at http://www.songfacts.com/detail.php?id=449 (accessed February 10, 2013).

10. *Never Mind the Buzzcocks* is a BBC2 pop-music panel quiz show parody—partly scripted and partly improvised—starring comedians Phil Jupitis and Noel Fielding as "team captains" and a guest host and four guest stars, usually two musicians and two non-musicians (one each per team). In the "Intros" round, Fielding and Jupitis, along with their musician guest, perform the instrumental intros of two hit songs a cappella, and the non-musician has to identity it; if failing to do so, the other team has a chance to identify it. For instance, the 250th Anniversary Episode was hosted by Richard Madeley, a former presenter of the long-running *This Morning* (ITV). Jupitis' team consisted of rapper Maverick Saber and comedian Andrew O'Neil; Fielding's team

consisted of pop singer Heidi Range and comedian Sean Flynn. Jupitis and Sabre did renditions of Marilyn Manson's "Beautiful People" (which O'Neill quickly identified) and Simply Red "Something Gotten Started" (which neither team identified). Fielding and Range performed Calvin Harris' "Ready for the Weekend" (neither team identified it) and Kool and the Gang's "Celebration" (which Flynn identified with some difficulty).

11. Waksman, *This Ain't the Summer of Love*, 61; emphasis original.

12. As quoted in McNeil and McCain, *Please Kill Me*, 47.

13. O'Neill, *Coming Apart*, 271; see also 289.

14. See Peck, *Uncovering the Sixties*, 168.

15. Attali, *Noise*, 147.

16. Buckley et al., *Rock: The Rough Guides*, 2nd ed., 833.

17. As quoted in Stambler, *Encyclopedia of Pop, Rock and Soul*, 444.

18. Passaro pleaded self-defense and was acquitted of murder charges when the footage of the incident from *Gimmie Shelter* was screened in court. It was clear that Meredith drew a pistol, but it was less clear whether Meredith drew the pistol without provocation and was attempting to shoot Jagger (as the defense claimed) or an act of self-defense during his altercation with the Hell's Angels.

19. Mailer, "The White Negro," 255.

20. O'Neill, *Coming Apart*, 262. In this respect, Norman Spinrad's parodic science-fiction novel *The Iron Dream* was published in 1972. Science fiction is often considered a "subversive" genre with its recurring themes of individual struggle, the dangers of technocracy, dystopian societies (usually authoritarian), etc. Spinrad's novel is set in an alternative history where Adolf Hitler emigrated to America in the 1920s and became a successful science-fiction writer, with much of *The Iron Dream*, the novel-within-a novel, *The Lord of Swastika*, written by Hitler. While *The Iron Dream* reveals the fascist elements of the fantasy and "sword and sorcery" genre, there are also references to Altamont. The protagonist's last name is "Jagger," and he enlists the aid of a motorcycle gang as his enforcers, dubbed "The Knights of the Swastika."

21. The question of stardom and authoritarianism was an underlying message of the Who's "rock opera" *Tommy* (1968) in which the title character becomes a messianic and ultimately totalitarian figure finally rejected by his youth movement followers. In *Pink Floyd—The Wall* (1982), the main character, Pink (Bob Geldof), is a rock star performing a concert whose mental collapse is paralleled by hallucinations that he is a dictator presiding over a political rally. In 1988, Laibach released an EP that contained *seven* mixes of their cover version of "Sympathy for the Devil" in their patented classical/industrial/martial style and their ongoing commentary on rock totalitarianism.

Chapter 4

1. See Simon Frith, "What Is Bad Music?" in *Bad Music: The Music We Love to Hate*, eds. Christopher J. Washburne and Maiken Derno (New York: Routledge, 2004), 21–22.

2. Frith, *Sound Effects*, 21; emphasis added. Here Frith's argument bears some elaboration and what have become some rather vulgar misinterpretations of Frith. Frith argued that black music in itself has serious contemplation value, in particular soul music and its use of nonverbal vocal signifiers and sound to convey meaning in the performance rather than lyrics and songs (see *Sound Effects*, 26). One of the more disingenuous responses was Alan Moore's assertions that "Firth talks dangerously of black music being 'felt,' perhaps implying that white music tends to be 'thought,' and therefore blacks are incapable of thought" (as quoted in Macan, 171). As much as the patent absurdity of Moore's suggestion that Frith has a view that "blacks as incapable of thought," Frith's argument is that rock music began to *assume* that black music was only felt and not thought and therefore required white music to make rock something that was thought. Moore is heavily relied on by Edward Macan in his attempt to refute critics such as Frith, yet Macan's view is that white music–specifically classical music and its role in progressive rock—elevated rock to music that was of higher artistic and intellectual quality from its musically and intellectually stunted origins.

3. As quoted in Tony Sclafani, "When 'Disco Sucks!' Echoed around the World." Archived at http://www.today.com/id/3183 2616/ns/today-today_entertainment/t/when-disco-sucks-echoed-around-world/#.UdcOc fnVDps (accessed July 5, 2013).

4. While the Rolling Stones conformed to the Bob Dylan "traditionalist" approach to rock, what might be termed the Beatles' "mod-

ernism" was exemplified by Frank Zappa and the Mothers of Invention. Equally influenced by modern classical (Igor Stravinsky, Edgard Varèse), jazz, doo-wop, and R&B, Zappa specialized in highly complex compositions that required considerable technical proficiency, large ensembles (incorporating horns, violin, tuned percussion instruments, etc.), social commentary lyrics that could be scathing and sophomoric (often at the same time), and using the studio as a compositional tool.

5. In *Postmodernism, or, The Cultural Logic of Late Capitalism* (Durham, NC: Duke University Press, 1991), Fredric Jameson argued that postmodernism in rock music was represented by "punk and new wave rock (the Beatles and Stones now standing as the high-modernist moment of that more recent and rapidly evolving tradition)" (1). Jameson's argument was challenged by Andrew Goodwin in his essay "Popular Music and Postmodern Theory," in *The Postmodern Arts: An Introductory Reader*, ed. Nigel Wheale (London: Routledge, 1991), 80–100. As Goodwin pointed out, "Jameson's analysis of music ... offers a reading that places the Beatles and the Rolling Stones ... as examples of 'high modernism' and the Clash, Talking Heads, and the Gang of Four ... as 'postmodern.' What this broad classification of music eludes, however, is the necessity of identifying musical differences within two historical moments which suggest more specific, if still crude parameters of rock 'realism' (the Clash) and rock 'modernism' (Talking Heads, Gang of Four), and of rock 'authenticity' (The Stones) versus pop 'artifice' (the Beatles). Historically, the music of the Beatles and the Rolling Stones articulated the social and political currents of the 1960s counter-culture. The Clash and the Gang of Four ... addressed political questions from a standpoint associated with punk rock—a quite different counter-cultural form which eschewed the peace and love message of the Beatles or the nihilistic hedonism of the Stones in favor of blunt left-wing critiques of life in Britain in the late 1970s. Looked at from the point of view of aesthetic form, the Beatles and the Rolling Stones need to be differentiated: if the development of modernism is at issue here, the increasingly artificial ... of the Beatles is modernist (self-conscious, ironic, knowingly artificial) in contrast with the 'authentic' rough-edged blues inflictions of the Stones and their lyrical themes of sexuality and violence" (84–85).

6. Stambler, *Encyclopedia of Pop, Rock, and Soul*, 4. A third brand of soul music emerged in the late 1960s with Philadelphia International Records and the "Philly soul" sound. Philly soul was an even more commercial "pop-soul" sound characterized by funk rhythms, soaring strings, and jazzy horns. In some respects, Philly soul was a precursor to disco.

7. This problem is more magnified when one considers that H-D-H were black, and the "Funk Brothers," Motown's stable of in-house studio musicians, were predominately black, with the notable exception of white guitarist Joe Messina. As Motown entered its "psychedelic soul" era, the Funk Brothers became more integrated with younger white musicians. Another issue was that Motown established a recording studio in Los Angeles ca. 1964 so that Motown performers could record sessions while in LA for concert or TV appearances. This sparked rumors that Motown "outsourced" songs and had backing tracks recorded in LA by well-known session musicians. In particular, bassist Carol Kaye claimed that many Motown classics were actually recorded in LA by session musicians, although many Motown performers, session musicians, and historians strongly disputed Kaye's contention.

8. Frith, *Sound Effects*, 35–6; emphasis added.

Chapter 5

1. As quoted in Reynolds, *Rip It Up*, 80.
2. Reynolds, *Rip It Up*, 159.
3. As quoted in Mark Mothersbaugh and Gerald Casale, audio commentary to Devo, *The Complete Truth about De-evolution*, Rhino Home Video, R2 970107, 2003.
4. Ibid.
5. Ibid.
6. See Reynolds, *Rip It Up*, 80.
7. As quoted in *Dada and Surrealist Film*, ed. Rudolf E. Kuenzli (New York: Willis Locker & Owens, 1987), 32.
8. As quoted in A.V. Club interview with Joe Garden. Archived at www.avclub.com/content/node/23325/print/1 (accessed January 7, 2009).
9. Unfortunately for Devo, the debut album was released in the shadow of two "post-punk" albums released months prior in 1978. One was the Talking Heads' *More Songs about Buildings and Food*, and the Talking Heads' postmodern merger of black music (disco, funk, reggae) and

white music (art rock, pop punk) was critically hailed. The other was the Cars' eponymous debut album, in which the influence of early Roxy Music avant-rock was translated into a commercially viable New Wave/stadium-rock hybrid (e.g., strange, affected crooning became self-conscious, ironic vocalizing; discordant guitar solos became hard rock guitar leads; synthesizer noises became quasi-progressive rock keyboard melodies).

10. Hegarty, *Noise/Music*, 70.

11. Robert Christgau, "Avant-Punk: A Cult Explodes ... and a Movement Is Born," *Village Voice*, October 24, 1977.

12. Hegarty, *Noise/Music*, 71; first emphasis added, second original.

13. As a reaction to the Moral Majority and emerging Reaganism in America, in the late 1970s Devo briefly performed concerts as "Dove the Band of Love"—a Christian New Wave band dressed in matching green polyester suits that performed tepid covers of gospel songs and MOR "born again" versions of Devo songs. According to *The Complete Truth about De-Evolution*, Dove played live three live shows and each resulted in the audience heckling and throwing objects at the stage. On a personal note, I had the opportunity to see one of Dove's few live shows at the M-80 festival in the fall of 1979, held on the University of Minnesota campus. They were (intentionally) awful.

14. See also Reynolds, *Rip It Up*, 82.

15. Dave Marsh, *Rolling Stone*, September 20, 1979. While Marsh did not call Devo fascist, in his infamous review of Queen's *Jazz* (*Rolling Stone*, February 8, 1979), Marsh claimed, "The group has come to make it clear exactly who is superior and who is inferior.... Queen may be the first truly fascist rock band." One suspects Queen's brand of operatic hard rock/metal was as much an affront for Marsh as the overall Continental pomp and circumstance.

16. By the early 1980s, Devo was also using sequencers on their recordings as well as live in order to keep the musical performance in synch with the video projections. This meant that Devo was also constrained in concerts in that they were playing along to a glorified metronome.

17. The father in "Satisfaction" was one of Devo's recurring characters named "General Boy," a symbol of the Cold War–era military-industrial complex and the authoritarian personality. General Boy was later seen in the Devo "Girl U Want" video orchestrating events behind the scenes of an *American Bandstand*–type dance show Devo is performing on, again suggesting that the mass culture of rock is under control of the system rather than opposed to it.

18. "Booji Boy" was another recurring character in Devo's music videos, notably "Beautiful World" in which Booji Boy is at the controls of a futuristic TV showing the video and intercut with said video shown full screen on the viewer's TV. The video is primarily made up of stock footage of fashion shows, sports, sexploitation film dance scenes, old war movies, Ku Klux Klan rallies, and the police beating civil rights demonstrators. Mothersbaugh also donned the Booji Boy mask in concerts to perform selected songs in Booji Boy's annoying infantile whine.

19. Theodor W. Adorno, "On the Fetish Character in Music and the Regression of Listening," in *The Culture Industry: Selected Essays on Mass Culture*, ed. J.M. Bernstein (London: Routledge, 1991), 56.

20. Herbert Marcuse, *One Dimensional Man* (Boston: Beacon Press, 1964), 70.

21. As quoted in Reynolds, 79; emphasis added.

22. Robert Christgau, "Devo Takes a Stand," *Village Voice* (1981). Archived at http://www.robertchristgau.com/xg/rock/devo-81.php (accessed April 12, 2009).

23. As quoted in *The Complete Truth about De-evolution*. It was fitting that Devo's ill-fated comeback in the late 1980s produced a music video for the song "Post Post-Modern Man." It was a parody of QVC with the band shilling various products, including Devo-related items like "Booji Boy" masks.

Chapter 6

1. Rob Sheffield, *Rolling Stone*, June 8, 2000; emphasis added.

2. Archived at http://www.rollingstone.com/music/pictures/rolling-stone-readers-choose-the-worst-cover-songs-of-all-time-20110818 (accessed January 17, 2013). Personally, I have great difficulty with the consensus that Miley Cyrus' cover of "Smells Like Teen Spirit" is the worst cover of all time, let alone the worst cover of "Smells Like Teen Spirit" when considering the wretched cover done by the Muppets Barbershop Quartet in *The Muppet Movie* (2011). Again, the list represents little more

than an attack on young, female pop performers who, as *Rolling Stone* readership would have it, inevitably corrupt the sanctity of classic rock.

3. Andreas Huyssen, *After the Great Divide: Modernism, Mass Culture, and Postmodernism* (Bloomington: Indiana University Press, 1986), 47.

4. In his essay "Commitment," Adorno argued, "Every commitment to the world must be abandoned to satisfy the ideal of the committed work of art—that polemical alienation which Brecht as a theorist invented, and as an artist practiced less and less as he bound himself more tightly to the role of a friend to mankind ... Kafka's prose or Beckett's plays, or the truly monstrous novel *The Unnamable*, have an effect by comparison with which officially committed works look like pantomime.... The inescapability of their work compels the change of attitude which committed works merely demand" (315–16). In this way, Kafka and Beckett's representation of the modern world is one that jolts the audience, whereas the Marxist polemics of Brecht ultimately end up as preaching to the converted. See Theodor W. Adorno, "Commitment," in *The Essential Frankfurt School Reader*, ed. Andrew Arato and Eike Gebhardt (New York: Continuum, 1982), 300–18.

5. Theodor W. Adorno, "The Culture Industry Reconsidered," in *The Culture Industry*, 106.

6. Norma Coates, "Teenyboppers, Groupies, and Other Grotesques: Girls and Women and Rock Culture in the 1960s and early 1970s," *Journal of Popular Music Studies* 15, no. 1 (2003): 68.

7. Charles Allen Mueller, "The Music of Goth Subculture: Postmodernism and Aesthetics" (dissertation, Ann Arbor: Proquest, 2008), 192. See also Norma Coates, "Revolution Now? The Potential Politics of Gender," in *Sexing the Groove: Popular Music and Gender*, ed. Shelia Whiteley (New York: Routledge, 1997), 50–65.

8. For a further discussion of Britney Spears as "oppositional culture," see my own *Teens, TV and Tunes: The Manufacturing of American Adolescent Culture* (Jefferson, NC: McFarland, 2012), chap. 8.

9. John Shepherd, "Music and Male Hegemony," in *Music and Society: The Politics of Composition, Performance, and Reception*, ed. Richard Leppert and Susan McClary (Cambridge: Cambridge University Press, 1989), 170–71.

10. In this context, one can consider the work of Antony Hegarty, a British transgender performer whose music draws extensively from classical music and pop—genres generally considered "feminine" and outside of rock—and lyrically addresses questions of gender identity, displacement, and transformation. In this framework, Hegarty also ruptures the boundaries between avant-grade and popular culture, incorporating elements of performance art, operatic aria, and pop music. His cover of Beyoncé's "Crazy in Love" performed in a white gown while accompanied by an orchestra is archived at http://www.youtube.com/watch?v=n8V94WQjMAw (accessed March 30, 2013).

11. John Strohm, "Women Guitarists: Gender Issues in Alternative Rock," in *The Electric Guitar: A History of an American Icon*, ed. André Millard (Baltimore, MD: Johns Hopkins University Press, 2004), 186.

12. The comparison here would be alt-rock performer Cat Power's cover of "Satisfaction" (*The Covers Record*, 2000) which is done as solo performance with Powers singing and playing acoustic guitar, where she sings the first verse, second verse, third verse, and the first half of the third verse. While the logic of rock ideology would dictate that Power's cover—a nexus of blues, folk, and jazz—is the more "authentic" cover to Britney Spears, it also reinforces rock ideology in two respects. One is that the acoustic guitar is played by Powers, a woman, and it remains the "feminine" foil to the "masculine" electric guitar. The other is that Power's performance suggests kind of adopted blackness and masculinity through the blues genre, not unlike Mick Jagger and the Stones.

Chapter 7

1. Frith, *Sound Effects*, 227.

2. As quoted at http://www.cracked.com/funny-60-led-zeppelin (accessed February 1, 2013).

3. Fast, *In the Houses of the Holy*, 196.

4. In one of several instances of Led Zeppelin "referencing" (read: plagiarizing) other songs, much of the verse lyrics and the vocal melody were lifted from Willie Dixon's song "You Need Love," originally recorded by Muddy Waters in 1962. Dixon eventually sued Led Zeppelin and, as part of an out-of-court settlement, received a co-writing credit for "Whole Lotta Love."

5. Fast, *In the Houses of the Holy*, 198.
6. Ibid.
7. This can be traced trough Elvis Presley's hip gyrations, Mick Jagger's "white negro" posturing, 1970s cock rock, and 1980s metal "hair bands." Conversely, popular music genres are vilified around an imposed feminine alignment and usually homosexuality: art-rock or progressive rock as "art fag" music, New Pop and New Wave as "Fag Wave," disco as "gay," and male metal musicians and fans as "closet cases."
8. As quoted in Fast, *In the Houses of the Holy*, 197.
9. In 1969, Stax's in-house musicians were informed by the label that they could only work exclusively for Stax Studios. Wayne Jackson and Andrew Love quit Stax and formed the Memphis Horns as an umbrella group that could bring in other horn players as needed for freelance concert and recording work.
10. This studio version is available on King Curtis, *Hi Five: King Curtis*, Rhino Records, B0012EGECG, 2006; and *Rock Instrumental Classics, Volume 3: The Seventies*, Rhino Records, B00003387, 1994, out of print. The *Fillmore West* version has more of a Memphis soul sound, in particular the prominence of Preston's organ and Purdie's intricate funk drumming. In contrast, the studio version is dominated by fuzz guitar, a more pronounced horn section, and a heavier driving drum beat comparable to the "psychedelic soul" sound emerging from Motown ca. 1970.
11. To note, probably the best-known song to use the reversed backbeat is, perhaps fittingly, the Temptations' "Ball of Confusion." However, two subsequent cover versions of "Ball of Confusion" from the 1980s—done respectively by Tina Turner and Love and Rockets—use a standard half-time beat by omitting the snare on the one.
12. In this respect, one can consider Edward Macan's detailed analysis of the Genesis song "Fifth of Firth" in *Rocking the Classics*, 106–12. Where Macan's analysis proves unsatisfactory is that it concludes by constructing a reductive Jungian analysis around music and gender: electric instruments, the rhythm section, and fast tempos are deemed "masculine" while acoustic instruments, the absence of the rhythm section, and slow tempos are "feminine" components in the song (see 112). The problem is that there is no real textual evidence offered to support this proposition. It instead accepts certain "natural givens" about music and gender to make the case.

13. Waksman, *This Ain't the Summer of Love*, 263.
14. See Waksman, *This Ain't the Summer of Love*, 5; Robert Walser, *Running with the Devil: Power, Gender, and Madness in Heavy Metal Music* (Hanover, NH: Wesleyan University Press, 1993), 129.
15. A similar translation occurs in Van Halen's cover of Roy Orbison's "Pretty Woman" (*Diver Down*, 1982). In Orbison's version, the song is performed from the perspective of a lonely man who sees a beautiful woman walking down the street and is trying to catch her eye. Within the pop-rockabilly setting, the song typifies Orbison's tendency toward the melancholy of unrequited love (e.g., "In Dreams" or "It's Over"), and the moment of redemption is that the "pretty woman" ultimately acknowledges him at the end of the song, manifesting the possibility that a relationship could develop. In Van Halen's version, the heavy metal "cockiness" and swagger suggests the male is simply seeking another carnal conquest when he sees the woman, and when she acknowledges the man there is confirmation that she cannot resist the macho vibe and the man is yet again successful in his mission of attaining sex.
16. In this respect, one can consider "Jamie's Cryin'" off *Van Halen*. While supposedly a "sympathetic" song about a woman regretting a one-night stand, the issue is how the structure of the song is designed to denigrate the woman. After Roth sings the title of the song in the chorus, Eddie Van Halen responds by interjecting a guitar lick that replicates a taunting mechanical voice saying "Wah! Wah!" and mocking the subject (Jamie) as a "crybaby." The guitar effect is achieved by using a wah-wah pedal, with a well-known brand being the Thomas Organ "Cry Baby" model.
17. Terry Eagleton, *Literary Theory: An Introduction* (Minneapolis: University of Minnesota Press, 1983), 189.
18. This Heat formed ca. 1975 with Charles Hayward (drums, vocals, misc.), Charles Bullen (guitar, vocals, misc.), and Garth Williams (organ, bass, vocals, misc). Hayward was a virtuoso drummer who played in the progressive rock band Quiet Sun, Bullen was working in avant-garde music, and Williams was a non-musician who had never played an instrument prior to joining This Heat. One of the more musically extreme post-punk bands, This Heat suggested a convergence of 1970s progressive bands like Soft Machine, King Crimson, and Henry Cow, the post-punk of the Pop Group

or Wire, and even the work of John Cage and Harry Partch. Their first album was not only co-produced by Cunningham, but he used the profits from the Flying Lizards' commercial success to set up an independent label, Piano Records, to release This Heat's debut album (*This Heat*, 1979). By 1981, post-punk had so effectively ruptured any distinctions between punk and avant-garde music that This Heat was signed to Rough Trade, the leading post-punk independent label at the time, for their second and final album *Deceit*.

19. See Reynolds, 168.

20. "Money" appeared on the UK release *With the Beatles* (1963) but was omitted from the substantially different U.S. release, *Meet the Beatles*.

21. Reynolds, *Rip It Up*, 188.

22. However, "Money" could be criticized as well in that the role of aristocrat indifferently voicing upper-class economic resentment is played by a woman, reinforcing the stereotype of the female consumerist.

23. As quoted in Reynolds, *Rip It Up*, 318; emphasis added.

24. Reynolds, *Rip It Up*, 351.

25. The Flying Lizard's second album *Fourth Wall* (1981) consisted of mostly original compositions by Cunningham and Robert and featured guest performances by Robert Fripp and Michael Nyman.

26. If Iggy Pop was "the Godfather of Punk," James Brown was not only "the Godfather of Soul" but "the Godfather of Post-Punk." One of the striking differences between punk and post-punk was the strong influence of, and reliance on, black music genres like reggae, disco, and especially funk. The Gang of Four, the Pop Group, and the Talking Heads were all highly influenced by Brown.

27. Eve Kosofsky Sedgwick, *Between Men: English Literature and Male Homosocial Desire* (New York: Columbia University Press, 1985), 1–2.

28. In the 1990s, Judas Priest lead singer Rob Halford came out as the first openly gay male in heavy metal. In retrospect, what was surprising was the extent to which Halford made little attempt to conceal his sexual orientation as far as his stage image—his leather outfits far more reminiscent of gay bar than biker—and songs like "Hell Bent for Leather" which could be heard as being about sexual desire for other men.

29. Fast, *In the Houses of the Holy*, 45; see also 41–47.

30. As quoted in Reynolds, *Rip It Up*, 60.

31. Cage's "intent" for *4'33"* was to point out that silence is impossible, and that accidental sounds were in fact the music generated in the performance of the piece (crowd noises, building noises, etc.). This also radically questioned audience expectations and demands of what should occur musically during a musical performance: that if the audience was expecting a piano performance, they should be rewarded with their money's worth. The expectation that something musically should occur on the piano, and the waiting for something that never happens, produces the musical "tension" that is only released when the performer walks off stage, having *not* played a note.

32. On the original version of "Anthrax" on the *Damaged Goods* E.P., Gill's recitation is a run-through of the various pieces of the studio equipment used in the sessions. In some ways it is more effective than the manifesto on the *Entertainment!* version in that Gill is listing the "means of production" of the song.

33. On Martha and the Vandellas' "Nowhere to Run" (1965), another song sung by women about being trapped in a bad relationship, H-D-H used snow chains as one of the percussion instruments.

34. Franklin's version of "You Keep Me Hangin' On" was recorded ca. the late 1960s–early 1970s but was unreleased until 2007 on *Rare and Unreleased Recordings from the Golden Reign of the Queen of Soul*, Rhino, B000S75BQI.

35. The Vanilla Fudge version was subsequently covered by Wilson Pickett in a slightly faster, funkier take on the song (*Right On*, 1970). Rod Stewart also covered the Vanilla Fudge version as an arena-rock version (*Footloose and Fancy Free*, 1977). Carmine Appice was the drummer in Stewart's backing band from 1977 to 1981. In this case one could say that the Supremes recorded the "original/standard version" whereas Vanilla Fudge recorded an "alternate standard version."

36. Odysseus' encounter with the sirens has produced a number of readings as far as music and society. In *The Odyssey*, rather than simply avoid the sirens, Odysseus devises a solution where he is tied to the mast while the oarsmen's ears are plugged with wax so that Odysseus can experience the music of the sirens while the oarsmen will be deaf to it and obliviously continue to row the ship on course. Jacques Attali interprets it as a moment of rupture when Odysseus becomes the powerless victim of sac-

rifice tortured by the noise produced while the oarsmen assume control of the ship as they are shielded from the sirens (see *Noise*, 29). Fredric Jameson argued that the moment represents class society with Odysseus the privileged individual experiencing music (art) while the oarsmen (the masses) are made oblivious to what is occurring; see *Late Marxism: Adorno, or, The Persistence of the Dialectic* (New York: Verso, 1990), 137.

37. Marty Wilde and Joyce Baker also played in the Wilde Three with future Moody Blues member Justin Hayward.

38. Kraftwerk pioneered the synthpop genre in the 1970s using only synthesizers and electronic percussion. However, given that early punk not only relied on a traditionalist minimalism but made progressive rock one of its many targets, keyboards and especially synthesizers were eschewed for punk's standard vocalist-guitar-bass-drum lineups (the notable exception being the Stranglers, a guitar-bass-drums-keyboard quartet). As post-punk emerged in the late 1970s, bands that featured keyboards, electronic drums, and drum machines emerged, minimizing or even abandoning conventional instruments, namely guitars—the instrument synonymous with rock. By the early 1980s, English synthpop/New Pop bands like the Art of Noise, Human League, Orchestral Manoeuvres in the Dark (OMD), Soft Cell, and Ultravox as well as American counterparts like Berlin established a foothold in the popular music market.

39. In 2007, the pop-punk band the Donnas covered "Kids in America" for the soundtrack of the film *Nancy Drew*. The Donnas' version becomes much more a rousing anthem to teenage rebellion, in particular the synthesizer arpeggios played by guitar harmonic overtones in the manner of heavy metal riffing. The lead vocals have a much more defiant edge and a distinctly Californian dialect as opposed to Wilde's reserved English accent, and the song ends with a triumphant chanting of the title as opposed to ironic pronouncements.

40. In 1981, Wilde stated, "The main thing is my music and no one needs to look beyond that: no message, no politics, no comment on society.... I will never be commenting on society. No politics in my songs. If you want to hear about that you'll have to read the papers." Originally published in *Hitkrant*, August 27, 1981. Archived at http://www.wilde-life.com/articles/1981/kim-wilde-i-dont-like-politics (accessed May 22, 2013). Here the issue is defining "political music" around whether the performer intends to make an overt political statement lyrically in a song. Political music also has to be considered around the music as much as lyrics and what kinds of "commentaries" are being made by the song as far as listening and interpretation.

41. Reynolds, *Rip It Up*, 380.

42. Ironically, a case in point would be the music video for Wilde's "Say You Really Want Me" (a later single released off *Another Step*), an R&B-influenced synthpop song. One scene in the video depicts Wilde lying in bed in a tight black dress seductively licking a long white pearl necklace she is wearing (and keeping in mind that "pearl necklace" is also a crude slang term for male ejaculation on a woman's neck); other parts of the video feature Wilde in said attire seductively dancing in front of a movie screen showing a film featuring Wilde in a black evening dress and gloves rolling around in bed with several half-naked men.

Chapter 8

1. Ornette Coleman, "Prime Time for Harmolodics," *Down Beat*, July 1983, 55.

2. As quoted in John Mulvey, liner notes to the Pop Group's *Y*, Rhino Records, 5101-19920-2, 2007.

3. As quoted in Leonard Feather, *The Encyclopedia of Jazz in the 1960s* (New York: Da Capo, 1966), 261.

4. Joachim E. Berendt, *The Jazz Book: From Ragtime to Fusion and Beyond*, trans. H. and D. Bredigkeit with Dan Motenstern (Westport, CT: Lawrence Hill and Company, 1981), 23.

5. Berendt, *The Jazz Book*, 23; emphasis added.

6. As quoted in Feather, *The Encyclopedia of Jazz in the 1960s*, 39.

7. Among Davis' contributors during the era were keyboardists Chick Corea and Joe Zawinul, saxophonist Wayne Shorter, and guitarist John McLaughlin. All became pivotal figures in the jazz-rock fusion movement of the 1970s: Corea with Return to Forever, Shorter and Zawinul with Weather Report, and McLaughlin as leader of the Mahavishnu Orchestra.

8. On a live version of "I Say a Little Prayer," Kirk plays tenor saxophone and manzello simultaneously. Archived at http://www.youtube.com/watch?v=-uRnvMwD6jM (accessed November 26, 2012).

9. As quoted in Berendt, *The Jazz Book*, 207. Another example is pianist Ramsey Lewis. His album *The In Crowd* (1965) won a Grammy and sold a million copies, whereas *Mother Nature's Son* (1969) consisted of instrumental covers of songs from the Beatles' *White Album* with George Stepney on Moog synthesizer and members of the Chicago Symphony Orchestra. In the 1970s, Lewis played electric piano on the Earth, Wind, and Fire instrumental "Sun Goddess" and delivered what was possibly the most dissonant solo ever heard on a hit record.

10. "King" and "Queens" veer toward more experimental jazz and are primarily duets with Nadi Qamar. Both begin and end with recitations by Harley ruminating on knowledge, consciousness, understanding, and other topics in vague rhetoric. On "King," Qamar plays intricate patterns on a *mamlukembia* (a type of thumb piano) while Harley plays a sprawling solo on bagpipes where the Coltrane influence is especially evident. "Queens" is a slower, fragmentary duet between Harley on soprano saxophone and Qamar on Madagascar harp.

11. Harley's cover of the Byrds' "Eight Miles High" is particularly intriguing in that it is strangely reminiscent of Can. The drums and bass maintain a "motorik" beat while the guitar—using effects like echo, phase-shifting, and wah-wah—intermittently punctuates the song with jagged riffing, occasional ringing chords, and sporadic lead runs, and the piano inserts fast, repetitive arpeggios and winding punctuations. Harley plays the vocal melody on bagpipes, using it as the basis for extended modal explorations.

12. Michael Kennedy and Joyce Bourne, *The Concise Oxford Dictionary of Music*, 5th ed. (New York: Oxford University Press, 2007), 659.

13. Fretless string instruments (e.g., violin, viola, cello, double-bass), fretless electric basses and guitars, and slide guitars can play microtonal notes. Reed and brass instruments can also play microtonal notes through various fingering positions (or placement of the trombone slide) and pitch control when playing the instruments. Synthesizers commonly have pitch modulation controls which allow for microtonal possibilities that pianos and organs lack. In order for acoustic keyboards to play microtonal notes, the instruments themselves have to be retuned.

14. In an episode of *King of the Hill*, the one blemish on straight-laced conservative Hank Hill's school record was a one-day suspension for refusing to sing "Flowers" in choir class.

15. While speculation, not releasing "Flowers" may have less to do with the specific political issue of war but with the fact that Harley's version of "Flowers" is so dissonant in places that it sounds badly played, and is therefore not an acceptable take as far as quality standards.

16. Kevin Boyle, *The UAW and the Heyday of American Liberalism, 1945–1968* (Ithaca, NY: Cornell University Press, 1995), 256.

17. Neil Young, liner notes to *Decade* anthology, Reprise 2257-2, 1977.

18. What is frequently overlooked regarding Kent State was a similar massacre at Jackson State University, a predominately African American college, on May 14, 1970. Responding to student unrest on the campus, police and National Guard fired over 450 rounds into a dormitory building. Two were killed and twelve injured.

19. Young's "Southern Man" and "Alabama" (*Harvest*, 1972) prompted Lynard Skynard to respond with "Sweet Home Alabama" (1974) in which they singled out Young by name and, in effect, told him to shut up. In this sense, the message of the song was telling northerners to sort out their own problems rather than lecture southerners (the song specifically mentions Watergate). However, the Neil Young/Lynard Skynard feud was far more humorous than it was malicious, and they were actually fans of each other's work. Lynard Skynard lead singer Ronnie Van Zant occasionally wore a Neil Young T-shirt in concert as well as on the cover of their album *Street Survivors* (1977); returning the favor, Crazy Horse bassist Billy Talbot wore a Lynard Skynard T-shirt in the concert film *Rust Never Sleeps* (1979). Moreover, Young wrote the song "Powderfinger" (*Rust Never Sleeps*) for Lynard Skynard who planned to record it for their album after *Street Survivors*. Tragically, Van Zant and two other members of the band were killed in a plane crash, and Lynard Skynard disbanded for a lengthy period.

20. Mitchell was invited to perform at Woodstock but, on the advice of her manager, declined in order to appear on *The Dick Cavett Show*, much to her regret. "Woodstock" was inspired by then-boyfriend Graham Nash's recollection of events.

21. Neil Nixon, "Crosby, Stills, Nash & Young," in *Rock: The Rough Guide*, 2nd ed., 235.

22. As quoted in Stambler, *Encyclopedia of Pop, Rock and Soul*, 133.
23. Vaneigem, *The Revolution of Everyday Life*, 170.
24. Jean-Pierre Depétris, "Ken Knapp, the Situationist International, and the American Counterculture." Archived at http://www.bopsecrets.org/recent/depetris.htm (accessed May 25, 2013).
25. As a personal example, one afternoon I was at a store where the counterperson was listening to arch-conservative Sean Hannity's Fox Radio show. The introduction of "Ohio" was used as the lead-in music coming out of commercial.
26. Vaneigem, *The Revolution of Everyday Life*, 31–32; emphasis added.
27. See Ted Robert Gurr, "Some Characteristics of Political Terrorism in the 1960s," in *The Politics of Terrorism*, 3rd ed., ed. Michael Stohl (Boca Rotan, FL: CRC Press, 1988), 35–36.
28. As quoted in Peck, *Uncovering the Sixties*, 228–29;.
29. As quoted in Peck, *Uncovering the Sixties*, 234–35.
30. One of the iconic counterculture films was *Billy Jack* (1971, dir. Tom McLaughlin). The title character is an ex–Green Beret, Vietnam vet, and martial arts expert now trying to live a life of non-violence and pacifism. However, the local rednecks continually harass the young, ethnically mixed, counterculture students at the local "Freedom School," and Billy Jack inevitably resorts to violent solutions, much to the dismay of the Freedom School principal. The situation comes to a head when one of the locals rapes one of the students and murders another, and Billy Jack murders the local. Poised for a final showdown with the police, the Freedom School principal convinces Billy Jack to peacefully surrender to the authorities. In this way, the message of *Billy Jack* is that non-violence is the superior form of political action over violence. However, the popularity of Billy Jack stemmed from a title character that was a spiritual hippie and also kicked ass.
31. Statistics taken from www.english.illinois.edu/maps/poets/s_z/stevens/africanamer.htm (accessed February 15, 2013).
32. Martin Luther King, Jr., "Beyond Vietnam," April 4, 1970. Archived at http://mlk-kpp01.stanford.edu/index.php/encyclopedia/documentsentry/doc_beyond_vietnam (accessed February 15, 2013).

33. A pop-oriented progressive rock band, the Electric Light Orchestra was much closer to the Beatles than ELP or Yes but considered prog-rock because of the lineup that included a violinist and two cellists. ELO covered "Roll Over Beethoven" on their second album (*ELO II*, 1973) and included quotes from Beethoven's works in the cover version, presumably to negotiate an objectivist musical treaty.
34. ELP, Yes, and Jethro Tull were extremely popular bands in the 1970s, while Genesis and King Crimson were moderately successful bands. Bands like Gentle Giant and Van der Graaf Generator had smaller but devoted followings. Genesis did not achieve their immense commercial success until the early 1980s, and by then had adopted a highly accessible "adult contemporary" pop-rock style.
35. Bangs, *Mainlines*, 50.
36. Attali, *Noise*, 109.
37. As quoted in Steve Dinsdale, "Emerson, Lake, and Palmer," in *Rock: The Rough Guide*, 2nd ed., 323.
38. Macan, *Rocking the Classics*, 173.
39. Ibid., 15.
40. "This third type is a hybrid form. Hand in hand with objectivism, this composer proceeds from the cognition of alienation. At the same time, he is more alert than the objectivist and recognizes the solutions of his colleagues as illusions.... In his effort, he employs the musical language belonging in part to the bourgeois musical culture of the nineteenth century, in part to present day consumer music. These means are used to reveal the flaws [the composer] detects. Through destruction of aesthetic formal immanence, this type of composer transcends into the literary realm.... It has been developed most consequentially in the works which Kurt Weill produced with Bert Brecht, particularly *The Three Penny Opera* and *Mahagonny*" (Adorno, *Essays on Music*, 396–97).
41. Macan, *Rocking the Classics*, 165; emphasis added.
42. While the advantage of the Mellotron was being polyphonic rather than monophonic like the early Moog and ARP synthesizers, the disadvantage was negotiating the time limitations and speed restrictions of the tape replay mechanism. These factors meant that the Mellotron was better suited as a "background" instrument simulating blocks of orchestra or choir, whereas monophonic synthesizers were primarily "lead" instruments used for soloing and punctuations.

43. Macan, *Rocking the Classics*, 77.
44. Frith, *Sound Effects*, 21.
45. Stu Hackel, "Yesterday's Dreams," liner notes to the Four Tops, *The Ultimate Collection*, Motown 314530825-2, 1997.
46. Boyle, *The UAW and the Heyday of American Liberalism, 1945–1968*, 229.
47. Another pioneer of political psychedelic soul was Curtis Mayfield, namely his 1970 hit "If There's Hell Below, We're All Gonna Go." The song combined a funk beat, insistent wah-wah guitar riffing, a menacing fuzz bass line, horns and strings, and falsetto vocals in a way that resembled a more ominous version of the Philly soul sound. As the title indicates, Mayfield gave a dire assessment of the current situation of American political life.
48. One also suspects that the popularity of Vanilla Fudge's "You Keep Me Hangin' On" was not lost on Motown. In fact, Rare Earth's cover versions charted higher than the Temptations' original versions.
49. As quoted in Hackel, "Yesterday's Dreams."
50. In *The Ultimate Collection* credits, the five members of the Moody Blues at the time are specifically listed as appearing on "A Simple Game." Given that Tony Clarke produced the recording sessions and the Moody Blues are credited, the assumption is that they are the backing band. However, accounts vary as to the extent the Moody Blues were involved.
51. As quoted in Hackel, "Yesterday's Dreams."

Chapter 9

1. As quoted in and archived at http://www.mtv.com/artists/laibach/biography (accessed January 8, 2013).
2. Glenn Gossling, "Laibach," *Rock: The Rough Guide*, 2nd ed., 591.
3. Robert O. Paxton, *Europe in the Twentieth Century* (Harcourt Brace and Jovanovich, 1975), 264–65.
4. Gregor Tomc, "A Tale of Two Subcultures: A Comparative Analysis of Hippie and Punk Subcultures in Slovenia," in *Remembering Utopia: The Culture of Everyday Life in Socialist Yugoslavia*, ed. Breda Luther and Maruša Pušnik (Washington, DC: New Academia Publishing, 2010), 177.
5. As a "collective" rather than a "band," Laibach has a flexible membership and frequently enlists outside musicians for recording and concert purposes as the specific "concept" entails. In this respect, three live versions of their cover of "Alle gegan Alle" are archived at YouTube (all accessed January 11, 2013): http://www.youtube.com/watch?v=LW1JhZFh54Q is ca. 1994–95; http://www.youtube.com/watch?v=nEbIk6vvF3Q is from 2007; and http://www.youtube.com/watch?v=RQEb3ZA2jJY is from 2012.
6. As quoted in Ian Shirley, "Laibach," *Record Collector* 412 (March 2013): 54.
7. An excellent discussion of Throbbing Gristle's musical and ideological complexities is Drew Daniel, *20 Jazz Funk Greats*, no. 54 in the 33 1/3 series (New York: Continuum, 2008).
8. Hegarty, *Noise/Music*, 120–21. Hegarty cites Throbbing Gristle and Whitehouse as industrial bands primarily concerned with transgression (breaking down the constructs of sexuality, violence, and morality), whereas Test Department was an industrial band that adopted an overtly left-wing political stance; Cabaret Voltaire could be added here as well, albeit with a political position derived from Foucault's "society of surveillance" as well as Marxism.
9. "Requiem pour un con," 51.
10. As quoted in *Situationist International Anthology*, 52.
11. Guy Debord, *The Society of the Spectacle*, trans. Donald Nicholson-Smith (New York: Zone Books, 1995), 145.
12. Guy Debord and Gil J. Wolman, "A User's Guide to Détournement," in *Situationist International Anthology*, 15.
13. Part of the "regimentation" of Laibach's live performances owes to the use of prerecorded tapes which are also synchronized with the barrage of video projections behind the band.
14. Alexei Monroe, *Interrogation Machine: Laibach and NSK* (Cambridge, MA: MIT Press, 2005), 7.
15. As quoted in Shirley, "Laibach," 54.
16. In their most overt comment on pop totalitarianism, Laibach's original song "Tanz mit Laibach" ("Dance with Laibach," *WAT*, 2003) was a pounding, martial-industrial song with a disco beat, grinding electronic noises, choral background vocals, and lead vocal barked in German including a chorus of "Eins, zwei, drei, vier!" Among the images in the music video for "Tanz mit Laibach" were extreme close-ups of stomping military boots, film negatives of dancing peasants, and animations of parading skeletons.

17. As quoted in John Hutnyk, *Critique of Exotica: Music, Politics, and the Culture Industry* (London: Pluto Press, 2000), 24.

18. Timothy D, Taylor, *Beyond Exoticism: Western Music and the World* (Durham, NC: Duke University Press, 2007), 134.

19. NSK State has established "embassies" in several Eastern European cities and issues its own currency, passports, and postage stamps. NSK State is not officially recognized by other nation-states.

20. "Montage [is] characterized ... by collision ... by the conflict of two pieces in opposition to each other.... The popularized description of what happens as a *blending* has its share of responsibility for the popular miscomprehension of the nature of montage." Sergei Eisenstein, *Film Form: Essays on Film Theory*, ed. and trans. Jay Leyda (San Diego: Harcourt Brace and Company, 1977), 37, 49; emphasis original.

21. As quoted in an interview with Stéphane Leguay, *Premonition* online magazine, August 2003. Archived at http://www.premonition.org/premor.php3?lien=actu/actu.php3X1X actuid=217002&ta=10 (accessed March 20, 2013).

22. The Federal Republic of Yugoslavia dissolved in 2003 with the establishment of the nation-state of Serbia and Montenegro in 2003. In 2006, Serbia and Montenegro divided into the nation-states of Central Serbia, Serbia (Vojvodina), and Montenegro. Kosovo became a nation-state in 2008 although its status remains in diplomatic dispute.

23. Laibach's immediate commentary on the collapse of the Soviet Union was *Kapital* (1992), which assembled elements of disco, hip-hop, industrial, and techno into a sound somewhere between Cabaret Voltaire and Public Enemy.

24. "We always liked repetition in music and disco was among our main inspirations. We are not crazy about techno, but it's a relevant and legitimate form and sometimes serves the goal" (Laibach as quoted in Shirley).

25. Given the almost "hyper-masculine" element of Laibach's early work, Laibach made a somewhat stunning change in 2003 by adding Eva Brezniker and Nataša Regnovic from the Slovenian girl group Make Up 2 on backing vocals and percussion (snare drums and crash cymbals). In live performances they would flank lead vocalist Milan Fras and stand in almost motionless attention while performing. In 2006, Mila Špiler from the Slovenian synthpop band Melodrom was added on lead/background vocals and synthesizer. All three can be seen in concert on Laibach, *Volk Dead in Trbovlje* (DVD, 2008). As of 2013, Špiler remains a member of Laibach; Brezniker and Regnovic are no longer in Laibach.

26. An avant-grade nexus of popular music and classical music was Portsmouth Sinfonia. Organized by Gavin Byars at the Portsmouth School of Art, the rules were that members had to be non-musicians or musicians playing instruments they were not trained on. They also had to play the pieces as best they could and not play intentionally badly. Their Brian Eno–produced album *The Portsmouth Sinfonia Plays the Popular Classics* (1974) includes a relentlessly atonal, two-minute rendition of Strauss' "Also Sprach Zarathustra" that sounds like Iannis Xenakis did the arrangement.

27. Walser, *Running with the Devil*, 104.

28. Tamara Žagar is credited as guest vocalist on "War," and the choir vocals may be Žagar singing on multiple tracks.

29. In 2010, Status Quo rerecorded "In the Army Now," and the proceeds were donated to war veterans groups. Not surprisingly, there were slight but considerable lyrical alterations that effectively converted it from an antimilitary song to a pro-military song.

30. Technically, it might be more correct to term "The Dogs of War" a David Gilmour song, as the song was co-written by Gilmour and Anthony Moore and Gilmour was the only member of Pink Floyd on the track and backed by guest musicians.

31. D.A.F. is an abbreviation of Deutsch Amerikanische Freundschaft (German American Friendship)

32. D.A.F.'s "Alle gegan Alle" is highly reminiscent of Suicide, a 1970s "post-punk" duo consisting of Alan Vega (vocals) and Martin Rev (keyboards, drum machine); Suicide performances could be as confrontational as any show by the Stooges or the Sex Pistols. Suicide's infamous *23 Minutes over Brussels* live recording ends with audience members confiscating Vega's microphone and refusing to return it, effectively ending the concert. Moreover, while stylistically dissimilar to Laibach, Suicide's music was also a "synthetic organization of greater efficacy" as a *détournement* of disparate genres ranging from Elvis Presley (a main influence on Vega's vocals which took Presley's gasping, moaning, and shouting to extremes) and rockabilly to lounge music, 1960s go-go music, electronic music, minimalist

music, and systems music—precisely at a time when early punk was reliant on traditional rock formalism.
33. Thomas Hobbes, *Leviathan* (New York: Touchstone/ Simon and Schuster, 1997), 100.
34. As quoted in Leguay, *Premonition*.
35. See *Situationist International Anthology*, 18.
36. *Situationist International Anthology*, 18; emphasis added.
37. Slavoj Žižek, "What the Hell Is Laibach All About?" Archived at http://www.youtube.com/watch?v=1BZl8ScVYvA (accessed January 11, 2013).

Chapter 10

1. Raymond Williams, *Marxism and Literature* (Oxford: Oxford University Press. 1977), 123.
2. Frith, *Sound Effects*, 24; emphasis original.
3. For an analysis of *School of Rock* and its conflation of rock history and rock ideology into rock mythology, see my *Teens, TV, and Tunes*, chap. 10.
4. Williams, *Marxism and Literature*, 122–23.
5. "Something" was the first and only Harrison song released as a Beatle's A-side single. More correctly, "Something" was released with Lennon's "Come Together" as a double A-side single.
6. In the wake of the Beatles official disbanding, two *Abbey Road* tribute albums appeared from genres outside of rock in 1970. Jazz guitarist-vocalist George Benson covered it on *The Other Side of Abbey Road* backed by jazz luminaries such as Herbie Hancock, Ron Carter, Freddie Hubbard, and Hubert Laws. Benson's cover of "Something," which began a medley that also included "Octopus' Garden" and "The End," was a jazz version with extended electric guitar soloing around the melody backed by electric piano, double-bass, drums, strings, and flute in which Benson only and rather eerily sings in the bridge—one of the ambiguous points in the lyrics that takes on even more ambiguity as to whether the object is "something" the performer has or wants to have—and the opening line of the song just as the song ends. Booker T. and the M.G.s did R&B instrumental versions of the songs on *McLemore Avenue* (the street Stax Studios was located on). Their version of "Something" begins with piano playing the melody over half-time drumming, and the chorus where the piano continues the melody while the drums shift to a brisk quarter-note rimshot beat (taking on the role of the organ in the Beatles' version). This goes into the bridge section, with the organ carrying the melody over half-time snare-ride cymbal drumming. Entering the verse, the lead guitar takes over the melody line accompanied by piano and the three of the half-time beat emphasized by the hi-hat and the guitar maintains the melody line when the song shifts to the chorus and quarter-note rimshots. Another verse follows with guitar, organ, and half-time drumming until the song suddenly kicks into an R&B shuffle beat and a long guitar solo followed by a piano solo. While Benson's version becomes a much darker interpretation of "Something" (the overall smooth jazz setting notwithstanding), Booker T. and the M.G.'s version of "Something" and *McLemore Avenue* as a whole suggests the covers are more of a way to celebrate the Beatles' illustrious career.

7. Ray Charles' version of "Yesterday" bears particular mention. The song is done in a gospel/blues setting with a string section and Charles on piano belting out the lyrics in a gruff, soulful baritone that teems with defeat and sorrow. At 1'41" and the point the second chorus begins, half-time drums and horns enter, and at the 2'08" the horns drop out in favor of the strings while the half-time continues for the rest of the song. It achieves an extraordinary power.

8. George Harrison remarked that his favorite cover of "Something" was James Brown's version, which was released as the B-side of Brown's single "Thanks" (1973). See "George Harrison—In His Own Words." Archived at http://www.superseventies.com/ssgeorgeharrison.html (accessed January 15, 2013). Brown's version is done as a Stax-style, slow R&B shuffle with ponderous half-time drumming, jagged funk guitar riffing, a wash of organ, and horn parts including a pronounced flute. Midway through, the song shifts into a funky, horn-dominated section that acts as the bridge and brightens the overall downhearted tone set in the preceding verse–chorus before the song returns to the verse–chorus to end with reestablishing the overall sense of despondency. Brown takes substantial liberties with the vocal melody as well as the lyrics, with the lyrics expressing that the "something" is what the women possesses that makes the man hope-

lessly attracted to her, and the recurring ad-libs are more overt in expressing the "something" he clings to is a desperate belief that she somehow loves him as well. Here the ambiguity of the lyrics becomes more unsettling to the extent Brown is not so much singing an ode to a loving partner who has "something" that immeasurably improves his life, but someone as a "something" that is an unattainable and painful void in his life.

9. Simon Frith, "What Is Bad Music?" in *Bad Music*, 19.

10. Early Moog synthesizers resembled an organ attached to a telephone operator's switchboard; they could only play monophonically, and the performer had to adjust knobs and repatch wires into different inputs to change sounds. *Switched-On Bach* (1968), an album of Moog synthesizer renditions of Bach compositions by Wendy Carlos, was something of a surprise commercial success and was pivotal in spurring popular interest in synthesizer music. A key development in synthesizer technology was the Minimoog in 1970—a much smaller, more portable synthesizer designed for concert performance as much as studio recording for jazz and rock musicians.

11. An electronic cover version of "Quiet Village" by Mark Mothersbaugh was used as a one-minute musical prelude for the opening titles of *Pee-Wee's Playhouse*.

12. "Crossover" artists are far from a unique phenomenon as far as American popular culture. Popular music performers ranging from Cher, Ice Cube, Ice-T, Reba McIntyre, Dean Martin, Elvis Presley, Frank Sinatra, and Barbara Streisand branched off into acting careers (to name only a few). However, this tends to be a one-way street. Well-known actors and celebrities tend to have much more difficulty finding acceptance in the popular music market, especially rock beyond the occasional hit song; one exception is Pia Zadora, who began her show business career starring in two critically savaged films, *Butterfly* and *The Lonely Lady*, before establishing her career as a pop singer in the 1980s. Part of this stems from an ethos in American popular music that a famous actor or celebrity who dabbles in rock or other popular music generally lacks "authenticity" while it is much more acceptable for an "authentic" rock musician to pursue acting (for example, Tom Petty did the voice of "Lucky," a semi-regular character on the animated sitcom *King of the Hill*).

13. A satirical humor magazine, *Spy* released three volumes of *Spy Magazine Presents* through Rhino Records. Volume 1 was *Spy Music* and was an anthology of hit spy movie themes and hit songs about spies and secret agents. Volume 2 was *White Men Can't Wrap* and featured spoken-word renditions of songs by male stars from the 1940s to the 1980s. Volume 3, *Soft, Safe, and Sanitized*, was essentially a *Golden Throats* album; in fact, several of the songs on *Soft, Safe, and Sanitized* appeared on previous *Golden Throats* anthologies.

14. There is one overt joke song on *Celebrities Butcher the Beatles*, Alan Copeland's "Mission Impossible Theme/Norwegian Wood" (1968). Copeland used session singers and musicians to set the vocals of "Norwegian Wood" (a 12/8 song) to the theme from the TV show *Mission: Impossible* (a 5/4 song)—a case of camping rather than Camp.

15. Lawrence Welk did a MOR instrumental cover of "Hey Jude" that appeared on his album *Galveston* (1969). It was not included on *Celebrities Butcher the Beatles* or other like-minded anthologies.

16. Susan Sontag, *Against Interpretation* (New York: Anchor/Doubleday, 1966), 292.

17. Ibid., 278.

18. Tony Bennett and Robert Sullivan, *Tony Bennett in the Studio: A Life in Art and Music* (New York: Sterling, 2007), 90.

19. Bennett's iconic status was solidified with *Duets II* (2011), an album of standards that paired Bennett with Lady Gaga, Amy Winehouse, Sheryl Crow, and Carrie Underwood, among others.

20. Sontag, *Against Interpretation*, 282.

21. In 2011, William Shatner released *Seeking Major Tom*, a collection of rock cover songs relating to the general theme of space travel (not surprising given Shatner's cultural iconography as James T. Kirk on *Star Trek*). They ranged from David Bowie's "Space Oddity" to Steve Miller's "Space Cowboy," Deep Purple's "Space Truckin'," Elton John's "Rocket Man," and Duran Duran's "Planet Earth." While the song instrumental arrangements were largely similar to the originals (as an exception, "Space Truckin'" was done on acoustic guitar and bongos), Shatner recited the lyrics with a self-aware, histrionic splendor. In this respect, *The Transformed Man* was Camp whereas *Seeking Major Tom* was camping.

22. In 2005, Paul Anka released *Rock Swings*, a collection of big-band cover versions of rock songs ranging from Soundgarden's "Black Hole Sun" and Nirvana's "Smells Like

Teen Spirit" to Van Halen's "Jump," Bon Jovi's "It's My Life," and the Cure's "Lovecats." While done with more "sincerity" than Boone's camping on *In a Metal Mood*, Anka's album was released well after the "lounge rock" fad had run its course and Johnny Cash's *American Recording* series set the new standard as far as older performers tackling rock songs.

23. See Howard Rosenberg, "Pat Boone Faces His Angry Peers," *Los Angeles Times*, April, 18, 1997. Archived at http://articles.latimes.com/1997-04-18/entertainment/ca-49837_1_pat-boone (accessed January 12, 2013).

24. Annalee Newitz, "What Makes Things Cheesy? Satire, Multinationalism, and B-Movies," *Social Text*, Summer 2000, 55.

25. Erik Anderson, "Sailing the Seas of Cheese," *Contemporary Aesthetics*, 2010. Archived at http://www.contempaesthetics.org/newvolume/pages/article.php?articleID=583 (accessed January 21, 2013).

26. See Frith, *Sound Effects*, 25, 29.

27. Aaron A. Fox, "White Trash Alchemies of the Abject Sublime: Country as 'Bad Music,'" in *Bad Music*, 51.

28. O'Neill, *Coming Apart*, 298.

29. The demise of Cash's TV show owed largely to a rebranding of the networks in 1971. After the success of *Rowan and Martin's Laugh-In* and *All in the Family*, the networks summarily canceled popular shows targeted at older and/or rural "conservative" demographics. CBS canceled *The Beverly Hillbillies, Green Acres, Hee Haw*, and *The Ed Sullivan Show*; ABC canceled *The Lawrence Welk Show* as well as *The Johnny Cash Show*.

30. The biopic *I Walk the Line* (2005), which focuses on Cash's life up to the early 1970s, was also central in constructing Cash's cultural iconography.

31. "Yesterday" was released on *Country Concert Live* (1966) and reissued as *Willie Nelson Live* (1976).

32. A particularly intense example of early industrial music is an outdoor live performance by Einstürzendie Neubaten achieved at http://www.youtube.com/watch?v=3cnaG3BX3lw (accessed January 13, 2013).

33. Marilyn Manson did 1990s "industrial" covers of 1980s synthpop hits like the Eurhythmics "Sweet Dreams (Are Made of This)," Soft Cell's "Tainted Love," and Depeche Mode's "Personal Jesus."

34. In this sense, Cash's cover of "Hurt" suggests an affinity to the Velvet Underground as the first proto-punk band.

35. The background information of the making of "Hurt" owes to Chet Flippo, "Nashville Skyline: Johnny Cash's 'Hurt' Video." Archived at http://www.cmt.com/news/nashville-skyline/1469972/nashville-skyline-johnny-cashs-hurt-video.jhtml (accessed January 23, 2013).

Conclusion

1. Friedrich Nietzsche, *Twilight of the Idols*. Reprinted in *The Portable Nietzsche*, ed. and trans. Walter Kaufmann (New York: Viking, 1968), 471.

2. As quoted in http://web.archive.org/web/20090416200238/http://www.songfacts.com/detail.php?id=3937 (accessed March 27, 2013).

3. As quoted in Colin MacCabe, *Godard: Images, Sounds, Politics* (Bloomington: Indiana University Press, 1980), 19; emphasis original.

4. Louis Althusser and Étienne Balibar, *Reading Capital*, trans. Ben Brewster (New York: Verso, 1997), 14.

5. Lawrence Grossberg, "Rock and Roll in Search of an Audience," in *Popular Music and Communication*, ed. James Lull (Newbury Park, CA: Sage, 1987), 177.

Bibliography

Adorno, Theodor W. "Commitment." In *The Essential Frankfurt School Reader*, 300–18. Edited by Andrew Arato and Eike Gebhardt. New York: Continuum, 1982.

———. *The Culture Industry: Selected Essays on Mass Culture*. Edited by J.M. Bernstein. London: Routledge, 1991.

———. *Essays on Music*. Edited by Richard Leppert. Translated by Susan H. Gillespie. Berkeley: University of California Press, 2002.

———. "On Tradition." *Telos* 94 (1993–94): 75–82.

Althusser, Louis. *For Marx*. Translated by Ben Brewster. New York: Verso, 1996.

———, and Étienne Balibar. *Reading Capital*. Translated by Ben Brewster. New York: Verso, 1997.

Anderson, Erik. "Sailing the Seas of Cheese." *Contemporary Aesthetics* (2010). Archived at http://www.contempaesthetics.org/newvolume/pages/article.php?articleID=583 (accessed January 21, 2013).

Attali, Jacques. *Noise: The Political Economy of Music*. Translated by Brain Massumi. Minneapolis: University of Minnesota Press, 1985.

Bangs, Lester. *Mainlines, Bloodfeasts, and Bad Taste: A Lester Bangs Reader*. Edited by Jim Morthland. New York: Anchor Books, 2003.

———. *Psychotic Reactions and Carburetor Dung*. Edited by Greil Marcus. New York: Anchor Books, 2003.

Bennett, Tony, and Robert Sullivan. *Tony Bennett in the Studio: A Life in Art and Music*. New York: Sterling, 2007.

Berendt, Joachim E. *The Jazz Book: From Ragtime to Fusion and Beyond*. Translated by H. and D. Bredigkeit with Dan Motenstern. Westport, CT: Lawrence Hill and Company, 1981.

Boyle, Kevin. *The UAW and the Heyday of American Liberalism, 1945–1968*. Ithaca, NY: Cornell University Press, 1995.

Buckley, Jonathan, Orla Duane, Mark Ellingham, and Al Spicer, eds. *Rock: The Rough Guide*. 2nd ed. London: The Rough Guide, 1999.

Cage, John. *John Cage: An Anthology*. Edited by Richard Kostelentz. New York: Da Capo, 1991.

Christgau, Robert. All articles and reviews accessible at http://www.robertchristgau.com. Reviews are best accessed at http://www.robertchristgau.com/cg.php.

Coates, Norma. "Revolution Now? The Potential Politics of Gender." In *Sexing the Groove: Popular Music and Gender*. Edited by Shelia Whiteley. New York: Routledge, 1997.

———. "Teenyboppers, Groupies, and Other Grotesques: Girls and Women and Rock Culture in the 1960s and early 1970s." *Journal of Popular Music Studies* 15, no. 1 (2003): 65–94.

Coleman, Ornette. "Prime Time for Harmolodics." *Down Beat*, July 1983.

Daniel, Drew. *20 Jazz Funk Greats*. No. 54 in the 33 1/3 series. New York: Continuum, 2008.

Debord, Guy. *The Society of the Spectacle*. Translated by Donald Nicholson-Smith. New York: Zone Books, 1995.

———, and Gil J. Wolman. "A User's Guide

to Détournement." Reprinted in *Situationist International Anthology*, 14–21.
Deleuze, Gilles. *Negotiations: 1972–1990*. Translated by Martin Joughin. New York: Columbia University Press, 1995.
Depétris, Jean-Pierre. "Ken Knapp, the Situationist International, and the American Counterculture." Archived at http://www.bopsecrets.org/recent/depetris.htm (accessed May 25, 2013).
Eagleton, Terry. *Literary Theory: An Introduction*. Minneapolis: University of Minnesota Press, 1983.
Eisenstein, Sergei. *Film Form: Essays on Film Theory*. Edited and translated by Jay Leyda. San Diego: Harcourt Brace and Company, 1977.
Fast, Susan. *In the Houses of the Holy: Led Zeppelin and the Power of Rock Music*. London: Oxford University Press, 2001.
Feather, Leonard. *The Encyclopedia of Jazz in the 1960s*. New York: Da Capo, 1966.
Flippo, Chet. "Nashville Skyline: Johnny Cash's 'Hurt' Video." Archived at http://www.cmt.com/news/nashville-skyline/1469972/nashville-skyline-johnny-cashs-hurt-video.jhtml (accessed January 23, 2013).
Foucault, Michel. *The History of Sexuality*. Vol. 1, *An Introduction*. Translated by Robert Hurley. New York: Vintage, 1978.
———. "What Is an Author?" In *Language, Counter-Memory, Practice: Selected Essays and Interviews*, 113–38. Edited by Donald F. Bouchard. Translated by Donald F. Bouchard and Sherry Simon. Ithaca, NY: Cornell University Press, 1980.
Fox, Aaron A. "White Trash Alchemies of the Abject Sublime: Country as 'Bad Music.'" In *Bad Music: The Music We Love to Hate*, 39–61. Edited by Christopher J. Washburne and Maiken Derno. New York: Routledge, 2004.
Frith, Simon. *Sound Effects: Youth, Leisure, and the Politics of Rock 'n' Roll*. New York: Pantheon, 1981.
———. "What Is Bad Music?" In *Bad Music: The Music We Love to Hate*, 15–38. Edited by Christopher J. Washburne and Maiken Derno. New York: Routledge, 2004.
Goodwin, Andrew. "Popular Music and Postmodern Theory." In *The Postmodern Arts: An Introductory Reader*, 80–100. Edited by Nigel Wheale. London: Routledge, 1991.
Greene, Doyle. *Teens, TV and Tunes: The Manufacturing of American Adolescent Culture*. Jefferson, NC: McFarland, 2012.
Grossberg, Lawrence. "Rock and Roll in Search of an Audience." In *Popular Music and Communication*, 175–97. Edited by James Lull. Newbury Park, CA: Sage, 1987.
Gurr, Ted Robert. "Some Characteristics of Political Terrorism in the 1960s." In *The Politics of Terrorism*, 3rd ed., 31–58. Edited by Michael Stohl. Boca Rotan, FL: CRC Press, 1988.
Hackel, Stu. "Yesterday's Dreams." Liner notes to the Four Tops, *The Ultimate Collection*. Motown 314530825-2, 1997.
Hebdige, Dick. *Subcultures*. London: Routledge, 1978.
Hegarty, Paul. *Noise/Music: A History*. New York: Continuum, 2007.
Hobbes, Thomas. *Leviathan*. New York: Touchstone/Simon and Schuster, 1997.
Hoberman, J., and Jonathan Rosenbaum. *Midnight Movies*. New York: Da Capo, 1991.
Hussey, Andrew. "Requiem pour un con: Subversive Pop and the Society of the Spectacle." *Cercles* 3 (2001): 49–59.
Hutnyk, John. *Critique of Exotica: Music, Politics, and the Culture Industry*. London: Pluto Press, 2000.
Huyssen, Andreas. *After the Great Divide: Modernism, Mass Culture, and Postmodernism*. Bloomington: Indiana University Press, 1986.
Jameson, Frederic. *Late Marxism: Adorno, or, The Persistence of the Dialectic*. New York: Verso, 1990.
———. *Postmodernism, or, The Cultural Logic of Late Capitalism*. Durham, NC: Duke University Press, 1991.
Kennedy, Michael, and Joyce Bourne. *The Concise Oxford Dictionary of Music*. 5th

ed. New York: Oxford University Press, 2007.

King, Martin Luther, Jr. "Beyond Vietnam" speech (April 4, 1970). Archived at http://mlkkpp01.stanford.edu/index.php/encyclopedia/documentsentry/doc_beyond_vietnam (accessed February 15, 2013).

Kuenzli, Rudolf E., ed. *Dada and Surrealist Film*. New York: Willis Locker and Owens, 1987.

Laibach. Interview with Stéphane Leguay. *Premonition* online magazine, August 2003. Archived at http://www.premonition.org/premor.php3?lien=actu/actu.php3X1Xactuid=217002&ta=10 (accessed March 20, 2013).

Leppert, Richard. "Music 'Pushed to the Edge of Existence' (Adorno, Listening, and the Question of Hope)." *Cultural Critique* 60 (Spring 2005): 92–132.

Macan, Edward. *Rocking the Classics: English Progressive Rock and the Counterculture*. New York: Oxford University Press, 1997.

MacCabe, Colin. *Godard: Images, Sounds, Politics*. Bloomington: Indiana University Press, 1980.

Mailer, Norman. *Advertisements for Myself*. Cambridge, MA: Harvard University Press, 1992.

Marcuse, Hebert. *One-Dimensional Man*. Boston: Beacon Press, 1964.

Marsh, Dave. "Devo, *Duty Now for the Future*." *Rolling Stone*, September 20, 1979.

McNeil, Legs, and Gillian McCain. *Please Kill Me: An Uncensored Oral History of Punk*. New York: Penguin, 1996.

Mendiola, Jim. "Anarchy in S.A." *San Antonio Current*, January 2, 2003. Achieved at www.randysrodeo.com/features/pistols/08.php (accessed May 19, 2008).

Monroe, Alexei. *Interrogation Machine: Laibach and NSK*. Cambridge, MA: MIT Press, 2005.

Mothersbaugh, Mark. A.V. Club interview with Joe Garden. Archived at www.avclub.com/content/node/23325/print/1 (accessed January 7, 2009).

_____, and Gerald Casale. Commentary. Devo, *The Complete Truth about De-evolution*. Rhino Home Video, R2 970 107, 2003.

Mueller, Charles Allen. "The Music of Goth Subculture: Postmodernism and Aesthetics." Dissertation. Ann Arbor: Proquest, 2008.

Mulvey, John. Liner notes. The Pop Group, *Y*. Rhino Records, 5101-19920-2, 2007.

Neate, Wilson. *Pink Flag*. No. 62 in the 33 1/3 series. New York: Continuum, 2008.

Newitz, Annalee. "What Makes Things Cheesy? Satire, Multinationalism, and B-Movies." *Social Text*, Summer 2000, 59–82.

Newman, Colin. Liner notes. *Rough Trade Shops: Post Punk Vol. 01*. Mute Records, CDSTUMM 224, 2003.

Nietzsche, Friedrich. *The Portable Nietzsche*. New York: Viking, 1968.

O'Neill, William L. *Coming Apart: An Informal History of America in the 1960s*. New York: Times Books, 1971.

Pareles, Jon. "Caution: Now Entering the War Zone." *New York Times*, February 24, 1991.

Paxton, Robert O. *Europe in the Twentieth Century*. New York: Harcourt Brace and Jovanovich, 1975.

Peck, Abe. *Uncovering the Sixties: The Life and Times of the Underground Press*. New York: Pantheon, 1985.

Reynolds, Simon. *Rip It Up and Start Again: Postpunk, 1978–1984*. New York: Penguin, 2005.

Rosenberg, Howard. "Pat Boone Faces His Angry Peers." *Los Angeles Times*, April 18, 1997. Archived at http://articles.latimes.com/1997-04-18/entertainment/ca-49837_1_pat-boone (accessed January 12, 2013).

Schiffer, Sheldon. "The Cover Song as Historiography, Marker of Ideological Transformation." In *Play It Again: Cover Songs and Popular Music*, 77–98. Edited by George Plasketes. Burlington, VT: Ashgate, 2010.

Sclafani, Tony. "When 'Disco Sucks!' Echoed around the World." Archived at http://www.today.com/id/31832616/ns/today-today_entertainment/t/when-disco-sucks-echoed-around-world/#. UdcOcfnVDps (accessed July 5, 2013).

Sedgwick, Eve Kosofsky. *Between Men: English Literature and Male Homosocial Desire*. New York: Columbia University Press, 1985.

Shepherd, John. "Music and Male Hegemony." In *Music and Society: The Politics of Composition, Performance, and Reception*, 151–72. Edited by Richard Leppert and Susan McClary. Cambridge: Cambridge University Press, 1989.

Shirley, Ian. "Laibach." *Record Collector* 412 (March 2013): 52–54.

Situationist International. *Situationist International Anthology*. Revised and expanded edition. Edited and translated by Ken Knapp. Berkeley: Bureau of Pubic Secrets, 2006.

Sontag, Susan. *Against Interpretation*. New York: Anchor/Doubleday, 1966.

Stambler, Irwin. *Encyclopedia of Pop, Rock and Soul*. New York: St. Martin's Press, 177.

Strohm, John. "Women Guitarists: Gender Issues in Alternative Rock." In *The Electric Guitar: A History of an American Icon*, 181–200. Edited by André Millard. Baltimore, MD: Johns Hopkins University Press, 2004.

Taylor, Timothy D. *Beyond Exoticism: Western Music and the World*. Durham, NC: Duke University Press, 2007.

Tomc, Gregor. "A Tale of Two Subcultures: A Comparative Analysis of Hippie and Punk Subcultures in Slovenia." In *Remembering Utopia: The Culture of Everyday Life in Socialist Yugoslavia*, 165–98. Edited by Breda Luther and Maruša Pušnik. Washington, DC: New Academia Publishing, 2010.

Vaneigem, Raoul. *The Revolution of Everyday Life*. Translated by Donald Nicholson-Smith. London: Rebel Books, 2006.

Waksman, Steve. *Instruments of Desire: The Electric Guitar and the Shaping of Musical Experience*. Cambridge, MA: Harvard University Press, 2004.

―――. *This Ain't the Summer of Love: Conflict and Crossover in Heavy Metal and Punk*. Berkeley: University of California, 2009.

Walser, Robert. *Running with the Devil: Power, Gender, and Madness in Heavy Metal Music*. Hanover, NH: Wesleyan University Press, 1993.

Williams, Raymond. *Marxism and Literature*. Oxford: Oxford University Press. 1977.

Young, Neil. Liner notes. *Decade* anthology CD. Reprise 2257–2, 1977.

Žižek, Slavoj. *The Sublime Object of Ideology*. New York: Verso, 1989.

―――. "What the Hell Is Laibach All About?" Archived at http://www.youtube.com/watch?v=1BZl8ScVYvA (accessed January 11, 2013).

Index

Adorno, Theodor W. 2, 27, 31, 68, 73, 76–77, 111, 124, 179c6n4, 184c8n40
African music 110, 114, 134
Aguilera, Christina 17, 22, 75
Alien Sex Fiend 163
alienation 9–10, 52–53, 55–56, 66, 78–79, 81–82, 96, 146, 160
Allen, Dave 99–100
Allman, Duane 103
Altamont 9, 56, 57, 58, 120, 133
alternative music 12, 161–162, 165
alternative TV (ATV) 37–38
Althusser, Louis 168
Amboy Dukes 62
American Federation of Musicians (AFM) 91–92
Americana 60–61, 159
anarchism 21, 29–30, 32, 42, 109
Anderson, Erik 159
androgyny 29, 94, 98
Animal House 121
Animals 104
Anka, Paul 47, 188–189c10n22
Anthony, Michael 93
anti-cover(s) 1, 8–9, 11–12, 19, 21, 34, 39, 42–47, 70, 95, 97, 101, 129, 132–133, 136, 140–142, 160, 167
anti-establishment 12, 21, 43, 55–56, 60, 62, 77, 82, 86, 119, 161
Apollo 100 137
Appice, Carmine 103
Arabic music 110
arena rock 133, 138
Armstrong, Billie Joe 167
Arrows 79
Asian music 114, 134
Association 47, 126
Attali, Jacques 20–21, 50, 56, 96, 123, 146, 181–182c7n36
authenticity 10, 62, 71–72, 77–78, 96, 154, 155, 159–160, 165

authoritarianism 9, 39, 56, 73, 160, 176c3n21
Authorship 7
avant-garde music 9, 22, 36, 40–43, 94–95, 111–112, 116, 131, 134
Ayers, Kevin 1
Ayler, Albert 110
Ayoade, Richard 144

Bach, Johann Sebastian 137
Bad Brains 2
Bad Company 45
Baez, Joan 80, 113
Baker, Joyce 104
Balibar, Étienne 168
Balin, Marty 57
Ballard, Florence 102
Band of Gypsys 121
Bangs, Lester 41, 45, 58, 123
Baraka, Amiri (LeRoi Jones) 111
Barb 56
Battle of Cer 142
Bauhaus 162
Baxter, Les 134, 152, 156
Beach Boys 46, 150, 153, 159
Beatles 10, 12, 32, 47, 51, 56, 59, 60–61, 91, 95–96, 112, 121, 124, 126, 133–134, 147–150, 152–155, 159, 161–162
Beckett, Samuel 2, 76
Beethoven, Ludwig van 7, 137
Beinhorn, Michael 22
Bennett, Tony 154
Benson, George 187c10n6
Benson, Renaldo "Obie" 125
Berendt, Joachim E. 110–111
Beresford, Steve 95
Berg, Alban 76
Berry, Chuck 51, 123
Biafra, Jello 42–43
Bieber, Justin 77
big band music 12–13, 63, 90–91, 149–152, 155, 157

Big Black 9, 43–45
Billy Jack 184c8n30
Bismarck, Otto von 135
Black Flag 2, 43–44
black music 9–10, 43, 51, 59–63, 65, 94, 111, 128, 134, 146, 155, 159, 176c4n2
Black Sabbath 1, 44, 46, 163
Blackmore, Ritchie 156–157
Blondie 156
Blue Man Group 68
Blue Öyster Cult 44
blues 17, 50–52, 54, 59, 60, 87, 111, 139
Blush, Steve 42
Bobby Fuller Four 42
Bogart, Tim 103
Boland 138
Bonham, John 86–88, 91
Booker T. and the M.G.s 63–65, 151, 187c10n6
Boone, Pat 12–13, 46, 59, 147, 154–157, 165
Bosnian War *see* Yugoslav Wars
bossa nova 111
Bowie, David 69, 162
boy bands 75, 77
Boy George 98
Boyle, Kevin 115, 126
Braxton, Anthony 111–112
Brecht, Bertolt 144
Britton, Benjamin 143
Brothers Four 113, 149, 152, 154
Brown, James 11, 17, 40, 50–51, 64, 97–99, 101, 109, 151, 181c7n26, 187–188c10n8
Brubeck, Dave 112
Bruce, Jack 54
Buffalo Springfield 60, 117
Bukowski, Charles 58
Burnham, Hugo 99–100
Butthole Surfers 9, 43, 45
Byrd, Bobby 97, 99, 101
Byrds 60, 117, 160
Byrne, David 67

Cabaret Voltaire (band) 162
Cage, John 2, 50, 100, 181c7n31
Cale, John 1–2
Camp 12–13, 46, 153–155, 157–159, 165
Camping (intentional Camp) 13, 46, 154, 155, 157–159, 165
Can 2, 36–37, 71
Canterbury Sound 172c1n17
capitalism 8, 21, 27–28, 41, 68, 71, 73–74, 76, 83, 97, 105, 123, 129–130, 133–136, 138, 142, 143, 144
Captain and Tennille 47
Captain Beefheart 2, 36, 38, 44–45, 68
Caribbean music 134
Carpenters 47

Casale, Gerald 67–68, 70
Cash, Johnny 13, 63, 147, 154, 157, 160–165
Cash, June Carter 164–165
Charles, Ray 149, 187c10n7
Cheap Trick 44
cheese/cheesiness 76, 158–159, 165
Christgau, Robert 5, 33, 44, 71, 73–74, 93–94, 132
Chrome 38
Churchill, Winston 135
Cinderella 98
Circle Jerks 9, 42–44, 47
civil rights 10, 65, 81, 110–111
Clapton, Eric 80, 123
Clark, Dick 39
Clarke, Tony 127
Clash 2, 30, 32
class/class politics 12, 26–27, 30, 46, 95–98, 119, 126, 128
classical music 8, 12, 24, 26, 61–62, 71, 88, 95, 123–124, 128, 132, 136–138
Clinton, Bill 28
Coasters 89
Coates, Norma 77
cock rock 10, 11, 18, 79, 86–87, 90, 94, 98–99, 168
Cohen, Leonard 97
Cold War 8, 12, 28, 129, 136, 138, 146
Coleman, Ornette 44, 89, 109
Collins, Judy 80
Coltrane, John 110, 112, 114
Combustible Edison 156
commodity function of music 10, 21, 40, 76–77, 79, 83, 119, 137
communism 21, 27, 29, 129, 131, 133, 136, 142–144
community 12, 19–20, 118, 125, 128, 135
Como, Perry 149
conformity 9–10, 26, 30, 41, 51, 55, 73–74, 77, 144
conservatism 27, 60, 110, 119, 133, 155, 157, 159–160, 167
consumerism/consumer culture 9, 41, 53, 55, 65, 70–71, 74, 78–79, 81–82, 119
contemplation value 61, 82
continentialism 10, 61, 159
Cook, Paul 30
Cooper, Alice 30, 41, 157, 163
Cooper, Jerome 110
Copland, Aaron 137
Coulter, Jessi 45
counterculture (1960s) 10–12, 17, 20–22, 28, 45, 55–56, 60, 62, 65–69, 91, 98, 118–121, 123, 127, 133, 136, 147, 150, 159–161
Country Joe and the Fish 60
country music 13, 16, 47, 50–52, 60, 81, 89, 116, 146, 149, 153, 159–162, 165, 167

Index

Covey, Don 51
Cox, Billy 19, 121
Cream 17, 20, 54
Creedence Clearwater Revival 44, 161
Croatian War for Independence *see* Yugoslav Wars
Cropper, Steve 63–65
Crosby, Bing 63, 152–153, 154
Crosby, David 115, 117
Crosby, Stills and Nash (CSN) 117–118
Crosby, Stills, Nash and Young (CSNY) 11, 57, 60, 115–118, 121
Crystals 97
cultural opportunism 10, 36, 74
culture industry 76–77, 126
Cunningham, David 95, 97
Curtis, King 10, 88–91, 180c7n10
Cyrus, Miley 3, 76, 77, 79

Dada 38, 45, 68, 144
D.A.F. (Deutsch-Amerikanische Friendship) 136, 140
Daltrey, Roger 86
Dammed 32
Davies, Ray 92–93
Davis, Clive 23
Davis, Miles 111
Days of Rage 120
Dead Boys 2
Dead Kennedys 9, 42, 43, 175c2n34
Dean, James 146
Debord, Guy 132, 144–145
Deep Purple 13, 45, 156–157
Deleuze, Gilles 45
Democratic National Convention (1968) 110
Denny, Martin 134, 152, 156
Deodato 137
Depétris, Jean-Pierre 119
Derek and the Dominos 161
Derrida, Jacques 94, 96
Descartes, René 60–61
détournement 12, 131–132, 135, 137–138
Detroit riots (1967) 126–127
Devo 2, 10, 38, 43, 67–74, 76, 80, 82–83, 95, 144–145, 177–178c5n9, 178c5n13, 178c5n16–18, 178c5n23
Diamond, Neil 45
Dickies 46–47
Die Kreuzen 2
Diller, Phyllis 153
disco 12, 16, 22–23, 37, 51, 60, 94, 99, 107, 131–132, 134, 137
dissonance 8, 11, 18, 19, 20, 26, 40, 43–44, 53–54, 94, 100, 107, 113–117, 139, 152, 162–163
Dohrn, Bernadine 120
Dolphy, Eric 112

dominant culture 12, 146–147
Donnas 182c7n39
Donovan 86, 104, 150
Doors 1–2
Dread Zeppelin 46
Duchamp, Marcel 144
Dunn, Donald "Duck" 63–65
Dupree, Cornell 89
Duran Duran 98
Dylan, Bob 5, 10, 52, 59–61, 121, 153, 155, 160–161

Eagles 41
Eagleton, Terry 94
Eastern Europe 12, 94, 129, 130–131, 136, 141
easy listening 46, 90, 134, 153
Edge, Graham 124
Einstürzende Neubaten 162
emergent culture 146–147
Emerson, Keith 123
Emerson, Lake and Palmer (ELP) 1, 123–124, 137
Emerson, Lake and Powell 137
Eno, Brian 1–2, 69–70
Entwistle, John 54
Esquivel, Juan García 156
establishment 12, 20–21, 52, 60, 77, 150
Europe (band) 136, 138
European Union 12, 130, 135, 142
Evans-Stickland, Deborah 95–96
Everly Brothers 51
exotica (music genre) 39, 131, 134, 152, 155, 157
experimental music 9, 22, 36, 40–43, 50, 61, 94–95, 131, 134

Fakir, Abdul "Duke" 125
fascism 12, 21, 41, 58, 72, 129, 131–133, 140, 144
Fast, Susan 6, 87, 97, 99
Faust 45
Feliciano, José 17
femininity 10, 18, 76–80, 86–87, 98–99, 106
Fergie 8
Ferguson, Maynard 112, 150
Fleetwood Mac 41
Flipper 43–44
Flying Burrito Brothers 57, 160
Flying Lizards 11, 46, 94–97, 101, 105
folk music 10–11, 13, 47, 60–61, 80–81, 113–114, 116–118, 121–124, 132, 142, 149, 152–153, 159, 160, 162
Ford, Tennessee Ernie 153
Foucault, Michel 55
Four Tops 12, 62, 92, 125–128
Fox, Aaron A. 160
Franklin, Aretha 22, 63, 89, 103

198 Index

Fras, Milan 138
Fraser, Andy 168
Free (band) 31, 168
free jazz 2, 19, 23, 37–38, 88, 95, 109–112
Fripp, Robert 69
Frith, Simon 5–6, 35–6, 38, 42, 59, 60, 64–65, 125, 146, 150, 159
funk 17, 22–23, 38, 43, 75, 94, 96–97, 99–100, 111, 134

Gale, Eric 112
Gang of Four 2, 31, 38, 44, 99–101, 134
Gaye, Marvin 25, 125
gender/gender politics 6–7, 10, 11, 27, 44–45, 52, 55–56, 65, 77–78, 79, 81, 86–87, 90, 92, 94, 98, 102–104, 106–108, 127, 136, 150, 168
generations/generational politics 1, 9–10, 12, 17, 26, 38, 118, 146–147, 150, 153–154, 158, 160, 168
Genesis 2, 123
Gentle Giant 2, 123
Gentry, Bobby 89
Gill, Andy 31, 99–100
Gilmour, David 139
Gilroy, Paul 134
Ginestara, Alberto 137
Ginn, Greg 44
glam 29, 98
Godard, Jean-Luc 38, 119, 167
Golden Throats 12, 152, 158
Goldman, Vivien 95
Goodwin, Andrew 177c4n5
Gordy, Berry, Jr. 62–63, 126
Gormé, Eydie 156
Gosling, Glenn 129
gospel music 17, 24, 26, 62, 80, 103, 111, 139, 153, 157, 162
Gramsci, Antonio 96
Grand Funk Railroad 62
Grateful Dead 20, 57, 159–160
The Great Rock 'n' Roll Swindle 34–36
Great Society 126
Greaves, John 97
Green (a.k.a. Green Gartsdale) 96
Green Day 167
Griffith, D.W. 133
Grossberg, Lawrence 168–169
grunge 75, 147
Guess Who 45
Guevara, Che 110, 160
guitar: gendering of 17–18, 79–80, 90, 106
Gulf War 8, 22, 24–26
Guthrie, Woody 60
Gypsy Sun and Rainbows 19

Hackel, Stu 125–126
Haden, Charlie 109–110

Haggard, Merle 60, 159–161
Hale, Jack 89
Halford, Rob 181c7n28
Hammill, Peter 36
Hannah Montana 3, 77, 154
hard rock 3, 11, 17, 43, 45, 62, 86, 90, 103, 116, 122, 132, 147, 168
hardcore punk 9, 41–43, 45, 147
Hardin, Tim 126
Harley, Rufus 11, 111–115, 183c8n10–11
Harmolodics 44, 109
Harris, Emmylou 80
Harris, Richard 151
Harrison, George 114, 148–150, 156
Harry, Deborah 94
Hayes, Isaac 64
Hayward, Justin 124–125
Heart 8
heavy metal 2, 12–13, 16, 34, 43, 47, 80, 86, 90, 92–94, 98, 107, 147, 155–158, 162
Hebdige, Dick 30
Hefner, Hugh 55
Hegarty, Antony 179c6n10
Hegarty, Paul 19–20, 71, 122, 131, 144
Hell's Angels 57–58
Hendrix, Jimi 8, 11, 17–22, 25–28, 80, 115, 121–3, 169; *see also* Jimi Hendrix Experience
Hendryx, Nona 23
Henry Cow 2, 97
heterosexuality 18, 55, 78, 80, 99, 101
Hi-NRG disco 11, 106, 107
Hickerson, Joe 113
Hilburn, Robert 20
hip/hipness 25, 51–52, 55–56, 58, 77–78, 153, 155
Hitler, Adolf 39, 58, 129
Hobbes, Thomas 140
Hoffman, Abbie 20–21, 172c1n8
Holland, Dozier, and Holland (H-D-H) 62, 101, 125–127
Hollies 117
Holly, Buddy 51, 89
Holst, Gustav 136, 142
homoeroticism 80, 99
homosexuality 55, 78, 98–99
homosocial (male relationships) 11, 98–99, 101, 104
Hopper, Hugh 23
Hopps, Roger 89
Horkheimer, Max 68
Horóscopos de Durango 3
Houston, Cissy 22
Houston, Whitney 8, 22–28, 154, 156, 169
Howe, Steve 123
Howlin' Wolf 59
Hughes, Langston 115

human-machine relationship 18, 71–72
humanism 69, 71–72, 76, 114, 119
Hunter, Meredith 57, 176c3n18
Hüsker Dü 43
Hussey, Andrew 31, 131
Huyssen, Andreas 76
Hyman, Dick 151–153

"(I Can't Get No) Satisfaction" 2, 8–9, 26, 50, 52–55, 64–66, 67, 69–73, 75–82, 106, 153–154, 168–169
Indian music 61, 110, 114, 134
individuality 10, 12, 19–20, 24, 27, 35, 42, 53, 55, 62, 67, 69, 71–73, 76–78, 105, 109, 118–119, 124–125, 128, 131, 144, 159–160
industrial music 2, 12, 75, 131–133, 136, 140, 143, 162, 165, 185c9n8
Island of Lost Souls 69
Isley, Ernie 121
Isley, Marvin 121
Isley, O'Kelly 121
Isley, Ronald 121
Isley, Rudolph 121
Isley Brothers 11, 17, 59, 121–123

Jackson, Al, Jr. 63–65
Jackson, Michael 78, 81
Jackson, Wayne 89
Jagger, Mick 50–52, 54–55, 57–58, 64, 70, 75–76, 78, 81
Jameson, Fredric 44, 177c4n5, 181–182c7n36
Jan and Dean 153
jazz 11, 17, 22–24, 43, 54, 96, 109, 111–114, 123, 134, 148, 150, 152
Jefferson Airplane 57, 60
Jeffreys, Garland 43
Jemmott, Jerry 89
Jenkins, Leroy 110
Jesus Christ 164–165
Jethro Tull 1, 123–124, 137
Jett, Joan 79
Jimi Hendrix Experience 17, 19, 21, 54, 111
jingles 39
Johnny Cash Show 161, 189c10n29
Johnson, Jimmy 112
joke band/joke song 46–47, 95, 155
Jones, Booker T. 63
Jones, Brian 52
Jones, George 161
Jones, John Paul 86–87, 91
Jones, Steve 30
Jones, Tom 97
Joplin, Janis 79
Joy Division 162

Kafka, Franz 2, 76
Kahn, Chaka 22

Kanter, Paul 57
Keith, Toby 167
Kennedy, John F. 111
Kent State (May 4, 1970) 11, 67–68, 115–116, 119, 121–122
Key, Francis Scott 16
Killdozer 9, 45–46
King, B.B. 112
King, Jon 101
King, Martin Luther, Jr. 122, 160
King Alexander 130
King Crimson 2, 44, 123, 137, 150, 160
King Mob 29
Kingsmen 53
Kingston Trio 113
Kinks 11, 27, 51, 91–92, 94, 150
Kirk, Rahsaan Roland 112
Kirkie, Simon 168
Kiss 74, 132
kitsch 30, 38, 134, 154
Klein, Allen 148
Kossoff, Paul 168
Kraftwerk 44, 46, 68, 70–72, 131, 151, 182c7n38
Kramer, Wayne 56
Krautrock 2, 45, 68, 71, 131
Die Kreuzen 2
Ku Klux Klan 133

Lacan, Jacques 96
Laibach 12–13, 21, 41, 46, 129–145, 185c9n13, 185c9n16, 186c9n23–5
Laine, Denny 124
Lake, Oliver 23
Laswell, Bill 22
Lateef, Yussef 112
Latin American music 17, 90–91, 134, 152, 156–157
Lavigne, Avril 76
Lawrence, Steve 156
Leary, Timothy 124
Led Zeppelin 1, 6–7, 10, 45–46, 86–91, 97–99, 154
Lee, Larry 19
Left Banke 126
Lennon, John 56, 89, 95–96, 148, 153
Lewis, Jerry Lee 63, 97, 123, 160
Lewis, Ramsey 183c8n9
liberal democracy 8, 19, 21, 26, 105, 115, 118–119, 128–130, 144
liberalism 25, 27–28, 72, 110, 115, 118–119, 126, 130–133, 160, 167
Liberation Music Orchestra (LMO) 109–110
Liberation News Service (LNS) 56
Little Richard 17, 59, 97, 123, 155
Lodge, John 124
London Musicians Collective (LMC) 95

Los Angeles Free Press 58
lounge music 90, 151, 155–158
Love, Andrew 89
lovers rock 96
Lydon, John 30–33, 36–38
Lynyrd Skynyrd 167, 183c8n19

Macan, Edward 123–124, 128
Madonna 27, 105
Maher, Fred 22–23
Mailer, Norman 51–52, 55, 58, 105, 153
Man Ray 68
Manifest Destiny 142
Manne, Shelly 111
Manson, Charles 120
Manson, Marilyn 162, 189c10n33
Mao Zedong 56
Mar-Keys 63–64
marches 12, 110, 132–133, 139, 143
Marcuse, Herbert 68, 73, 82
Marsh, Dave 60, 72, 80, 178c5n15
Marshal Tito (Josip Broz) 130–131
Marshall, Julian 97, 101
Martha and the Vandellas 62, 125
Martin, George 148
masculinity 10–11, 18, 52, 55–56, 59, 77–80, 86–88, 90, 92–94, 98–99, 106, 126–127, 160, 168, 180c7n7
mass culture 9–10, 76–78, 81–83, 92, 137; gendering of 26, 76–79
mastery 18, 27, 93
material 22–23
Matlock, Glen 30–32
Mayfield, Curtis 185c8n47
MC5 56, 62
McCallum, David 153
McCann, Les 111
McCartney, Paul 148, 156
McClary, Susan 21
McGuire, Barry 46
McLaren, Malcolm 29–31, 33–37, 74
McLean, Don 45–46
Meat Puppets 43–44
Memphis Horns 89, 180c7n9
Memphis soul *see* Southern soul
Mendiola, Jim 33
Merzbow 19
Meshuggah 3
"messthetics" 96
Metallica 157
Michael Zager Band 22
Middle Eastern music 110, 114, 134
Miles, Buddy 89, 121
Miller, Mitch 151, 153–154
minimalism 45, 68, 131, 140, 164
Ministry 162
Minutemen 2, 9, 43–44

Miracles 125
Mitchell, Jimmy 89
Mitchell, Joni 80, 117–118, 156, 183c8n20
Mitchell, Mitch 17, 19, 26
Modern Jazz Quartet 111
modernism 10, 61, 159, 177c4n5
Monkees 23, 126
Monroe, Alexei 133
Montenegro, Hugo 151–152
Monterey Pop Festival 18, 62–64, 92
Moody Blues 12, 46, 124–128, 160
MOR 9, 35, 47, 62, 149, 153, 156
Morales, Pancho 89
Morricone, Ennio 150
Morrison, Jim 2
Most, Mickie 104
Mothers of Invention 42, 156
Mothersbaugh, Mark 2, 67–70, 72–74
Motown (Records) 2, 10–12, 61–63, 89–90, 96, 101–103, 125–126, 128, 149, 177c4n7
Muller, Charles Allen 77
multi-media 68, 132
Murphy, Walter 137
music hall 61, 92, 148
musique concrète 38, 61, 131, 162
Mussorgsky, Modest 137
mutant disco 23
MX-80 Sound 38
Myers, Alan 70

Nash, Graham 117, 118
nation-state 10–12, 16, 24, 26, 130, 135, 145, 168
national anthems 16, 21, 132, 134
nationalism 12, 26, 123, 130, 133–134
Native Americans 141
NATO *see* North Atlantic Treaty Organization
NATO (Laibach album) 12, 135–144
Nazism 39, 41, 58, 130, 132
Nelson, Willie 149, 160–162
neoliberalism 8, 27–28, 135
Neue Slowenische Kunst (New Slovenian Art; NSK) 131, 134, 186c9n19
Never Mind the Buzzcocks 144, 175–6c3n10
New Democrats 28
New Pop 96, 98, 147
New Wave 9, 42, 95, 98, 105
New York Dolls 29, 31, 96
Newitz, Annalee 158
Newman, Colin 38
Nicks, Stevie 94
Nico 1–2
Nietzsche, Friedrich 167
Night Ranger 105
Nightingale, Wally 30
nihilism 32, 35–36

Nine Inch Nails (NIN) 13, 75, 161–165
Nirvana 12, 75, 147, 154
Nixon, Richard M. 118, 121
noise 8, 18, 19, 20–21, 26–27, 31, 40, 43, 46, 54, 94, 96, 100–101, 105, 107, 115–116, 123, 131, 144, 146, 162–163
Nolan, Jerry 29
non-verbal singing 64–66, 80–82, 97, 101, 143
non–Western music 2, 22, 110–111, 133–134
North Atlantic Treaty Organization (NATO) 135, 142–143
Nugent, Ted 62
Nyman, Michael 95

Obama, Barack 7
Ochs, Phil 60, 159
Oldham, Andrew Loog 53
O'Neill, William L. 17, 56, 160
oppositional culture 9–10, 22, 36, 41, 73, 77, 82–83, 86, 119, 144–145, 147, 152, 155
Opus 133
Orbison, Roy 63, 161
Orff, Carl 132, 140, 143
Otis, Johnny 61–62
outlaw mythos 42–43, 160–161

Pacific Islands music 134, 152
Page, Jimmy 18, 80, 86–88, 91, 98–99
Palladin, Patti 95
Pareles, Jon 25, 26
Parsons, Gram 160
Partch, Harry 38
Partridge Family 154
Passaro, Alan 58
Paxton, Robert O. 130
Payton, Lawrence 125, 127–128
Pere Ubu 2, 38, 105
Perkins, Carl 161
Perry, Mark 37–38
Peterson, Sally 97, 101
phallocentricism 94
phallogocentricism 94, 98
Phantom Tollbooth 8–9
Philly Soul (aka Philadelphia Soul) 177c4n6
Pinder, Mike 124–125, 128
Pink Floyd 1, 95, 136, 139, 156
Pizzicato Five 156
Plant, Robert 6–7, 86–88, 90–91, 98–99
Poison 98
Police (band) 134
polka music 46, 110, 112
Polkaholix 46
Pop, Iggy 69
Pop Art 38
Pop Group 2, 44, 109, 134
pop music 8, 10, 12, 22–24, 26, 41, 43, 47, 61–62, 75, 77, 102, 104, 111–112, 134, 150–152, 154
popular music 12–13, 15–16, 38, 40–41, 46, 51, 54, 61, 82–83, 95–96, 98–99, 101, 109, 123–125, 132, 137, 145, 154, 168
porn film music 75, 90
P-Orridge, Genesis 37
Portsmouth Sinfonia 186c9n26
post-hardcore 2, 8, 42–44, 147
postindustrial society 135
postmodernism 22, 67–68, 73–74, 132, 144, 177c4n5
post-punk 2, 9, 10–11, 22, 33, 36–38, 42–44, 46, 67, 92, 94–96, 99, 134, 147
prepared piano 50, 95, 101
Presley, Elvis 1–2, 18, 42, 45–46, 51, 63, 160
Press, Joy 6
Preston, Billy 89
Procol Harum 89, 137
progressive rock 2, 12, 32, 43, 47, 92, 123–124, 128, 137, 146, 160
proto-punk 30–31, 52, 62, 92
psychedelic rock 11, 17, 43, 45, 60, 103, 131, 147, 150, 152
psychedelic soul 10, 63, 90, 126, 128, 138
Public Image, Ltd. (PiL) 37
punk rock 2, 9, 10, 12, 16, 22, 29, 30–38, 41–43, 45–47, 52, 67, 71, 73, 92, 94–96, 132, 136, 140, 144–145, 147, 167
Purdie, Bernard "Pretty" 89

Queen 133
Quotation 132

race/racial politics 9–12, 17, 25–27, 51, 52, 55, 59–66, 78, 81, 86, 95, 110–111, 116, 119–124, 126–128, 146, 159, 168, 176c4n2
Radič, Stepan 130
Raiders (a.k.a. Paul Revere and the Raiders) 136, 141
Rainey, Chuck 112
Rammstein 46
Ramones 2, 17, 29–30, 33, 37–38, 46, 71, 97, 154
Rare Earth 126
Rascals 152
Reagan, Ronald 105, 120, 129
Reaganism 24, 27, 106, 120, 129
rebellion 10, 36, 43, 51, 55, 67, 72–73, 76–78, 82, 144, 155
Redding, Noel 17
Redding, Otis 9, 10, 63–66, 80–82, 103, 169
Reeves, Martha 62
reggae 37–38, 46, 94, 96, 99, 134
Reich, Wilhelm 99
Repressive Hypothesis 55, 73, 86
Residents 9, 38–41, 43, 46, 58, 68, 144–145, 174–175c2n29–30

residual culture 146–147, 158
reversed backbeat 89–91, 118
Revolutionary Ensemble 110, 112
revolutionary machismo 52, 56, 160
Reynolds, Simon 6, 36–37, 41, 95–97
Reznor, Trent 162–163
rhythm and blues (R&B) 50–52, 54, 59, 60, 62, 92, 95, 96, 103, 111, 121, 124–125, 146, 149, 155, 159, 160
Richards, Keith 50–54, 57, 59, 64
Rinde, Allen 57
Robinson, Smokey 62
rock ideology 9, 10–11, 18, 31–32, 41, 47, 56, 60, 71–72, 75–77, 79–81, 86, 144, 159–160
Rodgers, Jimmy 160
Rodgers, Nile 23
Rodgers, Paul 168
Rolling Stone 23, 25, 52, 72, 76
Rolling Stones 2, 8–9, 10, 17, 26, 41, 43, 50–58, 59, 64–66, 73, 77–78, 81–83, 86, 91, 127, 133, 154, 156, 160, 163, 168
Romanek, Mark 164
Ronstadt, Linda 78
Ross, Diana 62, 102–103, 107
Roth, David Lee 93–94
Rotten, Johnny *see* Lydon, John
Roxy Music 68, 105

Saccharine Trust 43
Safka, Melanie 80
Sainte-Marie, Buffy 80
samba 111
Sampedro, Frank "Poncho" 117
Sanders, Montego Joe 112
Santana 57
satire/parody 41, 43, 45, 47, 74, 94, 132, 140, 144–145, 157, 158, 160
Saturday Night Fever 137
Savalas, Telly 163
Schoenberg, Arnold 76, 110
School of Rock 147
Scott, Tom 156
Screamers 38
Scritti Politti 96–97
Sedgwick, Eve Kosofsky 98
Seeds 162
Seeger, Pete 60, 113, 161
Severinsen, Doc 150, 152
SEX (fashion boutique) 29, 30, 31
sex/sexual politics 6–7, 9–11, 18, 25, 27, 44–45, 47, 52, 55–56, 58, 73, 75, 78–81, 86–91, 97, 99–101, 131, 160, 161, 168
Sex Pistols 2, 29, 30–33, 36, 38, 68, 71, 74, 96, 131, 144–145
Shangri-las 137
Shankar, Ravi 114
Shapiro, Peter 52, 57

Shatner, William 155, 188c10n21
Sheffield, Rob 76, 159
Sheila E. 157
Shepherd, John 79
Shepp, Archie 23, 110
Shier, David 137
Shiffer, Sheldon 35
Silverstein, Shel 161
Simpson, Jessica 76
Sinatra, Frank 9, 12, 34–35, 112, 147, 148–151, 154–155, 164
Sirens (Greek myth) 104, 181–182c7n36
Sirone 110
situationist 12, 29, 31–32, 35, 36, 74, 131–132, 144
Situationist International (SI) 31, 35, 119, 131–132
Sledge, Percy 92
Sly and the Family Stone 111
Smith, John Stafford 16
Smith, Patti 6, 94
Socialist Realism 132
Soft Machine 23, 96
Solidarity 129
The Song Remains the Same 86
Sonic Youth 2, 43, 44
Sontag, Susan 153–155
soul music 8–11, 22–24, 26, 59, 61–64, 80, 89, 96, 102–103, 111–113, 121, 128, 136, 138–139, 150–151
Soundgarden 156
Sousa, John Phillip 26, 110
southern soul 62, 89–90, 103
Soviet Union 12, 27, 129–130, 136, 143–144
spaghetti western 151
Spears, Britney 3, 7, 10, 13, 26, 75–83, 106, 154, 159, 169
spectacle society 31, 35–36, 119
Spice Girls 75, 77, 154
Spicer, Al 37
Spinrad, Norman 176c3n20
Springsteen, Bruce 1, 72, 76–77
Spungen, Nancy 34
Square 51, 55, 77–78, 153, 155
Squirrel Nut Zippers 156
Stalin, Joseph 130
Stalinism 12, 144
Stambler, Irwin 51
"The Star-Spangled Banner" 8, 16–17, 19–22, 24–27, 115, 122, 169
Starland Vocal Band 47
Starr, Edwin 126, 136, 138
Starr, Ringo 148
Stars on 45 47
the State 19–21, 117, 119–122, 129, 134, 167; *see also* nation-state
Status Quo 136, 138

Stax Records 10, 61–63, 89
Steely Dan 44, 156
Stein, Mark 103, 104, 107
Steinberg, Lewie 63
Stereolab 156
Stiff Records 69, 174c2n25
Stills, Stephen 117–118, 121
Stockhausen, Karlheinz 45, 143
Stooges 31–32, 62
Strand (a.k.a. the Swankers) 29–30
Strauss, Richard 137
Strawberry Alarm Clock 152
Streisand, Barbra 154
Strohm, John 80
Strong, Barrett 95
Stubbs, Levi 62, 125–128
Suicide 38, 186–187c9n32
Sultan, Juma 19
Sun Ra 110–111
Super Bowl XXV (1991) 8, 22, 24–25
Supremes 11, 62, 101–104, 106–107, 125, 128, 149
surrealism 38
Swans 2, 43
symphonic soul 11, 62–63, 89, 126, 128
synthpop 11, 44, 67–68, 96, 105–107, 147, 163, 182c7n38

Talking Heads 38, 67, 134
Tangerine Dream 131
"Taps" 19
Taylor, James 121
Taylor, Timothy D. 134
techno 12, 132, 136, 138
technocracy 72–73
"technophallus" 18, 26, 93, 99–100
Tee, Richard 112
teen pop 10, 75–76, 78
teenyboppers 77
Temptations 62, 64, 125–126
Ten Day War *see* Yugoslav Wars
Test Department 162
Thatcher, Margaret 129
Thatcherism 129
Third Reich 131–132, 140, 144
Third Stream jazz 111
This Heat 95, 180–181c7n18
Thomas, Roy 124
Thomas, Thurman 89
Thompson, Tony 23
thrash music 42–44
Three Dog Night 63
Throbbing Gristle 37, 131, 162
Tito *see* Marshal Tito
Tomc, Gregor 131
tonality 23, 26–27, 109–111, 104, 116, 118, 163

Toop, David 95
Tormé, Mel 63, 150–152, 154
totalitarianism 12, 41, 51, 58, 131, 133, 135, 144, 145
tradition/traditionalism 8, 18, 22, 30, 31, 35, 37–38, 46, 51, 54, 72, 75–76, 79, 82, 112, 145, 147, 158–159, 165
Tribe 120
Trinity Broadcast Network (TBN) 157–158
Triumph of the Will 22, 25
Troggs 18
Tuesday's Child 120
Turtles 150–151
Twisted Sister 98

Ulrich, Lars 157
Upton, Michael 95, 101
utopianism 12, 28, 32, 71, 109, 125, 128

Valentinos 8
Valez, Jerry 19
Van der Graaf Generator 1, 2, 123
Vaneigem, Raoul 35, 119, 120, 144
Van Halen 1, 11, 18, 44, 78, 79, 92–94, 98, 150, 180c7n15–16
Van Halen, Alex 93
Van Halen, Eddie 27, 93, 100
Vanilla Fudge 11, 103–104, 106–107, 127, 169
Velvet Underground 163, 164
Vicious, Sid 9, 29, 32–35, 95, 173c2n12
Vietnam War 8, 11, 17, 19, 24, 45, 67, 110, 113–116, 122–23, 141
violence 43, 56–57, 107, 116, 119, 120–121, 131
Virgin Records 32, 33, 34, 69, 95, 173c2n13

Wagner, Richard 132, 140
Wakeman, Rick 32
Waksman, Steve 18, 53, 87–88, 90, 92–93, 98–99
Walker, Jerry Jeff 89
Walser, Robert 137
War of 1812 16, 26
Warhol, Andy 74
Warrant 98
Warsaw Pact 130
Warwick, Clint 124
Warwick, Dionne 22
Watts, Charlie 54, 64, 65
Weather Underground (WU) 120
Webb, Jack 46
Webb, Jimmy 151
Weil/Brecht 124, 184c8n40
"The White Negro" 51, 52, 66, 78
Whitfield, Norman 126
Who 17, 51, 54, 59, 77, 91, 154, 172c1n8
Wilde, Kim 11, 104–108, 169, 182c7n40, 182c7n42

Wilde, Marty 104–105
Wilde, Ricky 104–105
Williams, Andy 89
Williams, Hank 160
Williams, John 26
Williams, Larry 97
Williams, Raymond 146–147
Wilson, Ann 94
Wilson, Frank 127
Wilson, Mary 102
Wilson, Nancy 94
Wire 2, 32–33, 38, 44
Wolf Eyes 19
Wolman, Gil J. 132, 144–145
Wonder, Stevie 89, 125
Woodstock (festival) 8, 17, 19–22, 57, 117–118, 172*c*1*n*8
Woodstock (film) 22
Woodstock Nation 20; as symbol of counter-culture 20–22, 57, 122

world music 133–135, 152
Wyatt, Robert 23, 96
Wyman, Bill 54, 64
Wynette, Tammy 47

Yagsur, Max 117
Yardbirds 86, 104
Yes 123
Young, Neil 69, 115–117, 119–121, 161, 183*c*8*n*19
Young, Rob 109
Yugoslav Wars 12, 130, 135–136, 140, 142
Yugoslavia 130–131

Zager and Evans 136, 142
Zappa, Dweezil 156, 157
Zappa, Frank 37, 38, 40–41, 68–69, 74, 152, 156, 176–177*c*4*n*4
Žižek, Slavoj 145

www.ingramcontent.com/pod-product-compliance
Ingram Content Group UK Ltd.
Pitfield, Milton Keynes, MK11 3LW, UK
UKHW042003140426
5217IPUK00015B/953